MODERN ECONOMIC ISSUES

OTTO ECKSTEIN, Harvard University, General Editor

In this series the great public issues in economics are posed and put in perspective by original commentary and reprints of the most interesting and significant recent statements by experts in economics and government.

LAWRENCE H. OFFICER is a graduate of McGill University and received his Ph.D. from Harvard University where he is currently Assistant Professor of Economics. His published work includes papers in the area of economic theory, econometrics, and international economics and he is author of *An Econometric Model of Canada Under the Fluctuating Exchange Rate.*

THOMAS D. WILLETT is Assistant Professor of Economics at Harvard University and has also taught at the University of Virginia, where he received his Ph.D. He has written widely in the areas of economic theory, international finance, and social policy and is co-author with Gottfried Haberler of *Presidential Measures on Balance of Payments Controls* and *U.S. Balance of Payments Policies and International Monetary Reform.*

THE INTERNATIONAL MONETARY SYSTEM

PROBLEMS AND PROPOSALS

*Edited by Lawrence H. Officer
and Thomas D. Willett*

PRENTICE-HALL, Inc., Englewood Cliffs, N.J.

A SPECTRUM BOOK

To
GOTTFRIED HABERLER
Scholar and Gentleman

PREFACE

Our international monetary system is not working well. This volume focuses on two major questions:

1. What are the basic causes underlying the symptoms of international financial crisis and conflict?

2. What are the policy alternatives for improving the operation of our international monetary system?

Attention is paid almost exclusively to the actions and points of view of the industrial countries. This is not at all to imply that the financial problems facing the developing countries are unimportant, but rather that they are different from those with which we are primarily concerned here. There do exist several excellent discussions of the problems of international liquidity and international monetary reform from the point of view of the developing countries. See, for instance, items [30] and [37] in the bibliography at the end of this volume. A more general treatment of the problems of developing countries is found in another volume in this series (*Reshaping the World Economy*, edited by John A. Pincus).

We should warn the reader that while we have tried to report fairly the facts and logic surrounding the issues, we make no attempt to hide our own views, especially our preference for exchange rate flexibility.

We have many debts to acknowledge, especially to our students, former teachers, and colleagues, with whom we discussed the issues treated here. Otto Eckstein offered helpful criticisms and suggestions throughout the project, and Edward Tower and Jean Willett commented upon what proved to be substantially the final draft. We are grateful to our contributors and their publishers for permission to reprint their work. In many instances the authors agreed to update or adapt their papers for this volume. The American Enterprise Institute allowed the latter editor to draw upon his work with Gottfried Haberler in [26] and [27]. Our teaching loads were lightened during the period of this project by individual international studies grants from the Ford Foundation. We received considerable encouragement from Robert Martin of Prentice-Hall, Inc. and appreciate his willingness to deviate from several precedents in the Modern Economic Issues series. This volume could not have been completed on schedule without the excellent secretarial work of Miss Rosemary L. Carter and Miss Sharon E. Kiley.

Cambridge, Mass.   Lawrence H. Officer
                                                       Thomas D. Willett

CONTENTS

ix

THE INTERNATIONAL MONETARY SYSTEM

Problems and Proposals

PART I

What's Wrong With Our International Monetary System?

INTRODUCTION

What is happening to our international monetary system? Gold movements make front page headlines. High ranking officials scurry across the Atlantic to consult on international financial matters. The President of the United States imposes mandatory controls on U.S. overseas investment. Legislation is introduced before the United States Congress to reduce travel abroad by U.S. citizens, and Americans are asked to defer non-essential travel outside the Western Hemisphere.

In Britain one austerity program follows another. Special tariffs are placed on imports. Wages and prices are frozen. Finally, the pound is devalued. In Europe charges are levied that U.S. balances of payments deficits are exporting inflation and financing the takeover of European businesses by American concerns.

As President Johnson stated in his Balance of Payments statement on January 1, 1968: "To the average citizen, the balance of payments, and the strength of the dollar and of the international monetary system, are meaningless phrases. They seem to have little relevance to our daily lives. Yet their consequences touch us all—consumer and captain of industry, worker, farmer, and financier." This is true when international financial arrangements are working well and becomes even more evident when they are not.

In 1960 in a classic book entitled *Gold and the Dollar Crisis* [65], Robert Triffin predicted the breakdown of the present international monetary system. In "Neither Gold Nor the Dollar," the first reading in this volume, he pronounces its death and describes the events leading to its demise. While not all observers would argue that there is no life left in our international payments system, almost all would agree that such a system does contain inherent contradictions which lead to the symptoms of breakdown, the crises which have been reported on the front pages of our newspapers.

In the second reading, "The Present System and its Defects," Warren L. Smith describes the basic characteristics of our international monetary system and outlines the major problems confronting it. Following the Smith reading is a more extensive discussion of the international monetary system. This section provides a background to the structure and evolution of postwar international financial arrangements. The key issues surrounding the operation and reform of the world monetary system are outlined as an introduction to the remainder of the volume.

NEITHER GOLD NOR THE DOLLAR

Robert Triffin

Frederick William Beinecke
Professor of Economics,
Yale University

The devaluation of the pound might have opened a new era in monetary cooperation. For the first time in history, *meaningful* international
consultations determined the new rate, prevented a spiraling of mutually defeating devaluations by other major countries, and elicited from
them large credits in support of the new rate. It could have been a
great step forward in our groping for a new monetary order. Instead it
unleashed an unprecedented wave of speculation and even greater
doubts as to the survival of our international monetary system. Why?

Market analysts take note of the failure of the devaluation to restore
full confidence in the pound and bring back to London a substantial
portion of the short-term funds that flew from it in the preceding
weeks, months, or years. They see speculative unrest spreading from
the pound to other currencies, and particularly to the dollar. Private
gold purchases appear to have risen to record levels of possibly $1 bil-
lion, or more, in the month following the pound devaluation. Who is to
blame? And how long can this last without forcing an official, or un-
official, increase in the price of gold?

President de Gaulle kindly offers himself as a convenient scapegoat
for what happened. He started his gold purchases several years ago,
allowed—or stimulated?—press leaks that alarmed speculators, refused
to cooperate fully with others in financing the remedies which the U.S.
favored to get itself out of the hole. Others blame the British for having

From Robert Triffin, "Neither Gold Nor the Dollar," *The New Republic,* Vol.
158, No. 4 (January 27, 1968), 23–26.

waited too long, and for having bungled by not closing the exchange market on the day preceding devaluation, rather than on the following Monday. They ascribe the new wave of speculation which rocked the market from December 11 through December 18 to an unprecedented gate-crashing of the closed club, or Mecca, of central bankers—the Bank for International Settlements—by our Undersecretary of the Treasury, and to rumored U.S. proposals to seek agreement on various ways to close speculators' access to gold at the present price, thus inducing them to scurry before the door was locked in their face. The new and drastic U.S. balance-of-payments program unveiled January 1 was obviously timed to ward off a further speculative wave that might otherwise have been expected from the public announcement of the unprecedented gold drain from Fort Knox in December—$925 million in a month.

All this makes fascinating copy for newspapers but throws little light on the basic issues that will determine the ultimate outcome of the present crisis: the death throes of the present gold-exchange standard, aggravated and accelerated by the huge and persistent deficits of the two countries whose national currencies serve as international reserves for others, i.e. the United Kingdom, and primarily today the United States.

The gold-exchange standard is dead or dying, but nothing else has taken its place yet.

It rested uneasily yesterday on two sources of supply for needed increases in the world reserve pool, essential to sustain desirable and feasible rates of expansion in world trade and production: (1) gold, and (2) gold-convertible foreign exchange. Both have dried up in recent years.

Gold used to provide three-fourths, or more, of global reserve increases. In spite of increasing U.S.S.R. sales, its contribution dropped to only one-fourth in 1960–1964, and has now become negative. Indeed it was already negative even before the recent speculative wave. In the last twelve months for which estimates are available (July 1966 through June 1967), private purchases by industry, jewelers, dentists, hoarders and speculators ($1.7 billion) exceeded the total supplies coming to the market from new gold production in official gold holdings. Last month's events will, of course, dig further—probably by $1 billion or more—into the world pool of monetary gold.

Gold-convertible foreign exchange thus provided the lion's share of new reserve increases: 65 percent of the total over the years 1960–1964.

These foreign exchange reserves are overwhelmingly made up of dollar IOU's. They were at first accepted—or even eagerly looked for—by other countries, because they carried substantial interest earnings, unavailable on gold metal, and could be converted at will into gold by their holders, without any embarrassment.

This system was killed, several years ago, by our brilliant Undersecretary of the Treasury, Mr. Roosa, when he was forced—for very good reasons—to appeal to "international cooperation" in order to apply the brakes on gold conversions which might topple the system by raiding the gold cellars of Fort Knox. In 1949, these were overflowing with about $25.5 billion of gold and another $1.5 billion of net claims on the International Monetary Fund, while our gold-convertible debt to foreign central banks barely exceeded $3 billion. In the following years, our net monetary reserves dropped gradually from their 1949 peak ($22.8 billion) to $10.9 billion in 1959 and *minus* $3.2 billion in June of last year. The net reserves of both reserve centers together—the United States and the United Kingdom—and of the other countries were about equal (approximately $17 billion) in 1949, but the first had dropped by mid-1967 to *minus* $9 billion or $10 billion, while the second had risen to well over $50 billion.

Sterling, and even the dollar, no longer looked quite "as good as gold," and foreign countries became increasingly reluctant to pile up more—and less and less easily "gold-convertible"—sterling and dollar IOU's. They were more and more inclined instead to convert them into gold, if they could or dared, or into gold-guaranteed claims on the International Monetary Fund. In the two and a half years from the end of 1964 through mid-1967, they converted the entirety of their current reserve gains ($4.4 billion in round figures) and some ($0.2 billion) of their previously accumulated foreign exchange holdings into gold ($2.4 billion) and claims on the IMF ($2.1 billion). Foreign exchange liquidation by developed countries even reached the huge total of $2.8 billion ($0.8 billion by France and $2 billion by other countries).

Events have thus dramatically confirmed the reluctant and belated recognition by the official negotiators of the Group of Ten and the IMF that neither gold nor gold-convertible foreign exchange could be safely relied upon to sustain indefinitely the world reserve requirements of expanding levels of world trade and production. Indeed, now that both of these traditional sources of reserve increases have become negative, reliance on them threatens not only to unleash deflationary pressures or mutually defeating trade restrictions on the world economy, but also to destroy the stability of the two currencies which used to prop up the gold-exchange standard.

Four years of arduous negotiations finally succeeded, at the Rio de Janeiro meeting of the IMF, last September, in producing a blueprint for the deliberate creation of a truly international reserve asset, in the amounts necessary to supplement vanishing supplies of gold and foreign exchange reserves. This agreement, however, must still be written out in legal form and hatched—ratified—by scores of congresses and parliaments. And when the new bird finally breaks out of its shell, a special provision will still forbid it to fly, or even to walk until the United States and the United Kingdom have succeeded in diminishing substantially—or even eliminated entirely and durably—their huge and persistent reserve deficits.

I ventured to predict at the time that the Rio Agreement would do little or nothing to solve the more immediate problems raised by the storm already raging around the pound sterling, and by the tidal wave of bearish dollar speculation and bullish gold speculation which a sterling devaluation might unleash upon the world. I added optimistically, however, that these forthcoming crises would impel new international rescue operations which might finally force us to deal realistically with the problem which the negotiators had bravely tried to sweep under the carpet—the relationship of the proposed new reserve asset to the former ones, the role which gold, dollars and sterling would continue to play in future reserve creation, and particularly the inherent vulnerability of the system to sudden or massive conversions from foreign exchange into gold.

The much heralded opposition of views between the United States and France, which had blocked agreement for so long, revolved on this issue. The U.S. wanted, basically, to discourage the conversion of dollars into gold, but wished also to preserve as far as possible our chances to finance at least part of our future deficits through further dollar accumulation by foreign central banks, up to undetermined amounts. As long as we maintain that position, it will be difficult either to exact from European governments precise commitments for the creation and absorption of new reserve assets which might conceivably add to already excessive and inflationary levels of dollar accumulation, or to erect jointly appropriate safeguards against sudden or massive liquidation into gold of dollar reserves currently accruing to foreign central banks or already accumulated by them over the long years of functioning of the gold-exchange standard.

These financial disagreements have now been compounded by the political implications of continued dollar accumulation by foreign central banks. Our Secretary of the Treasury called for such accumulation, particularly by the surplus countries of Continental Europe, as an indispensable cooperation for the financing of our direct investments abroad and of the defense of the "free world" not only in Europe, but also in Vietnam. Negotiations aiming at offsetting the foreign exchange costs of the stationing of our troops in Germany ended up, last March, with a German "declaration of intention" promising apparently broader and unlimited dollar accumulation and retention to avoid undesirable disturbances in the gold markets. Substantial increases of foreign exchange reserves since last March, not only in Germany ($172 million through November), but also in Italy ($845 million), Belgium ($307 million), the Netherlands ($274 million), etc., in sharp contrast to previous reductions, suggest that similar bargaining pressures may have been exercised on these countries to bolster up their flagging interest in dollar accumulation and to deter them from excessive gold conversions.

We may be slipping unwittingly, by gradual steps whose ultimate outcome is hardly suspected—as in our Vietnam escalation—toward a most radical solution of our balance-of-payments difficulties. Influential banking voices have recently joined the chorus of academic writers calling for a demonetization of that barbarous relic: gold. We could do this unilaterally, by suspending formally gold purchases as well as gold sales, or, more informally, by raising various forms of restrictions —on capital, and even on current account transactions—against countries which insist on cashing their dollars for gold. Many countries might then prefer—according to this reasoning—to finance our deficits through unlimited dollar accumulation, since their refusal to buy and retain the dollar overflows would either expose their industries to severe U.S. restrictions, or to unbearable competition with U.S. producers whose costs would be slashed by the depreciation of the dollar in terms of their own currency. Other instruments of persuasion could even be brought into play, if necessary: sharp cuts in our foreign aid to some, in our military supplies to others, etc. The discriminations established by our new balance-of-payments program between three groups of countries might easily indicate a further, major step along this road, as they may induce countries to escape or alleviate our restrictions—shifting their status from "hell" to "purgatory" or "heaven"—by agreeing to limit their dollar conversions, or even to sell us gold against piling up dollar IOU's.

We could easily repeat in this manner the disastrous experience of Britain with her sterling area. We could force even more countries into a dollar area, large enough to absolve us of any future worries about our balance of payments.

At least, for a while! And at the cost, sooner or later, of a renewal of the divisive and destructive international monetary and economic chaos of the 1930's. Public opinion would soon awaken—or be awakened—to the political implications of such a system, *i.e.* the forcible financing by foreign central banks and their nationals of whatever deficits we may incur in pursuing policies unilaterally decided by us, even if these policies entered into conflict with their own views of world interests, or of their own national interests.

It is true that we similarly financed, in the Marshall Plan and early NATO days, the huge deficits of the European countries. These deficits, however, were associated with policies on which we all agreed: the reconstruction of a Europe ruined by the Second World War and left as a tempting prey for Stalinist aggression or subversion. It is abundantly clear that many Europeans do not agree today with the policies of our Administration in Vietnam, and that some of them strongly object to what they regard as an excessive penetration, or take-over, of their industries by American capital. They may be wrong, but it would be highly unrealistic to expect them to finance indefinitely policies on which they have not been consulted and with which they must at times deeply disagree.

The ultimate outcome of such short-sighted U.S. policies could only be to arouse sharp political, as well as economic, divisions between the United States and Europe, as well as many other countries. More and more countries would desert, sooner or later, the dollar area, and erect compensatory barriers against the "foreign-exchange dumping" associated with the downward drift of a floating dollar—no longer supported by central bank purchases—in the exchange market. Economic warfare *à la* the 1930's between a new gold bloc and a shrinking dollar-sterling bloc would replace the economic cooperation that has assured our joint prosperity ever since the end of World War II.

The agreement reached at the Hague between the EEC countries, and later expanded into the Rio Agreement of last September, was largely a sane, last-minute reaction to the abyss which was opening before the eyes of the negotiators as a result of the unreasonable and incompatible so-called "negotiating positions" previously adopted by France and the United States. Substantial concessions by the French rallied unanimity within the European Economic Community in favor of solutions acceptable to the United States, and far preferable to the "undermining" of the international monetary system alluded to by Secretary Fowler.

Having agreed, however, on the need for a new reserve asset, we should now try to accelerate—or anticipate—its creation, not so much to expand present levels of world liquidity, but to prevent their contraction through flights into gold by either speculators or central banks or both.

The new reserve asset can be made vastly more attractive to central banks, and more acceptable to their politicians and public opinion, than mere sterling or dollar IOU's. Contrary to widespread opinion, it can also be made as safe for them as gold itself.

As long as it is not available, however, for reserve accumulation, and as long as the practical choice for reserve holders remains constricted to either gold or dollars, President de Gaulle will not be alone in preferring gold, especially as our absurd and immoral venture in Vietnam perpetuates deficits of several billion dollars a year in our balance of payments.

The most urgent task confronting us at this juncture is not so much to expand immediately the world reserve pool; it is to arrest the contraction now triggered by wild flights into gold by speculators whom central bankers themselves might imitate tomorrow if they finally lost their nerve. The way to do this is *not* to close the private gold market, thereby transferring its activities to black or gray markets as in the late 1940's and early 1950's. It is to warn speculators that central banks no longer need gold as their ultimate reserve asset, are ready to use instead a new reserve asset jointly created and managed by them, and are therefore able and willing to dump in free gold markets the billions of dollars of sterile gold which they now hold.

This may well correspond to the ultimate objectives of the new gold pool plans rumored to have been proposed at Basle by Undersecretary of the Treasury Deming earlier this month. To make such proposals truly negotiable, however, we must stop overplaying our hand as we have done so often, and at such costs.

We cannot realistically expect to negotiate any agreement that would permit us to elude indefinitely the correction of our persistent balance-of-payments deficits either through bilateral palming-off of further dollar IOU's on foreign central banks, or through large and automatic earmarking in our favor (26 percent) of the new reserve asset proposed at Rio, but which is unlikely to see the light of day as long as our deficits continue on the present scale. We might be forced, *like other countries,* to accelerate the re-equilibration of our accounts, and to finance our tapering-off deficits through gold losses and recourse to our still huge drawing rights ($5.5 billion) on the International Monetary Fund. We can, on the other hand, reasonably expect to negotiate an agreement protecting us against the danger of massive conversions into gold of the huge indebtedness incurred by us over the last half century of this absurd Monte Carlo roulette game dignified under the name of "gold-exchange standard."

I am deeply convinced that the U.S. national interests, as well as those of the world, will be served far better in this way than by protracted delays and ultimate failure of negotiating aims unacceptable to other countries, or by short-sighted attempts to extract unlimited financing from reluctant partners in any "dollar area" scheme, or by the monetary chaos and economic warfare which either of these techniques would be bound to unleash in the end.

The new restrictions announced by the Administration on January 1 are primarily a hurried response to an immediate concern: plug the dramatically widening gold leak from Fort Knox. They may do so in the short run, even though the *net* "improvement" to be expected from them is likely to remain far short of the $3 billion optimistically aimed at. Direct investments financed abroad are exempt from the ceilings established, but much of this financing will come from foreign funds withdrawn from New York, or which otherwise have been placed in New York. Moreover, our hopes of improving our balance by $3 billion and Britain's hopes of improving its balance by $1.2 billion are unlikely to be matched by an accepted deterioration of $4.2 billion either in Continental Europe, whose surpluses totaled less than $700 million in the first three quarters of last year, or in the rest of the world where they barely reached $350 million. New troubles and spiraling of restrictions are likely to be forced upon other countries by our measures, just as they were forced upon us by the aftermath of the British devaluation.

As for our own longer run aims and policies, the new program confirms, but does not resolve, the dilemma highlighted above:

1. It can—and I hope should—be interpreted as a laudable and long overdue attempt to pave the way for a quicker and fuller agreement on a negotiable plan for international monetary reform, by meeting the European objections to our huge and persistent deficits. It even centers our proposed measures on an effort to reduce drastically the splurge of direct investments which some of them have denounced as a "take-over" of their industrial establishment by American capital.

2. The plan could also be interpreted, however, as a further move toward a "dollar area" solution, discriminating *in favor* of the countries which refrain from converting their dollars into gold—*i.e.* the under-developed countries, the United Kingdom, Canada, Japan, Australia, etc.—and *against* those, "principally Continental Western Europe," which refuse to finance our deficits in this way.

I suspect that the Administration itself remains deeply divided as to which of these two directions it will take in the forthcoming months. It might be forced into the second if the surplus countries of Continental Western Europe failed to respond constructively to the first. An international solution to what is, after all, an international problem will require their cooperation as well as ours. Neither is ensured as yet.

THE PRESENT SYSTEM AND ITS DEFECTS

Warren L. Smith

Professor of Economics,
University of Michigan

The basic principles of the international monetary system are as follows:

1. Each country is quite jealously insistent on its sovereign right to regulate internal demand for the purpose of maintaining suitable economic conditions at home in terms of employment and the behavior of its internal price level.

2. Free international movement of goods and of capital as a means of achieving efficient use of resources is a generally accepted goal, and substantial progress has been made in achieving it. In particular, since the advent of general currency convertibility in 1958, controls over the international flow of capital have been relaxed and investors have become increasingly inclined to shift funds internationally in response to differential changes in expected rates of return.

3. Trade is conducted under a system of fixed exchange parities at any particular time, with actual exchange rates fluctuating only within very narrow limits around these parities. The maintenance of fixed parities is a highly prized objective; nevertheless, provision is made for parity adjustments under the rules of the IMF as a means of dealing with "fundamental" balance-of-payments disequilibria.

4. Countries hold limited supplies of monetary reserves in the form of gold, dollar balances, and (to a lesser extent) sterling balances. In addition, lines of credit are available at the IMF; portions of these credit

From Prepared Statement of Warren L. Smith, in *Guidelines for International Monetary Reform,* Hearings before the Subcommittee on International Exchange and Payments of the Joint Economic Committee, 89th Cong., first sess., 1965 (Washington, D.C.: U.S. Government Printing Office, 1965), pp. 60–62.

lines are available virtually automatically and are practically the equivalent of "owned" reserves, while the remaining portions are available on conditions that become increasingly stringent as the amount borrowed increases. The reserves available and potentially obtainable set a limit—though a somewhat elastic one—on the cumulative size of a country's balance-of-payments deficit. Thus, each country operates subject to a "balance-of-payments constraint"—not in the sense that payments must always be in balance but in the sense that there is some limit on the size and duration of deficits that can be tolerated. It is important to note that there is no corresponding limit for surpluses.

A little more needs to be said concerning the goal of internal stability (item 1 in the above list). It is often said the countries seek the twin goals of "full employment" and "price stability." However, a more accurate way of describing the situation is as follows: There is in each country a "trade-off" between employment (or unemployment) and price stability; that is, over a considerable range the more unemployment is reduced by policies to expand the aggregate demand the higher is the price that must be paid in terms of inflation. This relation holds primarily because of the tendency for money-wage increases to outstrip increased in productivity even under conditions of substantial unemployment. The trade-off varies from country to country, depending on the organization, traditions, and aggressiveness of the labor movement, the price policies followed by industry, and so on, and from time to time depending upon the attendant circumstances. The trade-off may be influenced by policy measure—wage-price guideposts, income policies, etc.—but I am not aware of any cases in which efforts to change it have been notably successful. Not only does the trade-off between price stability and employment vary from country to country but so also do the relative weights attached to these two objectives in the hierarchy of values that govern the behavior of the authorities responsible for economic policy in the various countries. As a consequence, to the extent that each country is left free to decide what combination of price inflation and employment to select from the many choices open to it, price trends may vary from country to country.

Price stability is often given a high priority in the list of objectives of economic policy, not only for individual countries but for the world as a whole. It seems to me that the evidence is overwhelming, however, that price stability can really be attained on a continuing basis only at a cost in terms of unemployment and underutilization of economic resources that is not only politically unacceptable but probably socially undesirable in most countries. This is true not only because the wage-price determination mechanism tends to set in motion a "creeping" rise in the price level before an acceptable level of unemployment has been reached, but also because prices are much more prone to rise in times and at places in which demand for goods and services is rising than to fall under conditions where such demand is declining. I believe that the achievement of an acceptable rate of utilization of economic resources requires that the world be willing to accept—and, indeed, underwrite—a mild upward drift in the general level of prices, unless, of course, some as yet undiscovered means can be used to damp the tendency toward price and wage increases without reducing the overall level of demand.

There are three grave difficulties with the existing system as described above, admittedly in a slightly idealized way.

1. The first—and in many ways the most fundamental—difficulty is that the system contains no mechanism that can be depended upon to eliminate a balance-of-payments disequilibrium brought about by such disruptive forces as changes in tastes or technology. There are three possible ways of correcting a deficit or surplus by adjustment of the current account: through the use of trade or exchange controls, through an adjustment of exchange rates, and through internal price and income changes. Since all of these violate the principles of the system, they are ruled out. Consequently, when a country experiences a deficit, there is no assurance that the deficit will be eliminated before its limited supply of reserves is used up.

2. The system as it is now constituted is subject in extreme degree to destabilizing speculative tendencies which greatly complicate the problems of balance-of-payments adjustment. Although, as indicated above, fixed exchange rates appear to be one of the generally accepted goals of economic policy, we do not now have a system of really fixed rates. Indeed, the present arrangements, under which exchange rates are fixed within very narrow limits at any particular time but are subject to readjustment from time to time to correct "fundamental" disequilibria in national balances of payments, seem ideally calculated to encourage speculation. Since opportunities for the investment of capital, viewed broadly, do not ordinarily vary widely as between major countries, even a mild suspicion that a country may devalue its currency can cause a speculative outflow of capital from that country.

And, as more and more investors become familiar with the possibilities of transferring capital internationally, it seems probable that the potential size of speculative capital flows may become even larger. The result of this situation is that most countries will entertain the possibility of devaluation only in the most dire emergency, but the threat is nevertheless sufficient to induce speculation. And there is always the possibility that speculation will exhaust the country's reserves and force the devaluation that speculators are hoping for.

3. The third difficulty—and the one that I regard as least serious because easiest to correct—is that the present system contains no orderly arrangement for generating in a predictable way the increased quantities of international monetary reserves that are needed to meet the demands of a growing world economy. Increments to the world's monetary reserves are provided primarily by gold production (less the amount of gold that is absorbed in consumption and in hoards) and by additional dollars that are pumped into official reserves by U.S. deficits. Gold production is generally agreed to be capable of producing only a relatively small fraction of the additions to reserves that are needed, and the end to U.S. deficits, which may now be imminent, will shut off the flow of dollars.

The matter of speculative instability—the second of the three problems referred to above—merits some further amplification. The speculative threat to the stability of the system, which I believe is very serious, has two distinguishable aspects: (1) the threat imposed by the "overhang" of convertible claims against the monetary reserves of the reserve-currency countries—especially the United States—that are held by the monetary authorities of other countries; and (2) the danger of private speculative "runs" against currencies that are under pressure. The first of these dangers is present only in the case of reserve-currency countries. It has been an important factor in accentuating the difficulties of the United States, because as our continuing deficits have been settled partly in gold and partly through increases in the dollar holdings of foreign central banks, the ratio of our gold reserves to our outstanding dollar liabilities to foreign official agencies has declined, and fears that the dollar might have to be devalued have increased. This generates pressure for foreign central banks to convert outstanding dollars into gold and to insist on the settlement of current U.S. deficits in gold. This depletes U.S. gold reserves and weakens confidence in the dollar.

The second of the two dangers referred to above, that of private speculation against a currency that is under pressure, is, in my judgment, more fundamental and serious than the first and also more difficult to correct. In the first place, this threat is not confined to reserve-currency countries, although it may be more serious for such countries partly because it may be stimulated by reserve drains resulting from conversions of official holdings of reserve currencies. Under the present adjustable-peg exchange rate system, as long as there is some limit on the available supply of monetary reserves, any country whose currency comes under pressure as a result of a serious balance-of-payments deficit can easily get into a position where a devaluation of its currency (or the application of direct controls) is regarded as a serious possibility by private investors. This can quickly generate a speculative "run" which will reduce its reserves still further, thereby strengthening the fears of devaluation and leading to a self-generating increase in the rate of decline of its reserves. It is important to recognize that the entire stock of claims denominated in a particular currency is potentially available to participate in a private run on that currency. Since this includes claims held internally as well as externally, the possibilities are practically unlimited.

BACKGROUND NOTES: THE WORKINGS OF OUR INTERNATIONAL MONETARY SYSTEM

THE FOREIGN EXCHANGE MARKET

The most noticeable difference between domestic and international trade is that more than one national currency is generally involved in international transactions. Suppose a merchant in New York is trying to decide whether to purchase a shipment of wine from California or from France. He needs to know not only the price of the California wine in dollars and of the French wine in francs, but also the price at which dollars can be converted into francs and vice-versa, i.e., the exchange rate between the franc and the dollar.

In general, traders wish to receive payment ultimately in their own currency. Thus a sale of French wine to a merchant in the United States gives rise to a demand for French francs for payment. This would be true whether the sale were denominated in dollars or in francs. In the second case, the U.S. merchant would have to sell dollars to buy francs in order to meet payment. In the first case (which occurs more often), the French seller on acquiring dollars would probably want to convert them into francs, which could be used in his own country. Similarly, a demand for francs would arise if the New York merchant paid for the wine with francs he had in possession and then sought to replenish his foreign exchange holdings.

But what is the source of the supply of francs? The immediate source is foreign exchange dealers, which are usually large commercial banks. International exchange is always going on, and, therefore, there is a continual demand for currency conversion. Our New York merchant buys French wine and thus needs to buy francs (sell dollars), while a French firm purchases U.S. electronic equipment and thus has to buy dollars (sell francs). British firms are buying U.S. aircraft and demanding dollars (selling pounds) while purchases of Beatles' records by U.S. teenagers give rise to demand for pounds (supply of dollars).

17

Similarly, American firms acquiring subsidiaries in Europe supply dollars to obtain the foreign exchange for payment, and Canadians investing in the New York Stock Exchange need U.S. dollars to pay for the stocks they buy. These demands and supplies are matched up by foreign exchange dealers (usually large commercial banks), who act as intermediaries in the process of international exchange.

As may have been suspected by this point, there is a close connection between the aggregates of these demands and supplies in the foreign exchange market and a country's balance of payments, which records its international transactions. The question of what happens if all these demands and supplies don't balance is the same as that of what happens if a country has a balance of payments surplus or deficit. A country's imports of goods and services and its international investment, foreign aid, and military expenditures abroad, etc., give rise to demands for foreign currency (supplies of domestic currency). Its exports of goods and services, receipts of foreign investment and gifts, etc., give rise to supplies of foreign currency (demands for domestic currency).

In a free market, if quantity demanded exceeds quantity supplied at a given price, then the price of the good in question is bid up until the market is equilibrated, i.e., until quantities demanded and supplied are equal. The same would hold in a free market for foreign exchange. If the quantity of francs demanded exceeded the quantity supplied at a given exchange rate, then the competition of foreign exchange dealers for the scarce francs would bid up their price in terms of other currencies. Alternatively, we could say that an excess supply of dollars (the excess of dollars supplied over dollars demanded at the initial exchange rate) was forcing down the price of the dollar vis-à-vis the franc. Thus under a free market in foreign exchange, changes in exchange rates (the relative prices of currencies) would always equilibrate the foreign exchange market. There would be no need for concern over a country's balance of payments situation.

This is, in fact, the strongest argument in favor of countries leaving their foreign exchange markets free to provide such an equilibrating function. However, the situation is not that simple. It will be remembered that our New York merchant wanted to compare prices of foreign and domestic products in terms of a common standard, and for this he had to convert prices in francs into dollars. If there is a fixed price of the franc vis-à-vis the dollar, then it is no more difficult to compare the prices of California and French wines than it is to compare the prices of California and New York wines. If, however, the franc-dollar exchange rate is continually changing, then an additional uncertainty is brought into the merchant's decision. At an exchange rate of $.20 to the franc, French wine might be a very good buy, while if the rate of exchange were to be bid up to $.25, California wine might be preferred.[1]

Thus many feel that to reap the full benefits of international trade, exchange rates between currencies should be fixed. In fact, the question of whether exchange rates should be fixed or free to vary is one of the key controversies surrounding the operation of the international monetary system. The fixed versus flexible exchange rate question is explored in Part IV of this volume.

As was mentioned by Warren L. Smith, fixed exchange rates are one of the central aspects of our postwar international monetary system. This system has its basis in the agreements reached at the international conference held at Bretton Woods, New Hampshire, in 1944. Under this system, countries keep the value of their currencies pegged, i.e., fixed, in relation to the dollar within a narrow margin of the declared par value (one per cent in either direction). In turn, the price of the dollar is pegged to gold at $35 an ounce (again plus or minus a small margin).

Suppose there is a sudden drop in the demand for British exports. This would mean that at the original exchange rate, less pounds would be demanded than before. The price of the pound would begin to fall in the foreign exchange market. To keep the price within its prescribed limits of parity, the British authorities (the Bank of England) would have to enter the foreign exchange market, buying up the excess supply of pounds with sales of dollars. As with agricultural price supports or any other form of price fixing, the pegging authority must stand ready to buy all that is offered if the price sinks to its lower support limit and to sell all that is demanded if the price rises to its upper support limit.

It is important to realize that the ability of countries to maintain the price of their currencies is not symmetrical with respect to upward and downward pressures. National monetary authorities control the issue of their own currencies. Therefore there is no limit, except their own will or desire, as to how much of their currency they sell on the foreign exchange market in order to keep its price from rising above the upper limit.

However, in the case of keeping the price of a currency from falling below its parity floor, the authority must buy up the excess quantities of its domestic currency on the foreign exchange market, and this requires that it sell foreign exchange. Its ability to do this is dependent upon its command over foreign exchange, i.e., the quantity of international reserves that it owns or is able to borrow.

These excess demands and supplies that we have been discussing correspond closely to a country's balance of payments surplus or deficit as defined according to the official settlements concept.[2] Thus what we have been saying may be summarized as follows: Under the present international monetary system, surpluses or deficits in a country's balance of payments may occur because exchange rates are not left free to adjust to clear the foreign exchange market. There are no concrete limits to the amount and duration of a country's balance of payments surplus, but its ability to run a deficit is limited by the size of its international reserves and its ability to borrow. International reserves are not used to finance trade directly. They are used to settle payments imbalances.

ARE PAYMENTS DEFICITS GOOD OR BAD?

To any reader of newspapers in the United States or Great Britain, it is clear that payments deficits are considered to be a bad thing. But why? After all, the end purpose of international trade is to obtain goods from abroad at less cost than they can be produced at home. Imports are the fruits of international trade. A trade deficit (excess of imports over exports) means that more goods and services are being received from abroad than are being given up.[3] Surely this must be a good thing from the point of view of the deficit country! And it would be—if this were as far as the story goes. The problem is that the financing of such a deficit means that the country is losing reserves or is borrowing abroad (i.e., it is living off its savings or credit), and this may not be a comfortable situation.

Often the policies a country must undertake to correct a deficit, such as deflationary domestic financial policies, balance of payments controls, or devaluation of its currency, will conflict with one or more of its other major objectives, as was indicated by Smith. In other words, policy measures to adjust deficits in a country's balance of payments are often considered to be costly. Sufficient international reserves are desired to give a country a wide range of choice of methods to adjust its balance of payments, including ones which might take a long time for their favorable effects to occur. They also allow the country to ride out temporary deficits, such as might occur from shifts of short term speculative funds without the need to make adjustments which would soon be reversed.

Thus "the function of international reserves . . . is to render exchange-rate stability compatible with freedom for individual countries to pursue their national economic goals." [59, p. 4] However, such freedom for a deficit country would be complete only if it had unlimited reserves. By drawing down its reserves or using up its borrowing power, a deficit country reduces the immediate conflict between balance of payments equilibrium and other objectives, but at the same time it is increasing the potentiality for future conflict.

Given the advantages to deficit or potential deficit countries of large reserve holdings, why should there be any objection to the creation of such reserves in unlimited amounts? The reason is that countries that are accumulating reserves via balance of payments surpluses vis-à-vis deficit countries, do not have an unlimited demand for such reserves. The accumulation of reserves in this manner exerts an expansionary force on the domestic economy, and under the present system charges of "imported inflation" by surplus countries have been frequent.

In fact, this is the manner in which the international monetary system was supposed to operate under the old gold standard. Under the "rules of the game," national money supplies were to be tied to gold holdings. Since payments imbalances were settled by gold flows, countries in surplus would find that they were inflating as gold flowed in, while the countries losing gold because of their deficits would be contracting. The prices of goods in the surplus countries would increase relative to those in the deficit countries, and in this manner payments imbalances would be corrected.

In practice, because of wage and price rigidities, the deflationary pressures in deficit countries often resulted more in increases in unemployment than in decreases in prices. This is one of the major reasons why most countries today are not willing to accept this method of automatic balance of payments adjustment. We should emphasize that the problem is not that this "classical" method of adjustment will not work. Even with rigid wages and prices, deflationary policies will improve the trade balance; for as unemployment increases, income and the demand for imports will fall. The problem is that this method of adjustment is considered to be too costly in terms of other objectives, especially that of stabilizing income and employment.

To return to the point of view of surplus countries, in today's world of managed money supplies the inflationary effects of a balance of payments surplus can be offset by appropriate domestic financial policies. However, if such sterilization of the effects of surpluses is undertaken, then the natural forces tending to correct the surplus are held in check. Undesired surpluses of this kind represent inefficient resource use in the form of involuntary foreign lending. Such a surplus means there is an excess of domestic production over the domestic utilization of goods and services, an excess not consciously and deliberately lent to foreigners or given as foreign aid. "From the surplus country's own point of view it is a mere hoarding of resources that might have enhanced future output and welfare if added to domestic capital formation, or created present welfare if used to augment domestic consumption or government spending." [59, pp. 6–7]

In summary, under a system of fixed exchange rates, there is no mechanism for systematic balance of payments adjustment that does not conflict with other major objectives. Of course, if fixed rates are themselves an objective, then we are clearly in a situation in which all objectives cannot be obtained simultaneously, as was indicated by Smith.

BRETTON WOODS AND THE ADJUSTABLE PEG

The international monetary system set up at Bretton Woods was not designed to be based on immutably fixed exchange rates, as was the old gold standard. The structure of the system designed at Bretton Woods was strongly affected by the great depression of the 1930's and the resulting spiral of exchange controls and competitive currency depreciations (which in fact did little to change relative exchange rates). These events made the delegates to the Bretton Woods Conference skeptical both of a system of flexible rates, which they feared would facilitate competitive depreciation, and of permanently fixed rates because of the sacrifice of control over domestic full employment policies which they would imply.

In the hope of avoiding the anticipated evils of either extreme, an "adjustable peg" system was devised. Exchange rates were to be pegged (fixed) within narrow margins. An International Monetary Fund was established with a pool of currencies that could be drawn on for the temporary financing of deficits.[4] It was hoped that countries' foreign exchange reserves, international co-operation, and the lending facilities of the Fund would be sufficient to tide countries over most balance of payments difficulties.

The maintenance of employment and avoidance of controls over international *trade* (though not *capital* movements) were considered to be higher priority goals than perfect exchange rate stability. Thus, in the case of persistent or "fundamental" disequilibrium, a country would rely upon a change in its exchange rate to restore payments balance.[5] It was hoped that such a system would give the benefits of having fixed rates in the short run but flexible rates in the long run (via discrete changes in the values at which exchange rates were pegged).

As the "adjustable peg" system has actually operated, however, critics have claimed with considerable justification that it has combined the *worst* rather than the *best* features of the extremes of permanently fixed and freely flexible exchange rates. We might characterize this difficulty by observing that the exchange rate changes which give long run flexibility must always occur in some short run. One of the key features surrounding the operation of a fixed rate system, such as the gold standard or regional adjustment within a country, is the ease with which private capital can be attracted to help finance deficits. In other words, within a currency area or between countries the relative values of whose currencies are fixed, large quantities of private capital will move in response to small changes in interest rates.

Under an adjustable peg, however, the very time when a country desires most to rely upon such borrowing is when its ability to maintain the level of its exchange rate is under suspicion. A devaluation could wipe out the gains to foreign lenders from even a large interest differential in favor of the depreciating country.

Unlike freely flexible rates, the direction in which an exchange rate is to be altered is always clear under the adjustable peg system. Not only does this hinder the attraction of foreign funds during a period of balance of payments deficit, but the basic difficulty may be compounded by an outflow of domestic funds in anticipation of devaluation. In fact, such an outflow could lead to a devaluation that would otherwise have been unnecessary. Thus it can be argued that an adjustable peg system tends to maximize adverse ("destabilizing") speculation, the second problem mentioned by Smith.

Along with the problem of destabilizing speculation, a tendency has developed to consider changes in the par value of a currency as major political catastrophes. The resulting reluctance to devalue in the face of prolonged deficits has led to considerable dissatisfaction with the operation of our adjustable peg system of exchange rates.[6]

also ## INTERNATIONAL LIQUIDITY AND THE INTERNATIONAL MONETARY FUND *but too broad paper.*

Another criticism which has been raised against the present international monetary system is that its provision of international liquidity is unsatisfactory.[7] Both the composition or quality of liquidity and the capacity for its systematic growth over time in an expanding world economy have been questioned.[8]

Under the international monetary system that emerged from the Bretton Woods Conference, there were two sources of international reserves: gold and foreign currencies ("foreign exchange"). Hence the system has been given the name "the gold-exchange" or "reserve currency" standard. The role of the International Monetary Fund is not to create reserves. It is like a savings and loan association rather than a commercial bank. It can lend the funds which it has, but it cannot create new funds, as a bank creates deposits.

The Fund's resources consist of a stock of gold and a pool of currencies. Both are contributed by the payment of quotas by member countries. The amount of these quotas (determined by such factors as the size of a country's international trade, reserves, and national income) determines both a country's voting power and its borrowing power in the Fund. A member of the Fund has an automatic right to draw (borrow) funds up to the amount of its quota (generally 25 per cent) that it paid in gold.[9] This is called the "gold tranche." After that, a country normally may borrow an additional 100 per cent of its quota, subject to the stipulation that not more than 25 per cent (one "credit tranche") can be borrowed in any one year.[10] Conditions for borrowing become increasingly stringent at each additional credit tranche. The basis of these conditions is that the borrowing country follow suitable adjustment policies to cure its balance of payments deficit.

As Sidney E. Rolfe has commented:

In essence, the I.M.F. provides a progressively conditional source of liquidity for its members, the limit of which is a *fixed* quota. It does not supplant other sources of international reserves, nor does it allow any discretion on the part of its managers to adjust liquidity availability—except within the very narrow limits which allow flexibility in granting drawing rights. [56, p. 80]

Thus the IMF does not provide a source of systematically increasing liquidity. Quotas can be changed, and they were increased by 50 per cent in 1959 and 25 per cent in 1965. However, each increase must be negotiated anew with the entire membership of the Fund. Even with these quota increases, total United States drawing rights, for example, are in the same order of magnitude as many of the annual deficits which the U.S. has run since 1958.

The inadequacy of the size of the Fund to handle its task of fostering short run exchange rate stability was indicated clearly by the necessity of negotiating the "General Arrangements to Borrow" in 1962 and by the proliferation of bilateral "currency swap" agreements between countries designed to extend credit in the case of speculative pressure on the other country's currency. The General Arrangements to Borrow represent a multilateral arrangement under which ten major countries (including the United States and Britain) agree to lend funds to the IMF in times of exchange crisis. These funds would be made available for the support of the currency under attack. The total commitment under this agreement is $6 billion (although this figure overstates the effective size when it is the balance of payments of one of the member countries that is in difficulty). Such cooperative actions have proven to be quite effective in combating short-run speculative pressures, but they cannot serve as a full substitute for a systematic growth of reserves over time.

Nor have the other sources of international reserves provided a systematic increase in liquidity. As was indicated by Robert Triffin, the role of gold production in augmenting reserves has declined sharply, due largely to increasing private purchases by industrial users and by speculators and hoarders. The remaining source of additional liquidity has been increases in official holdings of foreign currencies. The vast majority of such balances are dollars and pounds, and official holdings of pounds have not increased at all in the postwar period. Thus increases in dollar holdings have served as the major source of additions to reserves.

This leads to two of the major sources of difficulties that have characterized the operation of the international monetary system in recent years: (1) Increases in liquidity have been closely connected with the size of U.S. deficits. (2) As the quantity of dollar holdings increases, the quality decreases. Before considering these problems in greater detail, however, we should consider why foreign central banks were willing to hold dollars rather than gold in the first place.

THE DOLLAR: GOOD AS GOLD?

At the end of World War II, it was clear that dollars were as good as gold. As was mentioned earlier, the United States agreed to meet its exchange rate obligations under the International Monetary Fund by standing ready to convert dollars freely into gold or vice-versa for foreign central banks at a fixed price of $35 an ounce. In the early postwar period, there was no doubt in the ability of the United States to fulfill this obligation. Between 1934 and 1940, some $16 billion of gold had flowed into the United States, giving it three quarters of total official gold holdings in the world. At the end of World War II, U.S. gold holdings were more than double its liquid liabilities to foreigners, while British liquid liabilities were almost three times gold reserves.

Not only were dollar holdings as good as gold; they were better, for they earned interest. While reserve holdings in other currencies also could earn interest, none of the corresponding capital markets (with the exception of London) possessed the breadth and efficiency and the scope of financial instruments available in the New York market. Furthermore, immediately following the war, the United States was the principal source of supply of goods for the reconstruction of Europe, and, of course, dollars could be converted directly into American goods and services. A still further factor was that the dollar is the primary intervention currency. As discussed earlier, it is dollars which foreign central banks must buy and sell in the foreign exchange market to uphold their IMF obligations.[11]

Thus, during the early operation of the Bretton Woods system, what was relevant to foreign monetary authorities was really not the convertibility of dollars into gold, but of gold into dollars. It is little wonder that the moderate U.S. deficits during the early and middle 1950's gave no cause for concern. In fact, most of the literature of that period was concerned with dollar shortage rather than glut.

This situation has changed, however, and since the late 1950's there has been considerable concern on both sides of the Atlantic over the size of U.S. deficits. This change in attitudes was a reflection of the sharp increase in the average size of U.S. deficits, combined with a growing feeling on the part of European countries that their reserves had been rebuilt to satisfactory levels.

As was indicated earlier, for non-reserve currency countries the discipline of a payments deficit is felt through the drawing down of one's limited reserves in support of the existing currency parity. However, when the United States runs a deficit, surplus countries are obligated to purchase excess dollars so that their currencies will not appreciate above the one per cent limit. To the extent that such purchases are not desired to build up a country's reserves, they represent involuntary lending to the United States.[12]

There is nothing that a surplus country can do directly to stop the accumulation of unwanted reserves, except to take measures to reduce its own surplus. Why would a country be hesitant to do this? Because, as Fritz Machlup argues:

. . . a country would have to pursue policies which it may want to avoid: appreciation of the currency, price and income inflation, or abolition of restrictions on imports. Currency appreciation is unpopular because it injures export industries (less able to compete in foreign markets) and industries competing with imports (becoming available at reduced prices); in addition, it reduces the value of gold and foreign assets held by the central bank (causing it a sometimes embarrassing capital loss). Domestic inflation is unpopular because of inequitable effects on income distribution and because of induced inefficiencies in the allocation of resources. The abolition of import restrictions is resisted by protected industries, their stockholders, workers and representatives in the legislature. [46, p. 28]

Of course, if the costs of a surplus exceed the costs of adjustment, then measures to reduce the surplus will be taken, such as the small German and Dutch currency appreciations in 1961. However, from the point of view of the surplus countries, the most desirable solution is for the deficit countries to take actions to correct their payments imbalances. The lower are the levels of their reserves, the greater is the pressure on deficit countries to adjust. Hence the traditional opposition of surplus countries to rapid expansion of international liquidity, and the advocacy of such expansion on the part of deficit countries.

The ability of the U.S. monetary authorities to pay out dollars to finance deficits is unlimited. In other words, if other countries were willing always to accept and hold the dollar outflows resulting from U.S. deficits, then the U.S. would have the ability to finance unlimited deficits. It could expand international liquidity as it desired. As Jacques Rueff states in a later paper in this volume, the United States would be in the position of an individual to whom merchants had agreed to return the amount of his bills on the day they were paid.

However, the U.S. *gold stock* is not infinite. Therefore the ability of the United States to finance deficits *via gold losses* is limited. By converting dollars into gold, other countries can put pressure on the U.S. to correct its deficit. (Of course, moral suasion also can be used for this purpose.) It is significant that the *percentage* of U.S. deficits settled by gold sales (or "losses," as they are commonly referred to in the press) have increased as the size of U.S. deficits has increased. In 1965, gold sales actually exceeded the size of the U.S. deficit, i.e., official foreign dollar holdings actually declined, as previously earned dollars were presented for conversion into gold.[13]

In fact, one can say that 1965 marked the end of the gold exchange standard as it had operated during the postwar period. To the extent that U.S. deficits are accompanied by corresponding gold sales, no increase in international liquidity takes place. Reserves are only redistributed.[14] Official foreign dollar holdings began to rise again in 1966, but this was due largely to the American appeals for international cooperation, mentioned by Triffin. These appeals were designed "to apply the brakes on gold conversions which might topple the system by raiding the gold cellars of Fort Knox." In other words, there was an increase in the trend toward what Sir Roy Harrod has termed inconvertibility by gentleman's agreement. "The financial or monetary gold-exchange standard was transformed into a political-exchange standard." [28, p. 165]

The reason for such actions was that by this time the prolonged U.S. deficits had led to a situation in which private and official foreign dollar holdings amounted to almost twice the U.S. gold stock. The U.S. no longer possessed enough gold to pay off its short term liabilities to foreigners if they all were presented at once.[15] Of course, one would not expect all foreign-owned dollars to be presented for conversion at once. As a world banker, the United States should be able to operate on a fractional reserve basis, as do commercial banks within a country. However, recognition of this point should not lead one to the other extreme, to the view that the U.S. bank cannot overextend its credit issue.

While the IMF and most major countries stand ready to help the United States in the case of an international run on the bank, such support is not unlimited. Under the present international monetary system, there is no lender of last resort with powers such as the Federal Reserve Banks have with respect to commercial banks in the United States today. Unfortunately, our present international monetary system is more analogous to the U.S. domestic banking system of the *previous* century, and the record of banking crises during that period is hardly reassuring.

The reasons why foreigners were anxious to hold dollars after World War II have been outlined. However, today many no longer feel that the dollar is as good as gold. While it is true that foreign dollar holdings now exceed the value of the U.S. gold stock (at the present price of gold), this is not the direct reason for the decline in preference for dollars relative to gold. The chief reason is that it is anticipated by many that the likely result of a massive conversion of dollars into gold would be an increase in the price of gold vis-à-vis the dollar and perhaps other currencies as well. As Leland B. Yeager has stated:

> Although it is more nearly true that gold gets its value from its link with the dollar than that the dollar gets its value from its link with gold, gold is first-class money and the dollar second-class money. The asymmetrical changeability of the link explains the paradox: Under present policies, gold is as good as dollars (except for not bearing interest) because the United States stands ready to buy it with dollars at a fixed price; and it seems even better than dollars because people believe that any change in its price can only be upward. International liquidity is defective nowadays not because dollars are used but because the dollars have an artificial second-class status, being precariously tied to gold on a fractional-reserve basis and therefore vulnerable to speculation. [32, p. 157]

As is considered in several of the readings in Part IV, if the United States responded to such a run by cutting the link between gold and the dollar instead, it is likely that the price of gold would *fall* instead of rising relative to the dollar. In fact, there is some indication that recognition of this possibility by foreign official dollar holders has been one of the reasons for their moderation in converting dollars. (Probably an even stronger reason, however, has been the fear of the political consequences of a breakdown in the system.)

We have reached a paradoxical situation in which the very susceptibility of the dollar has placed self-imposed constraints on the ability of
foreign official dollar holders to discipline the United States via gold
conversions. In making large-scale conversions of dollars into gold, foreign authorities would run the risk of precipitating a run on the dollar
with consequences that they may consider quite undesirable. Meanwhile, the continuation of large deficits by the United States runs the
same risk.

SUMMARY AND PREVIEW

Throughout most of its history, the Bretton Woods system has served
the world economy reasonably well. During the 1950's, remarkable
strides were made toward the reduction of trade barriers and payments restrictions. As Gottfried Haberler was able to write in 1965:

Broadly speaking and comparing the postwar performance with earlier
periods, especially the inter-war period, it would seem that the present system has done very well indeed. The world economy has developed quite
satisfactorily since the war. World trade has grown by leaps and bounds, not
only in value, but also in real volume (in terms of constant prices). The
annual compound rate of growth in real terms was something like 6 percent
a year, which is very high historically speaking, even if we allow for the
fact that the starting point at the end of the war was a very low one. [24, p.
2]

However, in a sense the system was operating during this period on
borrowed time. The "tearless deficits" of the 1950's have left a legacy
to the United States (and the rest of the world) in the form of the
large "overhang" of foreign dollar holdings, which threaten a confidence
crisis. Furthermore, the major source of expanding international liquidity has dried up. This occurred not via elimination of the U.S. deficit
(as many anticipated) but rather via diminution in the *quality* of the
dollar in the view of many foreign holders. The proliferation of balance
of payments controls imposed by the United States beginning in the
middle of the 1960's, further testifies to the costliness of balance of payments adjustment when exchange rate changes are ruled out. It is clear
that Triffin has considerable cause when he writes "the gold-exchange
standard is dead or dying."
As is further illustrated in Parts II and III of this volume, the need

for some kind of reform of our international monetary system is clear. In 1967 and 1968, several significant steps in the direction of reform were taken. Plans were established for the creation of a new international reserve asset (Special Drawing Rights) and the London gold pool was closed. In Part IV these steps and the other major proposals for reform are examined. Also considered are the likely consequences if agreement for reform is *not* obtained.

NOTES

1. In the United States, exchange rates are usually reported in terms of the number of dollars which it takes to purchase one unit of foreign currency. Thus our exchange rate with Britain is $2.40 = £1. Prior to the British devaluation of November 1967, the dollar-pound rate was $2.80. So it now takes 40 cents less to buy a pound than it did prior to that date. In other words, the pound was devalued by 40/2.80 = 14.3 per cent.
2. The various concepts of a balance of payments surplus or deficit are considered in the Introduction to Part II.
3. A qualification is in order, since countries realize mutual gains from trade. Thus even with balanced trade between two countries, both would be getting more benefit, in effect, than they were giving up. The point is that if one country's imports increased while its exports fell, then during that period it would be receiving even more benefit while giving up even less.
4. The Articles of Agreement of the International Monetary Fund were signed by 44 countries at the Bretton Woods Conference in 1944. There are now over 100 members of the Fund.
5. If the new par value of its currency is within 10 per cent of the *original* par value registered with the Fund, the country need not obtain the permission of the Fund for the change. If the 10 per cent margin is exceeded, the change is permitted only if the Fund gives approval, and it can do so only in the case of a "fundamental disequilibrium" in the country's balance of payments. Although this is the legal situation according to the Articles of Agreement of the International Monetary Fund, in practice approval appears to be given without regard to the presence or absence of a "fundamental disequilibrium." The term is not defined in the Articles of Agreement. Its meaning has not become clear through experience other than that it entails a large and persistent deficit or surplus in a country's balance of payments.
6. This topic will be treated further in Part III.
7. A country's international liquidity, i.e., its means to finance balance of payments deficits, consists of its actual holdings of international reserves and its borrowing power to acquire additional reserves. While borrowing power is a complex concept, it is clearly greater, the greater the availability and the less the cost of such borrowing. For an excellent outline of the problem of international liquidity, see [10].
8. There is considerable debate over just what the proper rate of growth should be. This question will be considered in Part III.
9. Actually, the loan takes the form of a sale and repurchase agreement. The borrowing country exchanges its own currency for foreign exchange, and

agrees to reverse the transaction in the future. The maximum duration of a loan is 3 to 5 years. There are interest costs (called "service charges").

10. If a country's currency has itself been drawn by other countries, its borrowing rights are extended by this amount. Furthermore, members may apply for additional drawing rights based on short term declines in earnings from merchandise exports. This export compensatory facility was established by the Fund in 1963, and was designed primarily for the use of the developing countries.

11. A few countries peg their currencies *indirectly* to the dollar, through the intermediary of another currency. Thus, countries in the sterling area use their holdings of U.K. pounds to intervene in the foreign exchange market, but the pound itself is pegged to the dollar.

12. Thus, there is some truth to the European charge that the United States is using its deficit to help finance the take over of European industry (or, less polemically, to finance U.S. long term investment abroad). No doubt, the frequency of this charge is partially due to the fact that the United States has traditionally run a surplus on current account (i.e., on goods and services) but an even larger deficit on capital account. But a balance of payments deficit merely tells that certain accounts have failed to balance in aggregate. There is no clear presumption whether one should say that the capital account deficit is too large or the current account surplus is too small. Thus, just as logically (though perhaps less appealingly), one could say that such involuntary lending is helping to finance European exports!

As to whether the extent of U.S. investment in European industry is a good or bad thing, we merely mention here the observation of the French economist Pierre Uri that a century ago European capitalists owned a much higher proportion of America's industrial assets than U.S. firms now own of European companies. And, as Uri goes on to say, "the U.S. didn't do too badly."—*The Boston Globe,* January 28, 1968.

13. In part, but not entirely, this was due to the decision of France to convert about $1 billion of its dollar holdings into gold.

14. Expressed alternatively, the conversion of foreign held dollars into gold destroys international liquidity.

15. Although the United States will sell gold only to official dollar holders, foreign private holders can exchange dollars for other currencies or for gold in private gold markets. In the former case, the dollars are likely to end up in the hands of foreign central banks, which have the right to convert them.

PART II

The United States as World Banker

INTRODUCTION

THE KEY CURRENCY STATUS OF THE DOLLAR

The dollar is often called a reserve currency. This refers to its use by foreign central banks and treasuries as a part of their international reserves. This role, combined with the widespread use of the dollar as a medium of exchange and method of holding wealth by traders, individuals, and institutions, has given rise to the *key currency* status of the dollar. (This term was coined by John H. Williams [73].) Alternatively, it is said that the United States serves as *world banker*.

Because one of the crucial features of the present system is the role of the key currencies, especially the dollar, the question of what future role the dollar would play is an important issue in judging among the many plans for international reform. As Herbert G. Grubel has argued: "Nearly all people who discuss what influence world monetary reform is likely to have on the American Position as the World Banker start from the implicit, but important, assumption that this status is desirable and socially profitable [from the U.S. point of view]." [18, p. 189]

In discussing the advantages (and disadvantages) of being world banker, it is important to keep in mind the distinction between the private and official uses of the dollar. Neither role was planned. As Robert Aliber has commented: "The dollar became an international currency neither by Act of Congress nor by Act of God, but rather because it met various needs of foreign official institutions and foreign private parties more effectively than other financial assets could." [4, p. 8]

33

Many of the reasons for the international use of the dollar by official holders and by private traders, individuals, and institutions are the same. However, the two uses need not necessarily go hand in hand. If the reserve currency role of the dollar were terminated, for instance, by the creation of a full-fledged international central bank or the initiation of flexible exchange rates, its use by private traders and institutions would almost certainly remain. In fact, such a reform could very well increase the private use of the dollar; for it might lead to the removal of the restrictions which have been applied in recent years to partially segregate U.S. financial markets from the rest of. the world.[1]

Like domestic money, the dollar serves many functions as an international currency. One of its major uses is as a *vehicle* or *transactions* currency. It is estimated that over half of world trade is financed—and probably even more denominated—in dollars. If one looks at any international (and many foreign national) publications, one sees the role of the dollar as a standard of measurement. "The dollar is the world unit of account—the standard in which foreign-exchange reserves, agricultural prices in the Common Market, contributions to the United Nations budget, and a host of other international monetary items, are measured." [40, p. 2]

As a store of value, the dollar is used by official institutions as a form in which to hold reserves and by foreign private individuals and institutions as a depository of their savings. And, of course, New York serves as a capital market for the world. Even many foreign-issued securities are denominated in dollars.

The role of the United States as a banker or financial intermediary for Europe is discussed in the reading "The Dollar and World Liquidity" by Emile Despres, Charles P. Kindleberger, and Walter S. Salant. One of their major arguments is that the use of the dollar as an international currency makes the normal accounting procedures for measuring balance of payments deficits inapplicable for the United States. While the general consensus, both in the United States and abroad, has been that the U.S. balance of payments has been in significant disequilibrium for some time, this view is no longer unchallenged. Another critic is Gunther Ruff, who has argued, "The 'dollar crisis' is a sham and a delusion. We have allowed ourselves to become the victims of misinterpretation by Europeans of our balance-of-payments presentation." [58, p. 7]

IS THERE REALLY A U.S. BALANCE OF PAYMENTS DEFICIT?

To this point, we have frequently referred to balance of payments deficits without defining precisely what the term implies. In fact, attempts to reach a consensus on a precise, rigorous definition have not succeeded. Yet, "There must be some sense in this mysterious numbers game; to deny it would seem presumptuous." [43, p. 163]

The balance of payments accounts are a record of all of a country's international transactions (i.e., those of its individuals, institutions, and government agencies) in a given period of time. They are usually broken down into several major categories: exports and imports of goods and services, unilateral transfers (such as private remittances and foreign aid), long term and short term capital, and monetary gold.[2] In an accounting sense, the balance of payments always "balances." If all items are considered, total receipts must equal total payments— a simple reflection of the fact that the balance of payments is based on double-entry bookkeeping. In defining a surplus or deficit, one distinguishes between "autonomous" or "independent" items, representing transactions undertaken for their own sake (such as merchandise trade and long term capital flows), and "financing" or "compensatory" items, representing transactions which are induced as the result of the balance on autonomous items (such as gold movements). The magnitude of these financing items is taken to indicate the size of a country's surplus or deficit.

The source of disagreement on how to interpret the balance of payments accounts comes down to which items are best classified as "autonomous" and which as "financing." In particular, the debate centers around the treatment of private and official short term capital movements. In the previous section, we quoted Ruff's comment that the United States has been the victim of European misinterpretation of its balance of payments presentation. If so, the official balance of payments statistics of the United States were not without guilt themselves in this matter.

Does it often seem from the reports of the balance of payments of the United States and other countries that perhaps the world as a whole has a balance of payments deficit? Of course, that is impossible, at least

in a real sense. Taken over all countries, balance of payments surpluses
and deficits should cancel out.[3] This is true, however, only if symmetrical definitions of surplus and deficit are used. For a long period, the
exclusive definition of the U.S. deficit presented in official United States
statistics did not have this symmetry property. This "balance on liquidity basis" was defined as the decrease in U.S. official reserve assets (pre-
dominantly gold and foreign currency holdings) plus the increase in
liquid liabilities (U.S. bank deposits, money market instruments, and
marketable government securities) to both official and private foreign
holders. According to this definition, a private short term capital outflow would contribute to the U.S. deficit, but if the recipient of these
funds turned right around and reinvested them in the New York money
market, no offset would be recorded in the deficit figure. In other words,
though no capital had left the country, the recorded U.S. deficit would
have increased. The use of this practice (which has aptly been labeled
"statistical masochism") means that the whole world could be running
a measured deficit.

In 1963, a review committee, with Edward M. Bernstein as chair-
man, was appointed by the Bureau of the Budget to examine the balance of payments statistics of the United States. The committee's *Report* [54] was issued in 1965, and it recommended an "official settlements" concept of the deficit: the "balance on official reserve transactions." This balance is the decrease in U.S. official reserve assets plus
the increase in liquid and certain non-liquid liabilities to foreign *official agencies*, and since 1965 has been presented in official statistics
together with the balance on liquidity basis.

The official settlements definition is symmetrical, and not the least
of its virtues is that it corresponds to the concept of private excess demands or supplies in the foreign exchange market (which was discussed in the Background Notes to Part I). However, even this definition need not always correspond to the distinction between autonomous and financing items for a reserve currency country such as
the United States. Official institutions may desire to build up their foreign exchange holdings. If so, then their purchases of dollars in the foreign exchange market would be autonomous rather than compensatory,
and the corresponding U.S. deficits on official settlements (and also on
the liquidity definition) would not represent a true disequilibrium.

This phenomenon is not just a theoretical curiosity, but rather seems
the best interpretation of the build up of foreign official dollar holding

during the early and middle 1950's. It explains the lack of concern over the measured U.S. deficits during this period. And it was argued by Robert Mundell in 1965 that this was still the case:

The United States counts, as part of the deficit, not only the gold loss but also the increase in short-term liabilities to private holders and foreign monetary institutions. The Bernstein Committee's recommendations would be an improvement because they exclude from the definition the additional claims of private holders, but they remain defective because they continue to count the additional claims of official holders, implying that the dollar is less than a full-fledged international reserve asset.

There is every evidence that the United States has miscalculated by allowing the fiction of an arbitrary accounting definition of her balance of payments, quite remote from one which reflects her true financial strength in the world, to condition U.S. economic policy and even international political attitudes. It is not just the old matter of the "tail wagging the dog"; the problem is that the tail has been confused with the dog. [50, p. 4]

Both the "liquidity" and "official transactions" definitions of the deficit are criticized by Despres, Kindleberger, and Salant in "The Dollar and World Liquidity." Their thesis is in turn examined critically by Edward M. Bernstein in the reading "Does the United States Have a Payments Deficit?" Bernstein concludes that there still is a meaningful U.S. deficit, despite the operation of the financial intermediary process emphasized by Despres, Kindleberger, and Salant.[4]

While there is no general consensus on any one statistical concept as the best measure of the U.S. deficit, another consensus does seem to be emerging, namely, that there cannot be any *single* measure which is adequate. As stated by Joseph Barr, Undersecretary of the Treasury, in a speech before the National Association of Manufacturers on September 21, 1965:

Equilibrium cannot be defined solely in terms of a figure, it is importantly a matter of confidence. Whether a given figure represents equilibrium depends on the particular circumstances at the particular time. Perhaps, then, the best indication of what equilibrium in the U.S. balance of payments is, is what the rest of the world thinks it is.

And in recent years the rest of the world has considered the U.S. balance of payments to be in substantial deficit.

THE COSTS AND BENEFITS OF BEING WORLD BANKER

We have considered some of the benefits to the United States from being world banker, and, implicitly in our discussion of the problems facing the U.S. today, also some of its costs. In Part II.B this topic is considered systematically.

Robert V. Roosa, in "Benefits and Responsibilities of the U.S. as World Banker," sees the benefits for the United States as three-fold. These are the economic and political advantages deriving from a successful payments system that contributes to worldwide growth in trade and incomes, greater flexibility in financing U.S. balance of payments deficits, and greater freedom in U.S. domestic and foreign economic policies. The reading selection is an excerpt from a statement submitted to the Joint Economic Committee in 1963 when Dr. Roosa was Undersecretary of the Treasury. (For further analysis concluding that the U.S. has received net benefits from the key currency role of the dollar, see the work of Robert Z. Aliber, one of the first to study this question, in [2] and [3].)

Herbert G. Grubel in "The Benefits and Costs of Being the World Banker" sees the flexibility provided to the U.S. by its world banker status as more apparent than real. He argues that, instead, the U.S. world banker role has constrained United States policy. In part of his article not included here, Grubel does examine the benefits for the United States emanating from the banking services and foreign investment provided by the use of the dollar as a medium of international transactions. However, Grubel concludes that these benefits do not outweigh the costs of being the world banker. "We therefore reach the conclusion that the U.S. has been serving as the World Banker and providing international reserve assets at a great social cost to her domestic economy." [18, p. 212]

Henry N. Goldstein, in "Does it Necessarily Cost Anything to be the 'World Banker,'?" argues that no real constraints have been imposed on the U.S. by its world banker role; rather, apparent constraints are due to poor policies on the part of the United States. He also argues that the European surplus countries rather than the United States should bear the burden of adjustment, and he suggests that the U.S. pursue negotiations to this end.

In "The Future of the Dollar Reserve System," William A. Salant points out that what is relevant for present decisions concerning reform are not the *past* benefits that have accrued to the United States from its role as world banker but the costs and benefits that accrue from its *continuance* in this role. He points to the "overhang" of foreign official dollar balances as the key as to whether U.S. policies will acquire flexibility or constraints from continual reliance on the dollar to perform this function. Actual large scale withdrawals are not necessary to constrain U.S. policy actions; the mere possibility of this action may suffice.

What can we say on balance? The United States did receive economic gains over the long period when it could run deficits without concern, but the years of the "tearless deficits" are over. Today the advantages claimed for being a reserve currency country seem to be more political than economic, and even these are open to dispute:

> Some Colonel Blimps even seem to regard it as a matter of national prestige to have their country's national IOU's float precariously in the coffers of foreign central banks. Yet, the constraints which possible conversions of such IOU's into gold metal impose upon the freedom of monetary and economic policy in the United States and the United Kingdom are likely to prove increasingly burdensome in the future, while the chances of any substantial piling up of further dollar and sterling balances in other countries' reserves are bound to become increasingly slimmer.—Robert Triffin [66, pp. 364–65]

In concluding this introduction, we should mention that gains to the United States from its role as the world banker need not imply corresponding losses to the non-key currency countries, since the financial intermediation role of the dollar can provide the basis for mutual gain. As Gottfried Haberler has observed:

> Interest earnings, convenience, easy access to major financial markets are the great advantages of the Gold Exchange Standard for the non-reserve countries. In the post-war period the accumulation of Dollar balances made it easier and cheaper for countries in Europe and elsewhere to build up an international reserve—an indispensable prerequisite for the introduction of convertibility. This was a very useful function, indeed. [23, p. 754]

Both these gains and the costs associated with being a non-key currency country under the present system are difficult to quantify. It is no small wonder, then, that there are so many conflicting views on the key currency status of the dollar. These views will be considered further in Parts III and IV.

NOTES

1. These restrictions are outlined in Part III.
2. Of course, in the actual balance of payments statistics, the values of many of these items have to be estimated on the basis of incomplete data. Thus, there is also an "Errors and Omissions" entry in actual U.S. statistics. Detailed treatments of the mechanics of balance of payments accounting may be found in almost any text on international economics or international finance. See, for instance, [54], and [77, Ch. 3] or [79, Ch. 3 and 4].
3. Actually there can be a net surplus, attributable to new reserve acquisitions such as gold production.
4. For further discussion of the Despres-Kindleberger-Salant thesis, see [68].

A. The Dollar and World Liquidity

THE DOLLAR AND WORLD LIQUIDITY

Emile Despres

Professor of Economics,
Stanford University

Charles P. Kindleberger

Professor of Economics,
Massachusetts Institute of Technology

Walter S. Salant

Senior Staff Economist,
Brookings Institution

The consensus in Europe and the United States on the United States balance of payments and world liquidity runs about like this:

1. Abundant liquidity has been provided since World War II less by newly mined gold than by the increase in liquid dollar assets generated by U.S. balance-of-payments deficits.

2. These deficits are no longer available as a generator of liquidity because the accumulation of dollars has gone so far that it has undermined confidence in the dollar.

3. To halt the present creeping decline in liquidity through central-bank conversions of dollars into gold, and to forestall headlong flight from the dollar, it is necessary above all else to correct the United States deficit.

4. When the deficit has been corrected, the growth of world reserves may, or probably will, become inadequate. Hence there is a need for

From Emile Despres, Charles P. Kindleberger and Walter S. Salant, "The Dollar and World Liquidity—A Minority View," *The Economist*, February 5, 1966, pp. 526–29. The Brookings Institution Reprint is used as the text, since it contains a few points that the authors consider important but that did not appear in *The Economist*.

planning new means of adding to world reserves—along the lines suggested by Triffin, Bernstein, Roosa, Stamp, Giscard, and others.

So much is widely agreed. There is a difference in tactics between those who would correct the U.S. balance of payments by raising interest rates—bankers on both sides of the ocean and European central bankers—and those in the United States who would correct it, if necessary, by capital restrictions, so that tight money in the United States may be avoided while labor and other resources are still idle. There is also a difference of emphasis between the Continentals, who urge adjustment (proposition 3 above), and the Anglo-Saxons, who stress the need for more liquidity (proposition 4). British voices urge more liquidity now, rather than in the future. But with these exceptions, the lines of analysis converge.

FOUR COUNTER PROPOSITIONS

There is room, however, for a minority view which would oppose this agreement with a sharply differing analysis. In outline, it asserts the following counter propositions:

1. While the United States has provided the world with liquid dollar assets in the postwar period by capital outflow and aid exceeding its current account surplus, in most years this excess has not reflected a deficit in a sense representing disequilibrium. The outflow of U.S. capital and aid has filled not one but two needs. First, it has supplied goods and services to the rest of the world. But secondly, to the extent that its loans to foreigners are offset by foreigners putting their own money into liquid dollar assets, the U.S. has not overinvested but has supplied financial intermediary services. The "deficit" has reflected largely the second process, in which the United States has been lending, mostly at long and intermediate term, and borrowing short. This financial intermediation, in turn, performs two functions: it supplies loans and investment funds to foreign enterprises which have to pay more domestically to borrow long-term money and which cannot get the amounts they want at any price; and it supplies liquidity to foreign asset-holders, who receive less for placing their short-term deposits at home. Essentially, this is a trade in liquidity, which is profitable to both sides. Differences in their liquidity preferences (i.e., in their willingness to hold their financial assets in long-term rather than in quickly encashable

forms and to have short-term rather than long-term liabilities outstanding against them) create differing margins between short-term and long-term interest rates. This in turn creates scope for trade in financial assets, just as differing comparative costs create the scope for mutually profitable trade in goods. This trade in financial assets has been an important ingredient of economic growth outside the United States.

2. Such lack of confidence in the dollar as now exists has been generated by the attitudes of government officials, central bankers, academic economists, and journalists, and reflects their failure to understand the implications of this intermediary function. Despite some contagion from these sources, the private market retains confidence in the dollar, as increases in private holdings of liquid dollar assets show. Private speculation in gold is simply the result of the known attitudes and actions of governmental officials and central bankers.

3. With capital markets unrestricted, attempts to correct the "deficit" by ordinary macro-economic weapons are likely to fail. It may be possible to expand the current account surplus at first by deflation of United States income and prices relative to those of Europe; but gross financial capital flows will still exceed real transfer of goods and services(i.e., involve financial intermediation, lending long-term funds to Europe in exchange for short-term deposits) so long as capital formation remains high in Europe. A moderate rise of interest rates in the United States will have only a small effect on the net capital outflow. A drastic rise might cut the net outflow substantially, but only by tightening money in *Europe* enough to stop economic growth; and this would cut America's current account surplus. Correcting the United States deficit by taxes and other controls on capital, which is being attempted on both sides of the Atlantic, is likely either to fail, or to succeed by impeding international capital flows so much as to cut European investment and growth.

4. While it is desirable to supplement gold with an internationally created reserve asset, the conventional analysis leading to this remedy concentrates excessively on a country's external liquidity; it takes insufficient account of the demands of savers for internal liquidity and of borrowers in the same country for long-term funds. The international private capital market, properly understood, provides both external liquidity to a country, and the kinds of assets and liabilities that private savers and borrowers want and cannot get at home. Most plans to cre-

ate an international reserve asset, however, are addressed only to external liquidity problems which in many cases, and especially in Europe today, are the less important issue.

With agreement between the United States and Europe—but without it if necessary—it would be possible to develop a monetary system which provided the external liquidity that is needed and also recognized the role of international financial intermediation in world economic growth.

EUROPE NEEDS DOLLARS

Analytical support and elaboration of this minority view is presented in numbered sections, conforming to the propositions advanced above as an alternative to the consensus.

1. The idea that the balance of payments of a country is in disequilibrium if it is in deficit on the liquidity (U.S. Department of Commerce) definition is not appropriate to a country with a large and open capital market that is performing the function of a financial intermediary. Banks and other financial intermediaries, unlike traders, are paid to give up liquidity. The United States is no more in deficit when it lends long and borrows short than is a bank when it makes a loan and enters a deposit on its books.

Financial intermediation is an important function in a monetary economy. Savers want liquid assets; borrowers investing in fixed capital expansion are happier with funded rather than quick liabilities. Insofar as the gap is not bridged, capital formation is held down. Europeans borrow from the United States, and Americans are willing to pay higher prices for European assets than European investors will, partly because capital is more readily available in the United States than in Europe, but mainly because liquidity preference in Europe is higher and because capital markets in Europe are much less well organized, more monopolistically controlled, and just plain smaller than in the United States. With unrestricted capital markets, the European savers who want cash and the borrowers who prefer to extend their liabilities into the future can both be satisfied when the United States capital market lends long and borrows short and when it accepts smaller margins between its rates for borrowing short and lending short. European borrowers of good credit standing will seek to borrow in New York (or in the Euro-dollar market, which is a mere extension of New York) when rates of interest are lower on dollar loans than on loans in European currencies, or when the amounts required are greater than their domestic capital markets can provide. But when interferences prevent foreign intermediaries from bridging the gap, and when domestic private intermediaries cannot bridge it while the public authorities will not, borrowing possibilities are cut, and investment and growth are cut with it.

The effects are not confined to Europe, or even to the advanced countries. Slower European growth means lower demand for primary products imported from the less developed countries. Preoccupation of the United States, Britain, and now Germany with their balances of payments dims the outlook for foreign aid and worsens the climate for trade liberalization. And the American capital controls are bound to reduce the access of less developed countries to private capital and bond loans in the United States—and indirectly in Europe.

2. It may be objected that no bank can keep lending if its depositors are unwilling to hold its liabilities. True. But savings can never be put to productive use if the owners of wealth are unwilling to hold financial assets and insist on what they consider a more "ultimate" means of payment. If the bank is sound, the trouble comes from the depositors' irrationality. The remedy is to have a lender of last resort to cope with the effects of their attitudes or, better, to educate them or, if neither is possible, to make the alternative asset (which, against the dollar, is gold) less attractive or less available. To prevent the bank from pursuing unsound policies—if it really tends to do so—it is not necessary to allow a run on it. The depositors can have their say in less destructive ways, e.g., through participating in the management of the bank of last resort or through agreement on the scale of the financial intermediation.

The nervousness of monetary authorities and academic economists is a consequence of the way they define a deficit and the connotations they attach to it. No bank could survive in such an analytical world. If financial authorities calculated a balance of payments for New York vis-à-vis the interior of the United States, they would find it in serious "deficit," since short-term claims of the rest of the country on New York mount each year. If they applied their present view of international finance, they would impose restrictions on New York's bank loans to the interior and on its purchases of new bond and stock issues. Similarly, the balance of payments of the U.S. financial sector consists almost entirely of above-the-line disbursements and therefore nearly equal "deficits." Between 1947 and 1964 the liquid liabilities (demand and time deposits) of member banks of the Federal Reserve System alone increased from $110 billion to $238 billion. This increase of $128 billion, or 116 per cent, was not matched by an equal absolute or even proportionate increase in cash reserves. Indeed, these reserves increased only $1.6 billion, or 8 per cent. Yet nobody regards this cumulated "deficit" of over $126 billion as cause for alarm.

The private market has not been alarmed about the international position of the dollar in relation to other currencies or the liquidity of the United States. Although there has been private speculation in gold against the dollar, it has been induced largely by reluctance of some central banks to accumulate dollars. The dollar is the world's standard of value; the Euro-dollar market dominates capital markets in Europe; and the foreign dollar bond market has easily outdistanced the unit-of-account bond and the European "parallel bond." As one looks at sterling and the major Continental currencies, it is hard to imagine any one of them stronger than the dollar today, five years from now, or twenty years hence. Admittedly, short-term destabilizing speculation against the dollar is possible, largely as a consequence of errors of official and speculative judgment. It can be contained, however, by gold outflows and support from other central banks, or by allowing the dollar to find its own level in world exchange markets, buttressed by the combination of high productivity and responsible fiscal and monetary policy in the United States. In the longer run, as now in the short, the dollar is strong, not weak.

3. Since the U.S. "deficit" is the result of liquidity exchanges or financial intermediation, it will persist as long as capital movement is free, European capital markets remain narrower and less competitive than that of the United States, liquidity preferences differ between the United States and Europe, and capital formation in Western Europe remains vigorous. In these circumstances, an effort to adjust the current account to the capital outflow is futile. The deficit can be best attacked by perfecting and eventually integrating European capital markets and moderating the European asset-holder's insistence on liquidity, understandable though the latter may be after half a century of wars, inflations, and capital levies.

An attempt to halt the capital outflow by raising interest rates in the United States either would have little effect over any prolonged period or else would cripple European growth. With European capital markets joined to New York by substantial movements of short-term funds and bonds, the rate structure in the world as a whole will be set by the major financial center, in this instance New York. Interest-rate changes in the outlying centers will have an impact on capital flows to them. Higher interest rates in New York will raise rates in the world as a whole.

The effort is now being made to "correct the deficit" by restricting capital movements. Success in this effort is dubious, however, for two reasons.

MONEY IS FUNGIBLE

In the first place, money is fungible. Costless to store and to transport, it is the easiest commodity to arbitrage in time and in space. Discriminating capital restrictions are only partly effective, as the United States is currently learning. Some funds that are prevented from going directly to Europe will reach there by way of the less-developed countries or via the favored few countries like Canada and Japan, which are accorded access to the New York financial market because they depend upon it for capital and for liquidity. These leaks in the dam will increase as time passes, and the present system of discriminatory controls will become unworkable in the long run. The United States will have to choose between abandoning the whole effort or plugging the leaks. Plugging the leaks, in turn, means that it must either get the countries in whose favor it discriminates to impose their own restrictions or withdraw the preferences it now gives them. Accordingly, the choices in the long run are between no restrictions, restrictions on all outflows, and establishment of what is in effect a dollar bloc, or a dollar-sterling bloc, within which funds move freely but which applies uniform controls against movements to all non-bloc countries.

In the second place, it is not enough to restrain the outflow of United States-owned capital. As Germany and Switzerland have found, to keep United States funds at home widens the spreads between short-term and long-term rates in Europe and also the spreads between the short-term rates at which European financial intermediaries borrow and lend, and so encourages repatriation of European capital already in the United States. For Europe, this effectively offsets restrictions on capital inflows. "Home is where they have to take you in." It would be possible for the United States to block the outflow of foreign capital—possible but contrary to tradition. If this door is left open, the $57 billion of foreign capital in the United States permit substantial net capital outflows, even without an outflow of U.S. capital. Although it would require powerful forces indeed to induce foreign holders to dispose of most of their American investments, they might dispose of enough to permit the "deficit" to continue for a long time.

4. Capital restrictions to correct the deficit, even if feasible, would still leave unanswered a fundamental question. Is it wise to destroy an efficient system of providing internal and external liquidity—the international capital market—and substitute for it one or another contrived device of limited flexibility for creating additions to international reserve assets alone? In the crisis of 1963, Italy borrowed $1.6 billion in the Euro-dollar market; under the Bernstein plan it would have had access to less than one-tenth of the incremental created liquidity of say $1 billion a year, perhaps $75 million in one year—a derisible amount. It would be the stuff of tragedy for the world's authorities laboriously to obtain agreement on a planned method of providing international reserve assets if that method, through analytical error, unwittingly destroyed an important source of liquid funds for European savers and of loans for European borrowers, and a flexible instrument for the international provision of liquidity. Moreover, agreement on a way of creating additional international reserve assets will not necessarily end the danger that foreigners, under the influence of conventional analysis, will want to convert dollars into gold whenever they see what they consider a "deficit."

But, it will be objected, the fears of the European authorities about the dollar are facts of life, and the United States must adjust to them. Several points may be made by way of comment.

EUROPE SQUEEZES ITSELF

In the first place, the European authorities must be learning how much international trade in financial claims means to their economies, now that it has been reduced. Europe has discovered that liquidity in the form of large international reserves bears no necessary relationship to ability to supply savers with liquid assets or industrial borrowers with long-term funds in countries where financial intermediation is inadequately performed and which are cut off from the world capital market. Financial authorities in Italy, France, and even Germany have lately been trying to moderate the high interest rates which reflect strong domestic liquidity preference and the wide margins between the rates at which their intermediaries borrow and lend, as well as (in the case of Germany) their own policies. Having scant success in getting households, banks or private intermediaries to buy long-term securities, these authorities are increasingly entering the market themselves. Investment is declining: in Germany with long-term interest rates touching eight per cent for the best borrowers, in Italy despite Bank of Italy purchases of industrial securities, and in France where government bonds are issued to provide capital to a limited list of industrial investors. It is ironic that United States firms seem able to borrow in Europe more easily than European firms, as they continue investing in Europe while abiding by their Government's program of voluntary capital restraint. Given their liquid capital strength in the United States, they have no objection to borrowing short, and command a preferred status when they choose to borrow long. But their operations in Europe put pressure on European long-term rates and enhance the incentive of other European borrowers and United States lenders to evade the restrictions.

Europe's own capital markets cannot equal that of the United States in breadth, liquidity, and competitiveness in the foreseeable future. Europe must therefore choose between an open international capital market, using fiscal policy to impose any needed restraints, and use of monetary restraint with an insulated capital market. The second alternative involves serious dangers. Without substantial European government lending to industry, which is unlikely, the terms on which long-term money would be available may cause industrial stagnation.

The first choice is the more constructive one, but it can work only if its implications are understood in both Europe and the United States. The United States, too, has failed to appreciate the role of New York in the world monetary system and has acquiesced in the Continental view of the U.S. payments position. It must be recognized that trading in financial assets with the United States means a United States "deficit"; United States capital provides not only goods and services, but liquid assets to Europe, which means European acquisition of dollars. Moreover, the amount of dollars that private savers in Europe will want to acquire for transactions and as a partial offset to debts in dollars, and for other purposes, will increase. This increase in privately held dollars will involve a rising trend in the United States deficit on the Department of Commerce definition, though no deficit on the Bernstein Committee definition.

But that is not all. The new liquid saving in Europe which is matched by European borrowing in the United States is not likely to be held largely in dollars, and certainly will not be held entirely so. Savers typically want liquidity in their own currencies, and so do banks. If household and commercial banks want to hold liquid assets at home rather than securities or liquid assets in dollars, the counterpart of foreign borrowing by industry must be held by the central bank of their country in dollars, or converted into gold. This implies a deficit for the United States even on the Bernstein Committee definition.

Whether householders and banks want to hold dollars or their own national currencies, the effect is the same: both alternatives now frighten the United States as well as Europe. They should not. And they would not if it were recognized that financial intermediation implies a decline in the liquidity of the intermediary as much when the intermediation is being performed in another country as when it is being performed domestically. An annual growth in Europe's dollar-holdings averaging, perhaps, $1½ to $2 billion a year or perhaps more for a long time is normal expansion for a bank the size of the United States with a fast-growing world as its body of customers. To the extent that European capital markets achieve greater breadth, liquidity, and competitiveness, the rates of increase in these dollar holdings consistent with given rates of world economic growth would of course be lower than when these markets have their present deficiencies. But whatever rate of growth in these dollar holdings is needed, the point is that they not only provide external liquidity to other countries, but are a necessary counterpart of the intermediation which provides liquidity to Europe's savers and financial institutions. Recognition of this fact would end central bank conversions of dollars into gold, the resulting creeping decline of official reserves, and the disruption of capital flows to which it has led.

It must be admitted that free private capital markets are sometimes destabilizing. When they are, the correct response is determined governmental counter-action to support the currency that is under pressure until the crisis has been weathered. Walter Bagehot's dictum of 1870 still stands: In a crisis, discount freely. Owned reserves cannot provide for these eventualities, as International Monetary Fund (IMF) experience amply demonstrates. Amounts agreed in advance are almost certain to be too little, and they tip the hand of the authorities to the speculators. The rule is discount freely, and tidy up afterwards, transferring outstanding liabilities to the IMF, the General Arrangements to Borrow, or even into funded government-to-government debts such as were used to wind up the European Payments Union. Owned reserves or readily available discounting privileges on the scale needed to guard against these crises of confidence would be inflationary in periods of calm.

LET THE GOLD GO

Mutual recognition of the role of dollar holdings would provide the most desirable solution, but if, nevertheless, Europe unwisely chooses to convert dollars into gold, the United States could restore a reserve-currency system, even without European cooperation in reinterpreting deficits and lifting capital restrictions. The decision would call for cool heads in the United States. The real problem is to build a strong international monetary mechanism resting on credit, with gold occupying, at most, a subordinate position. Because the dollar is in a special position as a world currency, the United States can bring about this change through its own action. Several ways in which it can do so have been proposed, including widening the margin around parity at which it buys and sells gold, reducing the price at which it buys gold, and otherwise depriving gold of its present unlimited convertibility into dollars. The United States would have to allow its gold stock to run down as low as European monetary authorities chose to take it. If they took it all, which is unlikely, the United States would have no alternative but to allow the dollar to depreciate until the capital flow came to a halt, or, much more likely, until the European countries decided to stop the depreciation by holding the dollars they were unwilling to hold before. If this outcome constituted a serious possibility, it seems evident that European countries would cease conversion of dollars into gold well short of the last few billions.

This strategy has been characterized by *The Economist* as the "new nationalism" in the United States. It can reasonably be interpreted, however, as internationalism. It would enable the United States to preserve the international capital market and thereby protect the rate of world economic growth, even without European cooperation.

While United States-European cooperation in maintaining the international capital market is the preferable route, it requires recognizing that an effective, smoothly functioning international capital market is itself an instrument of world economic growth, not a nuisance which can be disposed of and the function of which can be transferred to new or extended intergovernmental institutions, and it requires abandoning on both sides of the Atlantic the view that a U.S. deficit, whether on the Department of Commerce or the Bernstein Committee definition, is not compatible with equilibrium. Abandonment of this view, in turn, requires facing up to the fact that the economic analysis of the textbooks —derived from the writing and the world of David Hume and modified only by trimmings—is no longer adequate in a world that is increasingly moving (apart from government interferences) toward an integrated capital and money market. In these circumstances, the main requirement of international monetary reform is to preserve and improve the efficiency of the private capital market while building protection against its performing in a destabilizing fashion.

The majority view has been gaining strength since 1958, when Triffin first asserted that the dollar and the world were in trouble. Between 1958 and 1965 world output and trade virtually doubled, the United States dollar recovered from a slight overvaluation, and the gold hoarders have foregone large earnings and capital gains. Having been wrong in 1958 on the near-term position, the consensus may be more wrong today, when its diagnosis and prognosis are being followed. But this time the generally accepted analysis can lead to a brake on European growth. Its error may be expensive, not only for Europe but for the whole world.

DOES THE UNITED STATES HAVE
A PAYMENTS DEFICIT?

Edward M. Bernstein

President,
EMB (Ltd.), Research Economists

The concept of a deficit in the balance of payments is extremely complex and there is always considerable scope for reasonable differences of opinion on the amount of the deficit and, at times, whether there is a deficit. Unfortunately, it is not possible to say that the balance of payments of the United States is not in deficit at this time.

Professor Kindleberger emphasizes that the interpretation of the balance of payments cannot be the same for a country whose international transactions consist almost entirely of exports and imports of goods and services (a trader) and a country that not only engages in an enormous volume of trade but also is an enormous foreign investor and has large short-term foreign assets and foreign liabilities (a banker).

Banks [as distinguished from traders] are in the business of owing money. They have reserves, to be sure, generally of the order of 1 to 5 between their primary reserves and their demand liabilities. For the rest they are in the business of financial intermediation, or lending long and borrowing short. A definition which asserts that a bank is in disequilibrium every time its deposits rise without a parallel [equal?] rise in primary reserves would come as a shock to most bankers, although they do not protest when the Department of Commerce applies this definition to the United States.[1]

From Statement by Edward M. Bernstein, in *Contingency Planning for U.S. International Monetary Policy*, Statements by Private Economists submitted to the Subcommittee on International Exchange and Payments of the Joint Economic Committee, 89th Cong., 2d sess., 1966 (Washington, D.C.: U.S. Government Printing Office, 1966), pp. 3–5.

When a trading nation buys more goods and services than it sells, it can meet the excess of its payments by drawing down its reserves (gold and foreign exchange), borrowing from the IMF or other central banks (reserve credit), or by securing long-term or short-term credit from foreign financial centers. A trading country that meets its deficit on goods and services by borrowing long-term (through security issues) or short-term (through bank credit) is regarded as having a capital inflow. Its deficit on goods and services is offset by a surplus on capital account. The overall balance of payments is neither in surplus nor in deficit. On the other hand, when a trading country draws down its reserves or secures reserve credit, its overall balance of payments is in deficit.

The deficit of a banking nation is far more difficult to define acceptably. There are any number of definitions that may be used. The Commerce Department definition of the deficit (changes in reserves plus all changes in liquid liabilities to foreigners) is open to serious objection as being one-sided. As Kindleberger says: "All that count on the assets side are gold and convertible foreign exchange owned by the monetary authorities. All other assets are taken to be frozen, while all demand liabilities are regarded as just about to be presented for payment." The liquidity definition exaggerates the size of the deficit if that term is used as a measure of the payments problem.

There are other definitions of the deficit of a banking nation (reserve center) that are not open to this criticism, although they may be objectionable for other reasons. The reserve transactions deficit is measured by the decrease in reserve assets (gold, foreign exchange and claims on the IMF) plus the increase in liabilities to foreign monetary authorities (reserve liabilities). In this definition, an increase in foreign short-term claims in the United States, other than those of foreign central banks, is treated as a capital inflow, just as an increase in U.S. banking and other claims on foreigners is treated as a capital outflow.

The pragmatic test of a deficit is whether the balance of payments could be continued indefinitely with the existing relationship of the accounts. Obviously, a deficit on the liquidity definition could be continued indefinitely. Foreigners do want to accumulate dollar assets. As Kindleberger has emphasized, they are attractive assets, denominated in a currency whose foreign exchange value is assured, earning a good return, and easily bought and sold (or deposited and withdrawn) in a broad financial market. Even the Commerce Department experts recognize that a deficit on the liquidity definition of an average of $500 million to $800 million a year could be continued indefinitely—it is an equilibrium position requiring no change.

On the other hand, a reserve transactions deficit either depletes the reserves of a country (and cannot be continued indefinitely) or increases its reserve liabilities and confronts it with the risk of a sudden drawing down of its reserves in the future by conversions of foreign official holdings of its currency. This is an uncertain risk, although the United Kingdom has been confronted by it from time to time, and even the United States has had such conversions in 1965 and 1966. Nevertheless, it could be argued that there is a normal growth in foreign exchange reserves in the form of dollars that other countries would find necessary and acceptable, and such an increase in the holdings of a reserve currency could be regarded as capital inflow. Even so, for a banking nation that is a reserve center, there is no escaping the definition of the deficit as a decline in its reserve assets (including short-term reserve credit), for it cannot continue indefinitely a balance of payments that depletes its reserves.

The Kindleberger thesis is replete with description and analysis of the role of the United States as a financial intermediary—that is, a banker. There is much that is enlightening in this discussion. He fails, however, in his attempt to draw an analogy between the position of a commercial banker and the position of the United States as a reserve center. Of course, commercial banks are very happy to increase their liabilities and their assets—that is how they make profits as bankers. But a commercial bank could not continue to make loans (capital outflow in the balance of payments analogy) if it were to find that as a consequence of increasing its income-earning assets it were confronted with an unfavorable balance with other banks at the clearing-house or withdrawals of cash over the counter (reduction of reserves in the balance of payments analogy). It might have no objection to borrowing from the Federal or buying Federal funds (incurring reserve liabilities), provided it could do so without assuming undue risk. But if the Federal is reluctant to let it borrow and it cannot buy Federal funds, it will have to curtail its acquisition of income-earning assets, however profitable its lending and investment operations may be.

That is the situation of the United States. We have acquired a large amount of very valuable income-earning assets abroad. Our earnings from net exports of goods and services, after U.S. aid, have not been sufficient to pay for our foreign investments. This is true even after allowing for the increase of foreign banking claims in this country. As a consequence, we have been drawing down our reserves, and this no country (and no banker) can do indefinitely. It is futile to say, as Kindleberger does, "that the dollar has no need for adjustment, if financial intermediation is properly understood." This would seem to imply that foreign countries would always want to acquire as much dollars as the United States would wish to invest abroad in excess of its balance on other transactions—a thesis of doubtful validity. So long as the United States continues to pay out reserves, it has a deficit in its balance of payments, however much we may rationalize our role as a banker. The proof that we have a deficit is that we cannot continue the present balance of payments without ultimately being confronted with an exchange crisis.

NOTES

1. Charles P. Kindleberger, "International Monetary Arrangements," University of Queensland Press, St. Lucia, 1966. [Kindleberger here presents substantially the same argument as in the preceding article by Despres, Kindleberger, and Salant. —Ed.]

B. The Costs and Benefits of Being World Banker

BENEFITS AND RESPONSIBILITIES OF THE U.S. AS WORLD BANKER

Robert V. Roosa

Brown Brothers Harriman and Company

What special responsibilities and benefits accrue to the United States in the role of world banker? The special responsibilities of the United States as world banker stem from the fact that the dollar is the cornerstone of the world's exchange rate and payments system and is the principal reserve currency. This unique position of the dollar has been the result of a natural evolutionary process and does not stem from a conscious decision of the United States to have the dollar perform a role in international finance that would be consonant with its position as a political, economic, and military power. It nonetheless carries with it the responsibility of assuring that the strength of the dollar permits it to perform its functions that are essential for the viability of the free world's payment system and for the maintenance of a high level of trade which is essential for economic growth at home and abroad. This necessarily involves an obligation to pursue policies that contribute to domestic economic growth and avoid persistent balance-of-payments deficits.

The major benefit that has accrued to the United States as world banker relates to the broad economic and political advantages that have arisen from the successful evolution of a payments system in the postwar period—a system based on the dollar—that has contributed to the growth of trade and economic activity throughout the world. More specifically, the use of the dollar as a reserve currency by foreign monetary authorities has permitted the United States a greater flexibility in financing its balance-of-payments deficits and, until recently, gave the

From *The United States Balance of Payments*, Hearings before the Joint Economic Committee, 88th Cong., first sess., 1963 (Washington, D.C.: U.S. Government Printing Office, 1963), pp. 146–47.

United States greater freedom to follow desired domestic and foreign economic policies than would otherwise have been the case.

Had the dollar not been a reserve currency, the shape of postwar economic developments would have differed vastly from the pattern we have experienced. Had foreigners not been willing—indeed anxious until the last few years—to add to their dollar reserves we would have been forced long ago to face the disciplines imposed by the need to maintain reasonable equilibrium in our international accounts. It is of course impossible to detail what "might have been," but if we had not been a world banker, we might well have been forced long ago to cut down our imports (perhaps through deflation of our domestic economy), reduce materially our foreign investments, income from which makes a substantial contribution to our current balance of payments, and curtail, perhaps sharply, our military and economic assistance to our friends and allies. Had we taken these steps, our customers abroad would have sharply reduced their purchases in this country and we would now be confronted with discriminatory policies against the dollar in most countries of the world. Instead of the rapid growth of world trade, we would have witnessed stagnation that would have been harmful to our own prosperity and to that of the whole free world.

THE BENEFITS AND COSTS
OF BEING THE WORLD BANKER

Herbert G. Grubel

Associate Professor of Finance,
Wharton School of Finance and Commerce,
University of Pennsylvania

FLEXIBILITY AND ALL THAT

It has been argued that, as a result of being the World Banker, the U.S. has greater flexibility in the choice and timing of economic policies designed to bring domestic activity in line with the demands of external balance. The argument is based primarily on the historical observation that the rise in dollar balances owned by foreigners has financed 58 percent of the cumulative U.S. deficit since 1949, thus implying the narrow definition of the term World Banker. "Had it not been for our position as banker to the world, this credit would not have been extended to us." [1]

The connection between flexibility and the key currency status appears to be misconceived and based on a misinterpretation of an historical accident. The word flexibility implies the property of the repeated reversibility of a process; but there is hardly anyone who would want to argue that the $25 billion short-term credit extended by foreigners can be repaid without serious disruption of the world's payment system or that the flexibility available to the U.S. is as large as this $25 billion credit line. A much better interpretation of the events of the past thirteen years is that the world was hungry for liquidity and the U.S. was willing to supply it. America's stature and role in world trade, as well as the size of the gold stock at the beginning of this period, made her a natural choice for this role. It is doubtful that the

From Herbert G. Grubel, "The Benefits and Costs of Being the World Banker," *The National Banking Review*, Vol. 2, No. 2 (December 1964), 197–205.

world would have accepted an equally large cumulative amount of U.S. deficits had there been an adequate supply of gold, or had the need for liquidity been smaller. The benefits accruing to the U.S. from its role as a financial intermediary for the world, through the issuance of liquid liabilities in return for the deposit of illiquid assets by others, are distinctly different from those allegedly derived from flexibility.

If this point is valid, it follows that there is only very little connection between key currency status and flexibility. Any country with adequate reserves and reasonable stability in its exchange rate possesses flexibility in the sense that it has several first-line defenses on which it can rely before being obliged to take sharp corrective actions in the domestic economy. Such defenses are credits from trading partners, IMF drawing rights, and own reserves. They are available to every country, regardless of whether or not it serves as the World Banker. The absolute size of these defenses depends on a country's importance in the world economy, and on these grounds the U.S. possesses a great amount of flexibility. The ability to finance deficits by borrowing only indicates that someone has credit, and is not necessarily connected with the nature of the debtor's business. The Chase Manhattan Bank's credit may be better or worse than that of General Motors.

Being the World Banker has been claimed to have provided the U.S. with still another advantage. In Secretary Dillon's words, "Had it not been for our position as banker to the world . . . we would long ago have been faced with the hard necessity of . . . reducing foreign investment and cutting into the substance of our defense and aid spending abroad." [2] In that sense, the banking role is alleged to have enabled the pursuit of U.S. military and other political and economic objectives enhancing the country's position in the world in some immeasurable way. This allegation implies a rather curious interpretation of how the goals of investment and aid can be attained. In terms of traditional analysis, one is led to believe that the effectiveness of these policies depends on the quantity of resources effectually transferred. Yet, to the extent that the rest of the world was lending to the U.S., the actual transfer of aid from the U.S. was not achieved. Considered in this light, America is actually getting credit for the aid even though the real resources were supplied by someone else. [3]

It is true that the U.S. has made available international reserves equal to these $25 billion, most of which the recipient countries seem to have wanted and would have had to get in some other way had it not been for the willingness of the U.S. to be the World Banker in the narrow sense of the term. But this is not the original argument, and it cannot be used to defend the key currency position of the dollar without stating explicitly by what alternative methods countries could have obtained the reserves, or what quantity of reserves they would have required if the gold exchange standard had been replaced by some other monetary organization. A regime of flexible exchange rates, for instance, would have obviated entirely the need for reserves.

More important still is the presumption in Secretary Dillon's statement that, if the U.S. had not received these credits, the aid provided would have been smaller. In recent years, the U.S. has attempted to cut back aid and defense expenditures abroad in order to improve the balance of payments. This might have been the pattern in earlier years if international credit had not been available. But the pattern might also have been different. Devaluation, more effective maintenance of price stability, or sensible reform of the international monetary system might have been undertaken upon the realization that certain national objectives were unattainable within the existing institutional framework. In that sense, the world position of the U.S. might today be stronger in real terms than it is, if the country had not been the World Banker.

In sum, the argument that flexibility is due to the banking role and that it is beneficial to the U.S. does not stand up under close scrutiny. It appears rather to be an *ex post* rationalization of past developments and a defense of the *status quo*. The apparent flexibility of the past decade has actually been detrimental to the U.S., because it has encouraged complacency and allowed the development of a disequilibrium that is larger and more difficult to correct than it would have been otherwise.

CONSTRAINTS ON THE USE
OF FULL EMPLOYMENT POLICIES

All countries run balance of payments deficits from time to time, and consequently are required to undertake policy measures that may be undesirable and conflict with some important domestic policy objective. Therefore, in the following discussion we shall concentrate on how and to what extent there have been constraints on U.S. policies which can be attributed specifically to America's role as the World Banker and as the issuer of internationally acceptable reserve assets.

There are essentially three major constraints which can be so identified. *First*, the world's willingness to accept U.S. dollars has allowed the development of a balance of payments disequilibrium which was both larger and longer lasting than it would have been otherwise. The direct consequences of these developments are large divergences of prices from their equilibrium values and the accumulation of a large foreign short-term debt. *Second*, being the World Banker has severely limited the choice of tools that the U.S. can use to adjust her balance of payments, leaving only rather inefficient alternatives. And *third*, the existence of a large short-term debt increased the country's vulnerability to the outflow of short-term capital. As a result, monetary policy could not be used to get the economy to full employment. The need to use fiscal policy resulted in unemployment persisting longer, because of the normal time-lag characteristic of the enactment of fiscal policy changes. In the following we shall discuss these three constraints in greater detail.

It is a rather well-accepted fact that by about 1960 the U.S. balance of payments had turned adverse to such an extent that remedial action was needed. Because foreigners readily accepted dollars rather than demanding gold as settlement for U.S. deficits, the normal disciplines of the balance of payments did not affect American policy makers. They were able to show an almost complete disregard for the foreign trade implications of their domestic policies from the end of World War II through nearly the last year of the Eisenhower administration. As a consequence, whatever real forces were at work and had caused the imbalances to develop in the first place were allowed to go unchecked longer than they would have been otherwise. Partly as a consequence of domestic price increases, especially in steel, and partly because of the capital investments in the Common Market area, the U.S. found herself in a position where the balance of payments required remedial action in about 1960. But when it came to the choice of a specific line of attack, the position of the U.S. as a key currency country severely limited the choices open.

In the past, devaluation of the currency has been the one method whereby countries have chosen to redress their balance of payments quickly and efficiently after they found themselves in disequilibrium positions like that of the U.S. However, for the U.S. this method is not available. As Secretary Dillon said in his testimony before the Joint Economic Committee: "Our dominant role in world trade and finance has meant that we could not either prudently or effectively use many of the simpler and most direct types of action by which other countries have sometimes dealt with their payments deficits. Currency devaluation, import restriction, exchange control . . . are all out of the question." [4]

Because of these limitations, what choices were left for the U.S.? If the stated principles are not to be violated, there remains only one logical possibility, adjustment of the price level. Fortunately, in a dynamic world of rather universal and continuous price increases, no absolute reduction in the price level is required. Instead, it is only necessary that the U.S. rate of price increase be slowed down relative to the rest-of-the-world rate of change, which is much easier to achieve in an economy characterized by severe downward rigidities of wages and prices. That holding down the rate of price increase has been the prime official method of dealing with the problem can be seen from Secretary Dillon's statement: "Firm discipline in the maintenance of price and cost stability" is required to achieve the "substantial adjustments . . . in countless transactions by our private citizens and business firms, each responding freely and vigorously to new market incentives and opportunities." [5]

If we accept the proposition that such concern with price stability leads policy makers to accept higher levels of unemployment than would be considered desirable in the judgment of many people, then it follows that being the World Banker is responsible for real social losses in the form of unemployment and foregone output by closing off the opportunity to correct the balance of payments disequilibrium in any way other than by deflation. The large size of the required adjustment which is also due to the key currency role adds further to the social cost by making the period of deflationary employment levels longer than it would have been otherwise.

While the U.S. did not engage in any open currency devaluations, import restrictions, or currency control, various gimmicks were used which in practice amounted to doing the same things. The reduction of duty-free imports by American travelers abroad amounts to imposing a kind of import restriction by raising tariffs. The procurement orders for the military made it mandatory to purchase U.S. products for overseas use as long as the American price did not exceed the foreign price by more than 50 per cent. This procedure is equivalent to the application of a depreciated dollar rate of exchange to certain purchases, thus introducing in effect a multiple exchange rate system. The interest equalization tax, which is designed to curb the outflow of portfolio capital, amounts to a kind of currency control and in fact produces two quotations for the dollar. All of these interferences with the efficient working of the market reduce the freedom of choice of some individuals and lead to economic waste. As such, they must be considered a social cost. To the extent that being the World Banker has made it impossible for the U.S. to use the most direct approach to the adjustment of the balance of payments, the banking role is also responsible for these social burdens.

The key currency status of the U.S. is also responsible for some social cost in terms of unemployment. It is not necessarily contradictory that a country desires a slow rate of price increases and yet strives for a higher level of employment. For instance, the existing unemployment rate may be so high that a reduction is considered desirable, even though it implies a somewhat faster rate of price increases. This is especially so if the initial high unemployment is accompanied by almost complete price stability. Such a situation has existed in the U.S. at least from 1960 through 1964. The failure to achieve an acceptable level of employment is directly attributable to the large short-term capital obligations of the U.S. which the key currency status had brought about. These short-term obligations were a serious constraint on a really vigorous and adequate expansion of the money supply. "The Federal Reserve's anti-recession policy, for the first time since the early 1930's, was constrained by a serious balance of payments situation." [6] It is crucial for the argument to establish that the constraint on the use of monetary policy was not the increase in imports and prices which a higher level of income would have brought about, but that instead it was the fear that low interest rates and excessive liquidity would encourage interest arbitrage and add to the already large outflow of short-term capital.

Certain actions and statements by Washington officials support this interpretation of the situation. First, there was a change of technique in monetary policy explicitly designed to deal with the problem of short-term capital movements. This technique, known as "operation nudge," consists of trying to influence the maturity structure of interest rates by increasing the supply of short-term relative to that of long-term securities. In this way, it was argued, it would be possible to keep short rates competitive internationally, while allowing the longer rates to be lower, thus encouraging domestic investment. While monetary expansion was desired, the key currency status led to a complicated and less efficient method of getting the expansion.

The U.S. government was very much concerned about the interest sensitivity of these short-term funds, as the following statement by Secretary Dillon indicates: "Our conclusions, after studying this matter intensively, are that there are substantial sums of liquid funds that are potentially sensitive to differentials between interest rates here and interest rates in the Euro-dollar market, and also between rates here and those on British and Canadian Treasury bills and on other short-term paper in those, as well as in continental European money markets." [7] It is important to add that these funds discussed here are not owned by foreign governments but by private parties. It may be that these shiftable funds are relatively small as compared with the U.S. gold stock. But their importance goes far beyond their size, because of the swiftness with which they influence the balance of payments in any one quarter. The danger is that such sudden payments deteriorations will be interpreted as lack of confidence, and trigger speculative runs. It is in a sense not really important whether this interpretation of empirical evidence is erroneous or not, or whether it is misplaced at a time when agreements among central banks have considerably reduced the seriousness of the consequences of speculative runs on currencies. The fact that is important is that officials were concerned with the problem and considered it a constraint on policy. [8]

There is a second indication that the constraint on monetary policy was due to the short-term capital movements and not to the increased imports which normally accompany higher levels of employment. The push for a tax-cut was pursued vigorously throughout the Kennedy administration. Yet, during that period balance of payments deficits remained very large. What this means is that reductions in unemployment were considered so urgent that the accompanying deterioration in the balance of payments was acceptable.

Some supporters of the tax cut argued that domestic business expansion would actually benefit the balance of payments by making domestic investment more attractive relative to foreign investment and thus reducing the long-term capital outflows. Whatever the merits of this argument, it would be equally valid whether the domestic expansion was based on a tax cut or on monetary stimulation. This is one more reason to believe that expansionary monetary policy was not prevented by fears over price increases and deficits resulting from higher income, but by fears of triggering speculative runs through the inducement of large-scale interest arbitrage of short-term funds.

The evidence is therefore strong that being the World Banker has contributed to some real losses of output. *First,* the central position of the dollar has allowed the U.S. to get to a serious disequilibrium position and has then made it impossible to use devaluation as a method of return to equilibrium. *Second,* the large stock of U.S. short-term obligations put constraints on the use of monetary policy for the achievement of full-employment, so that there had to be resort to fiscal policy. The passage of the required legislation took several years, during which time unemployment remained high.

But there remains the question of quantifying these losses. Professor J. Vanek has estimated the loss as coming to between $15 and $20 billion in each of the four years between 1958 and 1962.[9] The Council of Economic Advisers has computed annual estimates of an "output gap," which can serve well as a gross figure of losses. This gap is defined as the income lost through the economy's failure to operate at capacity, which is considered to lie at an unemployment rate of four per cent. The output gap for the years 1957–1964 averaged approximately $35 billion a year. We shall not attempt here our own estimate of how much of this gap was actually due to the constraints on the use and timing of full employment policies which could be traced to the role of being the World Banker. The above discussion suggests that at least some portion of the gap can be thus allocated. But it should be noted that it does not require a large percentage for this real cost of America's banking role to exceed the benefits.

NOTES

1. Douglas C. Dillon's statement before the Joint Economic Committee, "The United States Balance of Payments," *Hearings,* Part I, Current Problems and Policies, Washington, D.C.: 1963, p. 28.
2. Dillon, *op. cit.,* p. 28.
3. This point was made by H. G. Johnson in his "Liquidity—Problems and Plans," reprinted in H. Grubel, ed., *World Monetary Reform: Plans and Issues* (Stanford: Stanford University Press, 1963), p. 373.
4. Dillon, *op. cit.*

5. Dillon, *op. cit.*, p. 17.
6. *Economic Report of the President*, and *Annual Report of the Council of Economic Advisers*, 1962, pp. 68–92.
7. Dillon, *op. cit.*, p. 24.
8. William Salant writes: "The sheer size of foreign dollar reserves, and the obvious availability of gold as an alternative form in which to hold reserves, suggest that the contingency of a reduction in the reserve can never be far from the minds of responsible officials in the United States." "The Reserve Currency Role of the Dollar: Blessing or Burden to the United States," *The Review of Economics and Statistics*, XLVI, No. 2 (May 1964), p. 169.
9. Jaroslav Vanek, "Overvaluation of the Dollar: Causes, Effects, and Remedies," in *Factors Affecting the United States Balance of Payments*, Compilation of Studies for the Joint Economic Committee, Washington, D.C.: 1962, pp. 272–73.

DOES IT NECESSARILY COST ANYTHING
TO BE THE "WORLD BANKER"?

Henry N. Goldstein

Associate Professor of Economics,
University of Oregon

In his recent stimulating contribution to this Journal,[1] Professor
Grubel maintains that "being the World Banker has severely limited
the choice of tools that the U.S. can use to adjust her balance of payments, leaving only rather inefficient alternatives."[2] Grubel's entire
cost/benefit analysis hinges on this assumption. As he notes, however,
the existence of such a constraint on U.S. policy has been pointed out
by no less than Secretary Dillon. According to Secretary Dillon:

> Our dominant role in world trade and finance has meant that we could
> not either *prudently* or *effectively* use many of the simpler and most direct
> types of action by which other countries have sometimes dealt with their
> payments deficits. Currency devaluation, import restriction, exchange con-
> trol . . . are all out of the question. [my italics][3]

As Grubel notes, the existence of this same constraint has also been
stressed by such authoritative academic observers as William Salant,
George Halm, Theodore Geiger, and Harry Johnson.[4]
Despite the official and academic credentials of those who have expressed this view, I do not believe that it withstands critical examination. Let me put my doubts in the form of a question. Has it been an
"institutional fact"—namely, the dollar's role as a reserve currency—
that has *compelled* the U.S. to follow "inefficient policies" in coping

From Henry N. Goldstein, "Does it Necessarily Cost Anything to be the 'World
Banker,'?" *The National Banking Review*, Vol. 2, No. 3 (March 1965), 411–15.

with its payments deficit in recent years? Or, should the responsibility for such policies be attributed more properly to timidity and lack of a "proper set" of social priorities on the part of those individuals who happened to have occupied positions of authority? To rephrase the question: has the failure of the U.S. economy to operate at a higher level of output and employment during the past five years reflected the "inevitable outcome" of the payments arrangements that have existed, *or* should that failure be attributed to the inappropriate policies of particular men working under those arrangements?

To assess the possible validity of this second hypothesis we have to suppose that a different attitude had dominated economic policy decisions in this country. For the sake of argument, then, imagine that during recent years different men had occupied the strategic "economic decision-making" positions in the Administration, the Congress, and the Federal Reserve System. Assume that these men had been less willing than the actual incumbents to tolerate excessive domestic unemployment in order to "keep the dollar as good as gold." And suppose, also, that they had been less apprehensive than the actual incumbents of the speculative after-effects of *equilibrating* adjustments in existing par values. With such men "at the controls," this country's macro-economic policies would presumably have differed from the policies actually followed in the following respects:

(1) we would have had an earlier and a larger tax cut;
(2) we would have had a larger volume of government spending;
(3) we would have had an easier monetary policy.

Presumably, these policies would have produced a higher level of employment, output and economic growth. But what would have been the probable balance-of-payments results?

In some respects, a higher level of domestic output and employment would have strengthened the U.S. external position. Relative to the rest of the world, the United States would have been a more attractive place for direct investments than, in fact, it has proved to be. Also, insofar as U.S. export and import-competing industries practice cost-plus pricing *and* have lower average unit costs at higher output levels, there would have been some tendency for these industries to be internationally more competitive than they in fact were.

On the whole, however, opposing influences would almost certainly have dominated. Under conditions of stronger general demand, costs and prices of U.S. goods would probably have risen more then they have in fact risen, and the willingness and ability of U.S. producers to provide prompt delivery and "fringe services" would have declined. Moreover, aside from reducing the competitiveness of U.S. goods in both price and nonprice terms, a higher level of U.S. national income would—through the "marginal propensity to import"—have stimulated a greater volume of imports. With the same exchange rates, therefore, the "basic" U.S. payments deficit would probably have been considerably larger than it actually has been. Correspondingly, the rest of the world would have experienced a larger overall payments surplus. In particular, the countries that have built up their gold and dollar holdings the most during the past six years—France and Germany—would have built them up even more.

All this, of course, assumes that continued confidence in existing parities could somehow have been maintained. But this possibility seems far-fetched. Before very long something would have had to give.

As Milton Friedman has pointed out, a country can cope with an underlying balance-of-payments deficit in four ways:

(1) it can reduce the external price of its currency;
(2) it can impose controls of one kind or another (and so "live with" a more-or-less permanent disequilibrium in the foreign exchange market);
(3) it can finance its deficit out of owned or borrowed reserves (so long as its stock of internationally acceptable assets or international credit hold out);
(4) it can deflate its economy.

But, as Friedman also emphasizes, these are the only four ways; there are no others.[5]

The U.S. policy makers who have actually been running our affairs have chosen to use a combination of methods (2), (3), and (4).[6] The dollar price of gold has been sacrosanct; and so have the par values of the currencies of those foreign countries whose surpluses have corresponded, in the main, to our deficit (the only exception was the 5 per cent revaluation of the DM and the guilder in March 1961). With a different set of U.S. policy makers at the helm, however, is it inevitable that this degree of rigidity in the exchange rates of the major industrial countries would have been maintained? Admittedly, it is likely that a different set of policy makers would also have been very reluctant to increase the dollar price of gold (for why provide an unnecessary windfall gain to the gold speculators, to the Soviet Union, and to the Republic of South Africa?). Nevertheless, it would surely have been possible to exert a great deal more pressure on Germany and France to revalue their currencies than was in fact ever attempted. Had this pressure been successfully exerted, there would presumably have been a quick restoration of reasonable balance in the flow of international payments between the U.S. and the Continental countries.

Had our policy makers striven to persuade the Europeans to revalue their currencies they could have utilized the following potent arguments:

(1) They could have pointed out to both the German and French governments, and to the governing authorities of the IMF as well, that a "basic disequilibrium" clearly existed. Had we pursued a full-employment policy with vigor, our deficits on current-account and long-term capital account plus net unilateral transfers would probably have exceeded $6 billion a year.[7]

(2) They could have pointed out that a change in the dollar price of gold (*unaccompanied* by a corresponding devaluation by the major surplus countries) would be the least desirable way of achieving the needed realignment of par values; for this mode of depreciating the dollar relative to foreign currencies would have played into the hands of gold speculators and also given windfalls to the Soviet Union and to the Union of South Africa.

(3) They could have pointed out that an appropriate realignment of par values would eliminate "imported inflationary pressures" on the Continent. (These pressures would have been even greater than those actually experienced if the U.S. had pursued more expansionary fiscal and monetary policies).

Admittedly, the surplus countries might have resisted our tactfully stated suggestions that they revalue their currencies. In that event, we may imagine the U.S. Secretary of the Treasury addressing his opposite numbers in the OECD in the following terms:

The maintenance of full employment and a high rate of domestic economic growth is as important an economic objective in my country as it is in yours. At the present, however, given the nature of our overseas com-

mitments, our price and cost structure, our level of "full-employment" national income, and our distaste for protectionism, we are compelled to admit
that the dollar is significantly overvalued relative to a number of your currencies. The exact extent of this overvaluation is uncertain; but our experts'
best guesses range from 10 to 15 per cent as against the following currencies—the DM . . . .%; the French franc . . . .%; the Austrian
schilling . . . .%, ...

In order to remove this disequilibrium, we urge your respective governments to revalue their currencies by the percentages just noted (with the
revaluations averaging 12.23 per cent on an "unweighted basis"). Should
your governments be unwilling to take this action, we shall feel compelled,
in order to meet our domestic and international responsibilities, to either increase the dollar price of gold by this same percentage, or—and this would
probably be our second choice—to cease buying and selling gold to foreign
official institutions altogether.

We appreciate the seriousness of either type of action. But we see no way
out except to deflate our economy or impose various types of open or disguised exchange controls, alternatives which we find even more distasteful
and which are also contrary to the spirit and letter of both the Bretton Woods
Agreement and the GATT.

Had U.S. policy-makers pursued this sort of line, is it altogether fanci-
ful to believe that the Europeans would have cooperated and adjusted their parities?

If this approach had failed, the U.S. would presumably have had
to go ahead with its threat and increase the dollar price of gold by an
amount ranging from 10 to 15 per cent of its present value. If the Europeans had not then "retaliated" and devalued their currencies by
offsetting margins, the dollar's devaluation would have represented an
effective resolution of the U.S. policy-dilemma, even though it would
have been considerably less optimal than an appropriate revaluation
of the strong European currencies.

Moreover, the possibility of "European retaliation" in these circumstances seems remote. For whereas the U.S. action would clearly
have been justified under the rules laid down in the Bretton Woods
Agreement, any European counter-action could only have been interpreted—under those rules—as an attempt to "beggar-their-neigh-
bor." If the U.S. had, in fact, increased the dollar price of gold following the refusal of the Europeans to revalue their currencies by appropriate margins, its determination not to allow a balance-of-payments

deficit to throttle its domestic economic growth or force it to adopt protectionist measures would have been evident, and counter-revaluations of European currencies would have appeared clearly unproductive and irresponsible. For similar reasons, it seems unlikely that the Europeans would have initiated any "run" on the U.S. gold stock following a devaluation of the dollar. Such an action might well have forced the U.S. to go "off gold" altogether—presumably the last thing any "responsible" European financial leader would want to see.

* * *

We have argued that a reserve-currency country has almost as much leverage in obtaining an equilibrating adjustment in exchange rates as a non-reserve currency country, *providing* that its policy makers have an appropriate set of social priorities and a suitable lack of respect for the "untouchability of existing par values." If our argument has merit, the case for abandoning the dollar's use as a reserve currency is weaker than Professor Grubel makes out.

Our argument does not imply, of course, that there is no merit in international monetary reform. Quite possibly, as Professor Grubel implies, a system of flexible exchange rates or—going to the opposite extreme—the creation of an XIMF [Expanded International Monetary Fund] would both prove superior to present institutional arrangements, even if these arrangements were managed in a better fashion than they have been. The main purpose of this note is simply to question the widely accepted assumption that a reserve-currency country is significantly more "constrained" than other countries in its efforts to achieve both internal and external economic objectives.[8]

NOTES

1. Herbert G. Grubel, "The Benefits and Costs of Being the World Banker," *The National Banking Review*, Vol. 2, No. 2 (December 1964), 189–212.
2. *Ibid.*, p. 200.
3. See Douglas C. Dillon, Statement before the Joint Economic Committee, "The United States Balance of Payments," *Hearings*, Part I, Current Problems and Policies, Washington, D.C.: 1963, cited by Grubel, *op. cit.*, pp. 201–202.
4. Appropriate references to statements by these observers are given by Grubel, *op. cit.*, p. 202.
5. See Milton Friedman, "The Case for Flexible Exchange Rates," reprinted in *Foreign Trade and Finance* (ed. by Allen and Allen), pp. 316–317.
6. Grubel argues (*op. cit.*, pp. 202–203) that the imposition of the Interest Equalization Tax and the partial tying of U.S. military purchases overseas may be

viewed as a disguised devaluation of the dollar for certain types of transactions.

7. In recent years, it has become fashionable in fiscal-policy discussions to use the term "full employment deficit" to refer to the estimated Federal budget deficit (or surplus!) at "Full Employment." My colleague, Reed Hansen, has suggested to me that a similar term might aid clear thinking in discussing balance-of-payments questions. A portmanteau term that has occurred to me is "the gimmick-free, full-employment payments deficit."

8. Professor Tobin has recently argued that—on grounds of "international morality" —the Europeans should either revalue their currencies or freely extend compensatory finance to enable the U.S. to "manage" its payments deficit at full employment. (See James Tobin, "Europe and the Dollar," *Review of Economics and Statistics,* May 1964, pp. 123–126.) As Tobin sadly observes, however, the Europeans have been quite unwilling to pursue such policies *voluntarily*—even though these policies would greatly benefit the United States and would involve no economic cost to themselves (rather, considerable economic benefit through the reduction of inflationary pressures). Moreover, in Tobin's view, the hands of U.S. policy-makers have been tied. As he puts it, "Once a banker has solemnly assured the world and his depositors that he will never fail, he is at the mercy of those depositors capable of making him fail" (*op. cit.,* p. 124).

Since the beginning of history, however, countries—great and small—have broken their "solemn promises" when circumstances have dictated. Consider, too, that in honoring our pledge to keep the dollar price of gold unchanged we find ourselves breaking our commitments under the Bretton Woods Agreement and the GATT to pursue policies that promote domestic full employment and free world trade (assuming that we are in fact placed in this "moral dilemma" by the unwillingness of the Europeans, *even under pressure,* to revalue their currencies). But, surely, it is a bit strained to "blame" the Europeans for not volunteering actions which—however appropriate from an internationally "moral" and economic point of view—would reduce their bargaining power and prestige, relative to the United States, around a host of international conference tables. Does not the blame belong, rather, to U.S. policy-makers who have failed to recognize their country's economic self-interest and to exercise the bargaining power at their disposal in negotiating with the Europeans?

THE FUTURE OF THE DOLLAR RESERVE SYSTEM

William A. Salant

The late William A. Salant
had a distinguished career in government service,
as an economic consultant,
and as a lecturer at Brandeis University.

For the purpose of determining policy, the relevant question is not whether the United States has gained or lost flexibility in its economic policy in the past by serving as an international reserve center. Nor is it whether the reserve currency function might result on balance in flexibility or in constraint in the abstract, if a blueprint for an international monetary system were worked out *de novo*, without any legacy from the past in the form of institutions, working relations, past experiences, and the dollar reserves now in existence. The question is rather whether flexibility or constraint will dominate in the future, if we begin where we now stand and go on from there. Thus the answer depends, in part, on the assumptions as to the conditions under which the dollar might serve as a reserve currency in the future.

Moreover, the answer requires a second term for the comparison. To say that United States policy is more flexible or more constrained when the dollar is used as a reserve currency implies a comparison with some alternative international monetary system. A large number of alternatives is possible; the result of the comparison depends on which one is selected. For example, it might be found that the United States would gain flexibility under a dollar reserve system as compared with a regime in which deficits were settled fully in gold, but would be more constrained than under a system which provided easy access to credit.

From William A. Salant, "The Reserve Currency Role of the Dollar: Blessing or Burden to the United States?" *The Review of Economics and Statistics,* XLVI, No. 2 (May 1964), 170–72.

Thus there is no single all-embracing answer to the question whether United States economic policies will be more or less constrained if the dollar continues to serve as a reserve currency than if it does not. The same observation applies to the broader question, whether the United States will gain or lose from the use of the dollar as a reserve currency if all the other factors that have not been discussed in this paper are thrown into the balance.

We shall glance at the relation between some of the major dimensions of variation in the international monetary mechanism and the degree of flexibility or constraint in United States economic policy.

I. The hazards of serving as a reserve center are greatly reduced if there is assurance that foreign holders will not withdraw their reserve balances, or at least if limits are placed on withdrawals. Such assurances might take a number of forms, formal or informal, multilateral or bilateral. A formal multilateral arrangement, for example, might specify the amounts, or the percentages of their total reserves, that participating countries would hold in the form of dollars.

II. Assurance against withdrawals would, presumably, require a *quid pro quo* involving some cost to the United States. Of the possible concessions that the United States might grant, two seem most important:

(a) A guarantee to foreign holders of dollar reserves against loss from devaluation. Such a guarantee would presumably take the form of agreement to maintain foreign reserve holdings at their former value in terms of either gold or some specified foreign currency in the event of a change in the dollar price of gold or in the relevant exchange rate. Although guarantees have won a good deal of outside support, the United States Treasury and Federal Reserve authorities have, at least in the past, been firmly opposed to them. Nevertheless, some form of guarantee may prove to be a necessary condition for European agreement to continued use of the dollar or other national currencies as reserve currencies.

(b) Increased consultation with reserve holding countries on United States financial and economic policies. Such consultation already exists. If assurances against withdrawal of reserve balances were granted (beyond any unpublicized assurances that may already be in effect), the United States would probably be required, in return, to intensify its consultation on policy. The cost to the United States would depend on (1) the extent to which consultation implied giving holders of dollar reserves an actual voice in the determination of United States policy, and (2) the extent to which United States views as to appropriate policy diverged from those of the foreign holders of reserve balances. In this connection, it is encouraging that foreign governments are said to be sympathetic to fiscal policy aimed at economic expansion in the United States. This represents a considerable improvement over the situation a few years ago when the appearance of a $12 billion federal budget deficit in fiscal year 1959, caused largely by a cyclical decline in tax receipts, gave rise to widespread concern abroad that the budget was "out of control" (perhaps reflecting in part similar concern expressed both in banking and administration circles in the United States).

III. The position of the United States under any new international monetary arrangement would be greatly influenced by the disposition of existing dollar reserve balances. Basically, there are three possibilities:

(a) Liquidation of the balances.
(b) Maintenance in their present form, in which they are convertible into gold at the option of the holder.
(c) Freezing, that is, restriction or termination of the right of withdrawal.

Numerous variations and combinations of these basic alternatives are possible, and restriction of the right of free withdrawal almost necessarily implies some provision for either gradual liquidation or amortization, or for guarantees.

One must rule out, as a practical possibility, the operation of the dollar reserve system as it existed in the 1950's, when foreign countries were happy to see a rapid build-up in their dollar reserves. The system has already been transformed, both by the changed attitudes of the holders of dollar balances arising from changed circumstances, and by the ingenious innovations introduced since 1960 to meet the new situation. These innovations include intervention by the United States in foreign exchange markets, mutual support through currency swaps, sale of Roosa bonds, and the stand-by arrangement to supplement the resources of the IMF, as well as periodic contact and consultations among officials responsible for financial and economic policy.

In making its choice among the available alternatives, the United

States should be guided primarily by the objective of seeking agreement on a payments system which combines adequate liquidity with stability. Narrower questions of United States interest must also be considered, however. Whether those interests will be better served if the reserve currency role of the dollar is maintained, shared, or eliminated, cannot be determined except by reference to the specific provisions of the available alternatives. Our discussion does, however, point to two general observations:

(1) The possibility of large scale withdrawal of reserve balances reduces the freedom of action of the United States in its economic policies. It would be highly advantageous to the United States if that possibility were removed or circumscribed, although any cost involved must of course be weighed against the advantage.

(2) This note has discussed only one aspect of the reserve currency function—its relation to the economic policy options available to the United States, and particularly the issue whether it is a source of flexibility or of constraint. Examination of the full range of costs and benefits associated with the reserve currency role of the dollar would suggest, in the judgment of the writer, that preservation of this role should not, in itself, be an important objective of the United States. If, as seems likely, other countries should make the curtailment or sharing of this role a condition of agreement to changes in the international reserve and payments system, the United States should acquiesce provided the changes achieve its broader objectives.

PART III

Balance of Payments Policies
Under the Adjustable Peg System

INTRODUCTION

One of the chief difficulties with the operation of the present adjustable peg system is the lack of low cost (efficient) methods of adjusting to payments imbalances. While there is fairly general agreement on this point, there is still strong disagreement over a number of issues surrounding the adjustment process. These tend to center around the following three questions: (1) Which countries have borne the greatest portion of the burden of adjustment in the postwar period? (2) In what proportion should the responsibility for adjustment be allocated among countries? (3) What are the best methods of bringing about adjustment, i.e., how should adjustment be undertaken? These three questions provide the basis for Part III.[1]

METHODS OF BALANCE OF PAYMENTS ADJUSTMENT

To improve its trade balance without resort to controls, a country's money income must be reduced relative to foreign money income as expressed in home currency. This may be achieved in three ways (singly or in combination). A country can follow policies which (1) lower its prices relative to those abroad, (2) lower its real income (output) relative to that abroad, or (3) lower the rate at which domestic currency is converted into foreign currency, i.e., lower its exchange rate (depreciate or devalue its currency).

The logic of the gold standard (which existed internationally in the 19th and early 20th centuries) was that price and income changes would be brought about automatically, under unalterably fixed exchange rates. As gold flowed out of a country as the result of a payments deficit, its money supply would contract and aggregate demand

79

would fall. Similarly, in the surplus country, gold inflows would bring expansionary pressure. Thus adjustment would be shared by surplus and deficit countries.[2]

However, deficit countries have not been attracted to this "classical medicine," i.e., deflation, in the face of balance of payments deficits. The existence of rigidities in domestic wages and prices means that deflationary policies often result more in unemployment than in price declines. Of course, increased unemployment itself will improve the trade balance, as less is imported out of lowered real income. Needless to say, such a method of adjustment sharply conflicts with important domestic objectives.

National policies are made on the basis of trade-offs between various competing objectives, but the trade-off between domestic employment and balance of payments adjustment through real income changes is a very bad one for countries in which foreign trade is small compared to the domestic economy. U.S. imports have been running at about 5 per cent of gross national product. If the same percentage of a change in income is spent on imports, it would take a $20 billion decline in gross national product to cut imports by $1 billion and a $60 billion fall to yield a $3 billion improvement in the deficit through this mechanism.

In recent years it has been emphasized that in a growing world economy adjustment without changing exchange rates need imply not absolute but only relative deflation. For instance, if the rest of the world is inflating at a rate of 3 per cent per annum and a given country can hold its own rate to 1 per cent, then it can realize a 2 per cent differential. The scope for such differential deflation is small, however, and sizable adjustment could take a long time.

We should stress that adjustment through relative rather than absolute deflation eases but does not eliminate the conflict with domestic objectives, except in circumstances in which the economy is overheated (and hence less expansionary policies are called for on both balance of payments and domestic grounds). They still force the economy to accept greater unemployment than is deemed desirable on domestic grounds. In other words, less expansionary policies lead the economy along its trade-off curve between unemployment and price stability (as described by Smith in Part I) toward greater unemployment. As was discussed in "The Costs and Benefits of Being the World Banker" (Part II.B), this description fits U.S. policy actions during the early 1960's and the corresponding high levels of unemployment. The U.S. efforts at wage-price guidelines and the British incomes policies are attempts to improve this trade-off (efforts which, we might add, have had only limited success).

Conflicts between the balance of payments and domestic objectives may be less than those between the trade balance and domestic objectives, however. A good deal of attention in recent years has been paid to improving the balance of payments via the capital account. While imports usually increase relative to exports during a domestic cyclical expansion (i.e., trade deficits accompany such expansions), the long term capital account generally improves. Cyclical expansion of output is accompanied by increased profitability, and hence there is a greater incentive for residents to invest at home and a greater attraction of funds from abroad.

Conceivably, the positive capital account effects of a domestic expansion could exceed the negative trade account effects, so that the overall balance of payments would improve. In fact, as Jeffrey G. Williamson shows in [74] and [75], this was the general case for the United States during the previous century. This reasoning was used by the Kennedy Administration in arguing for the 1964 tax cut, but, unfortunately, in this instance the strategy did not prove successful as a balance of payments cure. Considerable attention also has been given to the use of high interest rates to improve the short and long term (portfolio) capital accounts. Under this approach, the deflationary domestic effects of tight money are offset by expansionary fiscal policy. This idea was put forward by Robert A. Mundell in a highly influential paper [49]. However, further work, such as [1], [17], and [31], has indicated that such policies may lead to only short run improvements in the balance of payments and may conflict with other policy goals such as economic growth. Furthermore, such tight money policies can be a very expensive method of finance because of their high interest costs. (See [72].)

Thus it appears that in the absence of changes in exchange rates, there is no reliable method of market adjustment which does not conflict with major domestic objectives. As Otmar Emminger points out in a later reading in this Part, it is not that the classical medicine will not work, but that modern governments generally believe (quite rightly, in our opinion) that such a cure would be worse than the disease. In the terminology of the theory of economic policy, national governments do not have enough policy tools to meet effectively all desired economic goals if exchange rate variation is ruled out.[3]

Given that the priority goals of national macro-economic policy are growth and a good trade-off between employment and inflation, the choice of methods to correct or suppress a prolonged deficit usually comes down to the sacrifice of either the exchange rate parity or freedom of international exchange, i.e., to *devaluation* or *controls*.

U.S. AND BRITISH BALANCE OF PAYMENTS POLICIES

The "control or devalue" dilemma for deficit countries is clearly illustrated by the American and British experiences in the postwar period. Fritz Machlup points out in "The Adjustment Problem and the Balance of Payments Policy of the United States" that the emphasis of U.S. policy actions has been on financing rather than correcting the deficit. As Haberler and Willett conclude:

> United States balance-of-payments policy since 1959 may be characterized largely as a combination of short-sighted expedients with little emphasis on longer term solutions. Most of these policies were designed to buy time. Unfortunately little productive use has been made of this time as far as fundamental corrections are concerned. [26, p. 13] [4]

The United States for a long period relied on one of the major mechanisms implicit in the adjustable peg system. *They waited*, in hopes that the deficit would go away, i.e., in hopes that the factors causing the deficit would reverse themselves. Machlup refers to the "statements by our Presidents and Secretaries of the Treasury expressing their assurances and confident expectations that balance was just around the corner."

While there was clearly an element of wishful thinking involved in such predictions, the nature of the U.S. payments deficits is also an important explanation. There was no single factor causing the U.S. deficit, and hence diagnosis of future trends was difficult. Given the considerable costs to adjustment under a pegged rate system, it is not surprising that radical adjustment policies were delayed.

As to the cause of the U.S. deficits, a strong case can be made that it should be considered the lack of an adjustment mechanism rather than the various events and circumstances which have generated deviations from equilibrium. As Lionel Robbins has aptly stated:

"If a car fails to reach its destination, if it is continually running into the side, or if it is continually having to solicit hauls from passing lorries, we should not regard it as a sufficient explanation that the roads are not level and straight, that there are hills to ascend and corners to turn." [55, p. 16]; cited in [77, p. 393]

For the United States there have been many hills and corners, such as the postwar economic recovery of Europe and Japan, the depreciation of the currencies of nearly all major foreign countries in 1949, the French devaluation in 1958, shifts of liquid funds, inflationary developments in the United States (especially in certain key export sectors), and the Vietnam War.

Thus it is quite understandable that "The tendency to seek a single cause for the U.S. payments problem results in the sad finding that everyone is wrong." [38, p. 539] The controversy over the relative importance of hills and curves was also reflected in disagreement on the likelihood of the future reversibility of the factors giving rise to the deficit. While this does lead to problems in deciding when one should begin to administer cures, it need not be a problem for the choice of what types of cure to administer. Contrary to what strikes most of us as intuitively correct, ". . . only in rare cases can or should the cure of a deficit be tailored to the nature of the cause." [20, p. 126] (This point is considered further in the Emminger and Cooper readings.)

The policy actions taken by the United States are discussed by Machlup. Both controls and selective devaluations of the dollar for specific purposes such as foreign aid and defense procurements have been initiated.

The British responses to the recurrent difficulties of the pound since World War II have followed a similar course, with the exception that monetary and fiscal policies were used to a greater extent. As discussed by Grubel in Part II, U.S. financial policies were excessively deflationary from 1958 to 1964, partially in response to the balance of payments deficit. Yet U.S. policy was generally steady. In the U.K., monetary and fiscal policies were responsive directly to the short run state of the balance of payments. The British authorities responded with specific policies in an attempt to cure the deficit each time a crisis occurred. These measures involved a "stop-go" monetary and fiscal policy: contractionary policy in response to a balance of payments crisis, expansionary policy when the crisis passed.

In addition to macro economic policy, other measures were under-

taken in particular crises: exchange controls on the balance of payments, tariff surcharges, and controls on wage rates and prices. These
policies, too, have been alternatively strengthened and weakened in
response to fluctuations in the balance of payments. As Yeager comments: ". . . the rapid reversibility of British policy has been almost
comical at times." [77, p. 394] In fact it has been argued that U.K.
policy has accentuated or even caused the cyclical pattern in the British
balance of payments.[5]

However, there is no doubt that longer term forces have been at
work to cause balance of payments difficulties for Britain in the postwar period: a lagging educational system compared to other industrial
countries, a lack of drive and sales promotion for exports, poor quality
of management, and low productivity.

After a succession of crises in which the pound was bailed out by
reserve operations of official lenders (the IMF and foreign central
banks), it was decided that controls, special export taxes, etc., were not
sufficient to cure the British deficit. In November 1967, in the face of
another speculative attack on sterling, the pound was devalued by 14.3
per cent (from $2.80 to $2.40).

The British devaluation and the events surrounding it are discussed
by The Economist, a leading British publication. Their article, "Britain: Will the Bungle Work?" was written just after the devaluation.
These events provide a clear illustration of the confidence problems
which can plague the adjustable peg system.

ADJUSTMENT RESPONSIBILITIES

From the previous discussions, it is clear that both the United States
and Britain have reason to believe that they have borne rather heavy
costs of adjustment. The view has frequently been expressed that the
surplus countries should have done more to reduce the payments imbalances. (See for instance, Goldstein's paper in Part II.)

On the other hand, it is a common view among bankers and officials
in the surplus countries that the system has operated to their disadvantage, that the deficit countries have not borne their share of adjustment responsibilities and that the United States is in an especially privileged position of creating international liquidity to finance its deficits.
This view is espressed by Otmar Emminger in the reading "Practical
Aspects of the Problem of Balance-of-Payments Adjustment." He

argues that: "It may, from all the experiences in the postwar period, be safely said that our present international monetary system has a clear inflationary bias and a clear bias to the disadvantage of surplus countries."

What gives rise to these conflicting views?

How . . . can each country claim that it has borne the largest burden of adjustment? It is because there is, again, a half-hidden difference in national premises. Emminger can argue that "the burden of adjustment lay very one-sidedly on the shoulders of the European surplus countries" because the more rapid increase of European prices, fueled by imports of bank liquidity, was a high price for any European to pay for external balance. Yet Americans can claim that the United States bore too large a share of the total burden, for though there was "no significant deflation on the U.S. side," public policies to cut back unemployment were delayed or modulated by the fear that they would worsen the balance of payments. To be brief but blunt, we have not yet devised a way to compare the social costs of inflation and unemployment inside a single country and are further still from any way to balance an inflation in one country against unemployment in another country.—Peter B. Kenen [38, p. 539]

While it is certainly true that no satisfactory scientific method of comparing the costs of inflation and unemployment has been devised, many feel that on both equity and efficiency grounds any trade-off between the two should be heavily weighted toward inflation. Even if a consensus were reached at this point, however, it is not clear that it would be efficient to place all of the responsibility of adjustment on surplus countries:

The realization that demand deflation, depressing business activity and lowering employment, is more wasteful and painful than demand inflation, overstimulating business activity and raising prices, may suggest the conclusion that for all countries taken together the cost would be smallest if adjustment were induced only by demand expansion in the surplus countries. The error of such a precept lies in the neglect of the possibility that making adjustment costless to deficit countries may increase the temptation to pursue policies leading to deficits, which in turn may increase the need for adjustment, and hence the cost of adjustment over longer periods.—Fritz Machlup [41, p. 80].

Another criterion which suggests itself is to apportion adjustment responsibilities according to responsibility for having caused the imbalance, but as has been indicated in this introduction, determining the cause(s) of payments imbalances is no easy task.

Should we say that the deficits resulting from the reserve currency status of the dollar were caused by the United States or by Europe? And were these deficits harmful to Europe? In this regard, James Tobin's comments are instructive:

> The United States has provided a reserve currency. In the late 'forties no other international and intergovernmental money was available except gold, and the supply of gold was not keeping up with the demand. U.S. deficits filled the gap with dollars. It is true that this gave the U.S. a favored position among countries. Anyone who can print money can choose how new money will be first spent. The U.S. did not seek this privileged role; it arose by accidental evolution rather than conscious design. As it happens, the U.S. did not exploit it to live beyond our means, to make the American people more affluent. We used it rather for broad international purposes. No doubt in the long run the creation of new international money should be a privilege and responsibility more widely and symmetrically shared. But once the U.S. and the world are adjusted to the creation of international money via U.S. deficits, it is scarcely reasonable suddenly to ring a bell announcing that the world's financial experts have now decided that these deficits—past, present, and future—are pernicious. [64, p. 156]

In the same vein, Haberler has remarked:

> A tiny tail threatens to wag a huge and rapidly growing dog! The true dimension of the problem should be pondered by foreign critics who complain that the role of the dollar as an international reserve currency enables the United States to "live beyond its means" by extracting "involuntary loans" from other countries. In reality, the so-called "involuntary loans," as measured by the dollar holdings of the complaining foreign central banks—balances on which they earn a good interest—are a small fraction of the United States' transfers abroad for economic aid, government loans, military assistance, private capital investments abroad which contribute to the growth and development of the recipient countries. [25, pp. 432–33]

It has been held by some that the existence of a payments deficit is in itself evidence of excessive expansion on the part of the deficit country; for absolute or relative deflation would always have corrected the deficit. As Machlup has pointed out, however, to apply a rule based on this argument is to confuse "cause" and "failure to avert" and to make ". . . the existence of a deficit tautologically identical with responsibility for it. Such 'guilt by tautology' cannot reasonably be accepted." [41, p. 81]

The apportionment of responsibilities for adjustment is a critical issue. It has been the subject of considerable international consultation, especially under the auspices of the Organization for Economic Cooperation and Development (OECD). This body set up a Working Party (No. 3) in 1961 to analyze balance of payments adjustment and to suggest improvements.[6]

It is now generally agreed that there is mutual responsibility for adjustment. However, there is still considerable disagreement over how this responsibility should be shared, both on the basis of equity and on the basis of efficiency criteria. Perhaps one of the clearest areas of agreement is that, as the Report of Working Party No. 3 states: "Wherever possible, it is desirable that adjustment should take place through the relaxation of controls and restraints over international trade and capital movements by surplus countries, rather than by the imposition of new restraints by deficit countries." [76, p. 25][7]

LIQUIDITY CREATION AND ADJUSTMENT PRESSURE

The disagreement between surplus and deficit countries over adjustment responsibilities is mirrored in their attitudes toward the proper rate of expansion of international liquidity. As was indicated in the Background Notes to Part I, the greater are the reserves available to deficit countries, the less is the pressure on them to adjust. Thus, in attempting to answer the question "what is the optimal amount or rate of increase of international liquidity?" we are right back to the difficulties of agreement among countries discussed in the previous section. This holds also for the question of the composition of international liquidity as between owned and borrowed reserves, i.e., between the provision of additional reserve assets or additional credit facilities.

Recall the distinction between the two economic purposes for holding reserves: to allow time to be taken in curing a fundamental disequilibrium so that adjustment might be less costly, and to render adjustment unnecessary in the face of temporary reversals in the balance of payments. Where the size of such possible short run fluctuations is quite high (due, for instance, to the volatility of huge masses of private speculative funds), the provision of sufficient owned reserves or unconditional borrowing rights to handle this problem might entail levels of reserves that from the surplus countries' point of view would place insufficient pressure on deficit countries to correct their balance of payments. Thus, at least from the surplus countries' point of view, the perfect solution to such a dilemma between risking the stability of the system and weakening the incentives for curing deficits is to provide easy access to credit for deficit countries, allowing them to weather short run crises, while maintaining stringent conditions for the creation of owned reserves.

It is largely because of these conflicting points of view that there has been no general agreement on whether there exists a shortage of international liquidity. In other words, as Gottfried Haberler has pointed out: "While a real scarcity of international liquidity would almost certainly manifest itself in balance-of-payments deficits of some countries, not every balance-of-payments crisis, even of a reserve currency country, can be regarded as a symptom of an international scarcity of liquidity." [24, p. 10] There are extreme circumstances in which universal agreement over a shortage of liquidity could probably be reached. As Haberler goes on to argue, if almost all countries at the same time were undertaking policies designed to build up reserves—such as restricting international trade and investment, following deflationary domestic policies, or devaluing their currencies—then we clearly could speak of a genuine shortage of international liquidity.

In contrast to the clear adverse effects of a genuine global shortage of international reserves, the results of "too rapid" an increase in reserves are not as clear. The general charge is that rapid increases in reserves will be inflationary. But this is not so in the direct sense that a rapid expansion of the domestic money supply in a fully employed economy will be inflationary; for, as was stressed earlier, international reserves are held by national governments, not by private traders and investors.

However, it is true that a higher average level of world inflation generally would result from a rapid expansion of international reserves, because of the removal or weakening of constraints on monetary expansion in deficit countries caused by their balance of payments positions and the concomitant shifting of a greater portion of the burden of adjustment onto surplus countries. Nevertheless, it is not clear that surplus countries would react to surpluses resulting from the creation of international reserves in the same manner as they would to surpluses vis-à-vis deficit countries. In both cases it is true that accumulating reserves entails the opportunity costs of the foreign goods and services that they could be used to obtain; but in the second case obtaining reserves would not entail giving up domestic resources as it does in the first. Hence it seems likely that accumulation of reserves will have less inflationary impact on the country receiving them when they come from allotments of created reserves than when they are "earned."

Support for such a view that the inflationary impact of international reserve creation often may have been exaggerated is found in Fritz Machlup's extensive survey [46] of the relationships between countries' reserve levels and the variables, such as the volume of the country's imports and the variations in its trade balance, which generally are taken as the primary determinants of the demand for reserves. Machlup concludes from his study that there is serious doubt ". . . that the size of reserves is among the major targets or goals of economic policy, except where reserves are so *dangerously low* that a false step may bring the roof down or where reserves, though respectably high, show a *decline.*" [46, p. 25]

Shortly before this study was published, Machlup had offered what has become known as "the Mrs. Machlup's Wardrobe Theory of Monetary Reserves."

What then are foreign reserves needed for? They are not "needed" at all, strictly speaking. But monetary authorities make a fuss if they do not have all that they think they ought to have. Let me explain this by comparing the typical central banker with my wife, though this might be too flattering for most central bankers. How many dresses does my wife need? One, seven, 31, or 365? You may think that one dress is all she really needs—and even this is only because of our "culture pattern." I assure you, however, that she thinks she needs more. Whether she wants 25 or 52 depends on her upbringing and on the Joneses with whom she wishes to keep up. Perhaps she wants to maintain a fixed ratio of dresses to the family income. If that ratio declines, she will fuss and fret, and if I were to keep her from getting additional clothes, she would impose restrictions and controls affecting my home life and our external relations with friends and acquaintances. I conclude that the right amount of clothes owned by my wife is that which keeps her from fussing and fretting and spares me the danger of unpleasant restrictions.

Before I leave this analogy between women and central bankers, let me point out that "rights" to borrow dresses from friends or from rental agencies would not take care of the matter in the least. Most women want to own their dresses, not to borrow them. I wish that my friends at the IMF would take full cognizance of the psychological difference between owning and borrowing.

Central bankers look not at their clothes closets but at their balance sheets, and they like to see among their assets foreign reserves far in excess of what they would need to cover their nudities; they would like to maintain certain ratios of foreign reserves to total liabilities. The ratio may be merely a matter of tradition or of fashion or, if you will, of religious doctrine. There is no point quarreling with such normative matters. The point is that most central bankers start fussing when the reserve ratio declines. Their liabilities have got to increase year after year, because notes and deposits, the domestic money supply, must increase if deflation is to be avoided. With labor force and productive facilities increasing continuously, and money wages refusing to go down, central bankers have to provide the additional money to avoid continuous deflation and increasing unemployment. Being used to certain traditional reserve ratios, they want their foreign reserves to increase roughly in proportion with their total liabilities. Not that they need it in any sense other than my wife needs more clothes. But if the central banks lose foreign reserves, and even if they find their reserve ratios declining, there will be demands for policies conducive to the inflow of reserves. I conclude that the "need" for reserves is determined by the ambitions of the monetary authorities. I submit we ought to see to it that they get foreign reserves in amounts sufficient to be happy and satisfied; in amounts, that is, that will keep them from urging or condoning policies restricting imports or capital movements. [42, pp. 168–69]

To the extent that central bankers do behave in this manner, there seems a presumption that from a global point of view, to the extent that one must err in reserve creation, it should be on the high rather than low side. However, a "global" point of view seems to be noticeably lacking in international financial negotiations. James Tobin has remarked that: "Memories are short, and gratitude is not a consideration respected in international relations, especially when money is involved." [64, p. 155]

Along with short memories, there seems to exist an equally strong propensity for short foresight. The same conflicts between prospective surplus and deficit countries discussed above were also present at the Bretton Woods Conference in 1944. It is ironic that the United States, foreseeing the period of chronic dollar shortage immediately ahead, opted for a more conservative system, which placed the greater part of the burden of adjustment on deficit countries, while Britain and the Continental countries favored the Keynes plan, which provided for the creation of substantially greater international liquidity.[8] Today the situation is reversed. The United States favors more rapid expansion of international liquidity, while the Continental countries are much less convinced of this need. Such experience suggests that agreement on international monetary issues might be much easier to obtain if negotiating officials would take a longer run point of view, one not based entirely upon the balance of payments position that their countries happen to occupy at the time of negotiations.

NOTES

1. Discussion is limited here to adjustment under the adjustable peg system. Exchange rate flexibility will be considered in Part IV.
2. Recent research has indicated that the historical gold standard actually seldom operated according to the conventional textbook version. See, for example, [8], [67], and [71].
3. For further exposition of this problem, see [61].
4. For a more sympathetic view of United States balance of payments policy, see [69].
5. For a discussion of the British balance of payments crisis in 1964–1965, see [14, Ch. 18].
6. The countries in Working Party No. 3 are Canada, France, Germany, Italy, Japan, the Netherlands, Sweden, Switzerland, Britain, and the United States.
7. There is also strong reason to believe that, on efficiency grounds, smaller, more open economies should bear more of the adjustment, and in fact, under an automatic adjustment mechanism this is what would occur. (See Robert A. Mundell [51].) Further discussion of the proper apportionment of adjustment responsibilities is found in [63].
8. At the Bretton Woods Conference, the two rival approaches considered as the basis for postwar international monetary relationships were: the American plan, propounded by Harry Dexter White, the principal U.S. negotiator, and the British plan, developed by John Maynard Keynes. The United States had the strongest bargaining position because of its economic and military power, and it is not surprising that the White Plan served as the basis of the IMF Articles.
   In contrast to the adopted plan, the Keynes proposal provided for much greater amounts of international liquidity in the form of individual countries' quotas. Furthermore, Keynes envisaged a higher "quality" of liquidity than provided by the IMF: drawings by a member country would be automatic rather than at the discretion of the international institution. Other distinct features of the Keynes plan were the provision of penalties on countries in balance of payments disequilibrium—both surplus and deficit countries—and the one-way conversion of gold into deposits with the international institution. (A country would not be permitted to exchange its deposits for gold.)

A. *The Difficulties of the Dollar and the Pound*

THE ADJUSTMENT PROBLEM AND THE BALANCE OF PAYMENTS POLICY OF THE UNITED STATES

Fritz Machlup

Walker Professor of Economics
and International Finance,
Princeton University

The problem of adjustment arises mainly in connection with persistent imbalances of payments. When a serious deficit in the balance of payments has reduced the net monetary reserves of a country and no reversal in the net flow of payments is in sight, it becomes imperative for the country to adopt policies to restore external balance. The 1968 Report of the Council of Economic Advisers discusses this problem under two headings, "Adjustment Process" and "The U.S. Balance of Payments." Their analysis of the problem suffers from a failure to distinguish different kinds of approach to the problem of reducing or removing an imbalance of international payments.

They do distinguish "temporary measures" from policies that are "long term in character," but this leaves open the question whether the temporary measures have only temporary effects or long-lasting effects. If I discover a leak in a pipe and press my thumb against the hole, this is a temporary measure with only temporary effect: as soon as I remove my thumb, the leaking resumes. If I discover a bleeding cut on my finger and put a band-aid over it, this temporary measure may have lasting effects, because the wound may heal, the lesion of my skin disappear. The difference between these temporary measures is essential; to call both of them "leak-stopping policies" and be silent on the question whether they are palliatives or cures is not very helpful.

For some 250 years economists studying international finance have

Excerpts from a Statement of Dr. Fritz Machlup before the Joint Economic Committee Hearings on the 1968 Economic Report, on Monday, February 19, 1968.

known the process of economic adjustment that would remove imbalance and restore balance. This adjustment involves changes in relative prices and incomes in the countries concerned, resulting in changes in the allocation of productive resources and in the international flow of goods and services. The process has been conceived as an automatic one, but it can be fully automatic only under monetary institutions that no longer exist. Hence, adjustment policies have to produce the effects which the conceivably automatic mechanism would have produced. These policies do not, however, include every type of measure, including direct controls, that may be instituted for the purpose of removing a payments deficit.

In medicine, no one would doubt for a moment that there is a difference between a surgical operation or some other painful treatment and a disappearance or removal of the need for it. There may be some alternative therapeutic techniques that could remove the need for the painful one; or perhaps the affliction may disappear all by itself. The same possibilities exist for balance-of-payments troubles: with luck, the troubles may go away or some other therapy may make it unnecessary to go through the operations which economists have called the adjustment process. I use the term "compensatory corrections" or "correctives" to indicate those things that are considered as alternatives to the adjustment process.

REDUCING THE PAYMENTS DEFICIT: ALTERNATIVE METHODS

We need even more distinctions. There are measures that do not remove deficits but facilitate financing them. For example, if an increase in interest rates attracts short-term capital from abroad, one may not want to regard this as a credit item in the balance of payments that removes a deficit, but may prefer to regard it as a temporary stopgap, a way of financing an existing deficit for a while. (As soon as the attractive interest differential is terminated, the inflow of short-term capital will stop and what has been received will flow back.) In addition, we should separate measures that work on the flow of goods and services from those that work on the flow of capital funds. The adjectives "real" and "financial" can be used for this purpose.

We thus distinguish real adjustment, real correctives, financial correctives, corrective management of government transactions, and external financing.

To *finance* a deficit is to pay for it by reducing the net monetary reserves or by increasing liquid liabilities to foreigners incurred just for this purpose. (If an increase in foreign liabilities arises from an increased foreign demand for dollar balances and other dollar assets, it should be treated as an autonomous capital inflow, not as a debt incurred in order to finance a deficit. Unfortunately, we usually lack the information required for this distinction.)

To reduce or remove a deficit by *real adjustment* is to induce such changes in relative prices and incomes as will alter the allocation of real resources and cause such changes in the international flows of goods and services as will improve the current account to match the balance on capital account and unilateral payments. We distinguish aggregate-demand adjustment, cost-and-price adjustment, and exchange-rate adjustment.

Real correctives influence the international flow of goods and services through selective impacts on particular goods, industries, or sectors. *Financial correctives* influence the international flows of private capital funds. *Corrective management of government transactions* may affect foreign expenditures, loans, and grants by the government.

REAL ADJUSTMENT

Economists trained in the classical or neoclassical tradition—the present writer included—have a deep-seated prejudice in favor of real adjustment: (1) it relies largely on market forces rather than selective "interventions" by the state; (2) it is more likely to operate indiscriminately, avoiding differential treatment of particular industries or firms; and (3) the chance of its working, of achieving its objectives, is greater.

On the other hand, practical-political considerations militate against real adjustment: (a) policies to check the expansion of aggregate demand are apt to reduce business activity and employment; (b) policies to check increases in wage rates and prices are resented by some of the strongest groups in society; and (c) policies to adjust foreign-exchange rates are opposed by leaders in business and finance, here and abroad, for reasons good and bad; most understandable is the opposition abroad to a successful adjustment in the flow of goods and services, since it would hurt the business of some of the industries abroad.

Aggregate-demand adjustment is not without advocates among practical men: some highly respected bankers here and abroad advise the United States to "put its house in order" and "halt inflation"; and they intimate that this can be done by means of higher interest rates, higher taxes, and economies in government programs.

Their practical advice is unexceptionable if it refers merely to avoiding inflation of incomes and prices. As a matter of fact, high interest rates, higher taxes, and budget cuts are badly needed to prevent a further deterioration of the imbalance of payments. But it would be far too optimistic to expect that containment of further expansion would restore external balance, especially since the major industrial nations of Europe are likewise pursuing anti-inflationary policies, some even more successfully than the United States.

If the conservative advice goes beyond mere avoidance of inflation and suggests in effect that aggregate demand in this country be *reduced* to such a level that our imports fall and exports rise sufficiently for the export surplus to match all other outflows of dollars—then the advice is not acceptable. A deflation of such force could have well-nigh catastrophic consequences for domestic employment and world trade.

Real adjustment by means of demand deflation in the United States is out of the question; adjustment by means of demand inflation abroad is not likely to be accepted, nor would it be advisable. Now, if the adjustment of levels and structures of costs and prices cannot be expected to occur either through reductions in the United States or through increases abroad, the only remaining possibility of real adjustment lies in alignments of foreign-exchange rates. Yet, the resistance to any moves in this direction seems too strong to allow it to be contemplated. I shall, however, not be inhibited and will return to this only chance for a workable adjustment.

PARTIAL DEVALUATIONS

Among real correctives the policies most appealing to advocates of selective measures are what I have for years called "disguised partial devaluations of the dollar." Open and uniform devaluation being ruled out, measures are recommended to reduce the value of the dollar for particular purposes or in chosen sectors of the economy.

The United States has resorted to such makeshifts several times, for example, when it in effect devalued the dollar used for foreign military expenditures. This was done by trying to save foreign exchange whenever the cost of buying at home was at first not more than 25 per cent, later 50 per cent, above the cost in foreign currencies calculated at the official exchange rate. In other words, in decisions whether to buy abroad or at home, foreign currencies were to be given a higher value than would correspond to the official parity.

Through tying foreign aid to purchases of our products, the United States reduced the value of its foreign-aid dollar. Countries receiving aid had to buy in this country even if they could have bought at lower prices elsewhere. It cost some of them about 30 per cent more, which corresponds to a devaluation of the aid-dollar by about 23 per cent.

In July 1963, the United States began taxing purchases of foreign long-term securities at a rate of 15 per cent. This is the equivalent of devaluing the dollar used for buying foreign securities. This partial devaluation, designed to reduce capital outflows, is a financial, not a real, corrective.

In January 1968, the Administration proposed a tax on foreign travel and tourism, which would be the equivalent of devaluing the tourist's dollar. In addition, there are nonofficial proposals for taxes or tariff-surcharges on imports—the equivalent of devaluing the dollar for imports—and for subsidies or tax-refunds on exports—the equivalent of lowering the value of the dollar to foreign buyers of our exports.

If these disguised devaluations of the dollar were uniform, affecting proportionally all imports, all exports, and all other international transactions, they might work indiscriminately and perhaps efficiently. As it is, however, they are selective, disproportionate, and inefficient. They discriminate against some sectors and in favor of others, distort the structure of prices and the allocation of productive resources, and are usually incapable of effecting their purpose. (For example, the tourist who stays at home because of the disguised devaluation of his dollar will spend more at home and will thereby cause imports to increase, and exports to decline, with importers and exporters not calculating at the same, if any, rate of devaluation.)

Partial devaluations can improve particular items in the balance of payments, but may worsen others in the process, partly because of the substitution of purchases for which the dollar is not "devalued," partly because of foreign and domestic repercussions to the reduction of purchases for which the value of the dollar is reduced.

DIRECT CONTROLS

Partial devaluations have at least one advantage: they work through price incentives and disincentives, and leave the markets essentially free. The bureaucratic mind, however, prefers a more direct approach, a more direct attack on the "item" that has been found irritating or insalubrious: it prefers direct controls, which give to some governmental authority the power to prohibit, to restrict, to license, or to permit, according to its unfailing judgment of what is or is not warranted in the national interest.

Direct controls can be employed as real correctives or as financial correctives of the payments deficit. As real correctives they may involve discretionary subsidies to exporters, quotas and other nontariff restrictions on imports, licensing of foreign travel or fixing the amounts that travelers may spend abroad. As financial correctives they may restrict bank credits to foreigners, direct foreign investment, portfolio investment and foreign loans of various types.

The effectiveness of controls that are not comprehensive, not all-inclusive (as general foreign-exchange controls, comprising all foreign transactions would be) is limited by the possibilities of avoiding, evading, and circumventing the restrictions. The elasticity of substitution among different forms of capital outflow, for example, is not sufficiently appreciated; there are also those offsetting changes in other items that are classed as repercussions, though in some instances substitutions and repercussions shade into one another.

It should be easy to understand that portfolio investment, bank loans, trade credit, and direct investment may be substituted for one another. Restrict one and you will see the others expand. Yet, many overlook that there is also substitution between foreign and domestic funds. Restrict the outflow of American capital funds and you will see foreign funds withdrawn from the United States.

This is not retaliation or an unfriendly act, but the operation of normal market forces: if American funds are kept from going abroad, interest rates abroad will rise and, naturally, foreign funds will "go home." Or, if American firms are forbidden to use their own money for direct investment abroad, but are permitted to raise foreign funds in foreign markets, foreigners holding American securities may decide to sell them in New York and buy the more attractive new securities offered by the American subsidiaries abroad. Thus, a legitimate outflow of capital takes the place of a forbidden one. Call it repercussion or call it substitution, it severely limits the effectiveness of the financial correctives.

If financial correctives are effective in reducing the outflow of capital, they may set forth offsetting reductions in the trade surplus. These repercussions or feedbacks may be small or large, but will rarely be zero. They can be zero only if the reduction in the flow of capital does not affect the use of funds either in the domestic or in the foreign markets. Assume that an American, A, is prevented from lending his money to a foreigner, F; only if A then decides to sit on his money and not to spend, lend, or invest it at all, and if F manages to disburse abroad exactly the same amount of money that he would have disbursed thanks to the receipt of A's funds, only then will imports and exports be unaffected by the financial corrective. In all probability, A will use some of his funds at home and F will have less to spend abroad, and the United States will have larger imports and smaller exports as a result.

FOREIGN PROGRAMS OF THE GOVERNMENT

In the search for "guilty items" in the balance of payments, foreign disbursements by the U.S. Government are the most popular targets. According to one's political philosophy, one will argue for cutting military expenditures abroad or for cutting foreign aid. The question whether these funds for fighting wars and fighting poverty abroad are desirable expenditures is often confused with the question whether the reduction of these funds would cure the imbalance of payments.

Both hawks and doves are inclined to exaggerate the effects which a reduction of expenditures for military operations in Viet-Nam would have on the payments deficit. If the war ends and military expenditures in Viet-Nam are reduced, there will probably be an increase in economic aid to Viet-Nam, in an effort to rebuild what has been destroyed and to show the world that our intentions all along had been to help the country maintain its freedom and develop its economy. If, none the less, total expenditures abroad are reduced when military operations cease, then the Vietnamese will have less money to purchase goods and to import from abroad. The reduction of their imports may not always directly reduce exports from the United States, but through triangular trade and multilateral repercussion our exports may still be affected.

In addition, there is the probability that defense expenditures in the United States will be replaced by expenditures for other purposes. Programs in our domestic war against poverty have been cut because of the rising cost of the war in the Far East. If, with the end of military operations, we escalate expenditures for domestic programs, imports from abroad are likely to increase. Hence, with all these repercussions on the flow of goods and services, one must not count on an improvement of the balance of payments by anything near the full amount by which our military expenditures are reduced.

THE INEXORABLE DEFICIT

I may well be accused of undue pessimism. Is there any historical or theoretical support for my warnings about the ineffectiveness of the various corrective measures adopted or proposed? Is the deficit really impervious to all efforts to deal with it through corrective measures?

Our actual experience can really make us rather fatalistic. Year after year, at least since 1960, we have done all sorts of things to work on the balance of payments; we have picked one item after another for special treatment; yet, we have failed. I have prepared a list of quotations from statements by our Presidents and Secretaries of the Treasury expressing their assurances and confident expectations that balance was just around the corner, that the deficit would disappear within the year, or the next one. Yet, the deficit is still with us and one cannot even say that it is substantially smaller than it used to be.

I am not including this list of assurances in my testimony, because to do so would not be charitable. After all, the President and the Secretary of the Treasury were courageously battling a Hydra: they did not realize that for every head cut off two grew in its place. They did not know that you cannot decapitate a Hydra; you have to dehydrate her if you want to get rid of her. (Incidentally, the metaphoric dehydration need not be an absolute reduction of domestic liquidity. It suffices to reduce liquidity relative to foreign countries, calculated at current exchange rates.)

A review of the statistical balance of payments from 1950 to the present shows that the financial transfers from the United States have regularly exceeded the real transfers. The financial transfers have consisted chiefly of our military expenditures abroad, remittances and pensions, grants and net capital exports of the Government, and net outflows of private capital of U.S. residents. The real transfers have been the surpluses of exports over imports of goods and services. The difference between financial and real transfers is called the "transfer gap."

If we succeeded in achieving full adjustment, the surplus in the balance of goods and services would match the net deficit on the other accounts. Why full adjustment has not been attained and why, therefore, a transfer gap has remained throughout the years is a controversial question. Probably several factors have accounted for the lack of adjustment.

Virtually all theoretical analyses of the transfer problem include as necessary conditions for full adjustment relative price and income deflation in the paying country and relative price and income inflation abroad. Perhaps these conditions have not been met, chiefly because we have, for very good reasons, been unwilling to allow production and employment in the United States to be sufficiently depressed to "push out" enough of our products to achieve an adequate export surplus. Likewise, foreign nations have been unwilling to allow a rate of inflation sufficient to "suck in" enough goods from the United States.

Another important factor in the incomplete working of the adjustment process may have been the policy of some countries to offset the external effects of their price and income inflations by devaluations of their currencies. France, for example, devalued the franc in 1957 and 1958 with the result that the franc became undervalued and France could within a few years accumulate a gold reserve of almost $6 billion.

THE TRANSFER PROBLEM

It is sometimes said that the theory of the adjustment mechanism—a theory explaining how the trade balance adjusts to remove imbalances of payments—was not designed for countries or periods in which large amounts of financial transfers disturbed the balance of payments. This is not so. The classical debate of this problem of adjustment started when Britain had extraordinarily large military expenditures on the Continent during the Napoleonic Wars.

The discussion of the adjustment to large financial transfers was resumed when France had to pay indemnities after the Franco-Prussian War, and again when Germany had to pay reparations after the First World War. It was in connection with the discussions of the German transfer problem that some economists raised doubts as to whether the balance of goods and services could ever be flexible enough to allow adjustment to large transfer commitments.

The transfer problem of the United States may likewise be seen in our inability to raise our export surpluses to the size of our net financial transfers. It is significant that all the figures in question are minute fractions of our GNP. Exports of goods and services, in the period 1950–1966, varied from 4.7 to 6.0 per cent of GNP. Imports (excluding military expenditures) varied from 3.6 to 4.6 per cent. The export surplus is, of course, a still smaller fraction. It varied from 0.7 to 2.0 per cent, of GNP.

The financial transfers varied from 1.5 to 2.3 per cent of GNP. It may be worth pointing out that there has been no consistent increase in financial transfers relative to GNP. On the contrary, from 1964 to 1966 they declined from 2.2 to 1.5 per cent of GNP. The transfer gap varied only between 0.3 per cent of GNP (in 1951, 1957, and 1966) and 1.2 per cent (in 1950).

The smallness of these figures is most impressive. For it shows what minimal transfers of productive resources in the economy from domestic industry to export industry would suffice to achieve full adjustment. That we should have been incapable of achieving it seems to indicate that anonymous forces involving market prices and incomes can be strong enough year after year to frustrate the aspirations and expectations of this wealthy nation. I hope my observation will not be mistaken for a plea to restrict the forces of the free market. It is meant, on the contrary, as a warning that these forces should be treated with more respect.

THE BALANCE-OF-PAYMENTS PROGRAM OF 1968

After seven years of unsuccessful corrective measures, the Government has now embarked on a new program. It is, again, not a program to promote real adjustment in the economic sense; instead, it relies on selective correctives operating on hand-picked items of the balance of payments. The President, the Secretary of the Treasury, and the Council of Economic Advisers hope that the country will save at least $1 billion by a "mandatory program" to restrain direct investment abroad and to bring home larger parts of foreign earnings from past investments; another $500 million by a "tightened program" to restrain foreign lending by banks and other financial institutions; another $500 million by discouraging "nonessential travel outside the Western Hemisphere"; and again another $500 million by reducing the foreign-exchange cost of keeping troops in Europe.

In summary, $1.5 billion are to be saved by financial restrictions, $500 million by a corrective measure operating on the private demand for foreign travel, and $500 by corrective management of government disbursements abroad. The last of these may turn out to be the only continuing saving, if troops are brought back from Europe or if compensating payments are received from NATO allies. The other $2 billion are nothing but stop-gaps.

Even if the three stop-gap measures succeeded in improving the balance by the full $2 billion, and even if this improvement eliminated the deficit for the time the restrictions are in force, it would not restore balance; it would only suppress imbalance. As soon as the restrictions are lifted, the deficit will reappear, for there is nothing in the program that has any adjusting, remedial or curative effects. The demand for foreign travel will not be reduced by restricting for a few years the chance of satisfying it. The flow of capital funds from this country to Europe is determined by relative incomes, prices, profit rates, interest rates, and saving ratios. None of these underlying conditions is altered by the restrictions. The flow is likely to resume, perhaps even to broaden, when the restrictions and prohibitions are taken off.

But that these selective controls are only temporary, and that they have no lasting effects, is not all. An additional question arises concerning the effects that they will have even temporarily. The possibilities of substitution and of repercussions must not be disregarded. Permitted outflows may be substituted for the prohibited ones, and repercussions in the trade balance may offset some of the savings achieved in the selected items. I shall presently provide explanations for these warnings. But I must first deliver myself of an observation on the principle of restrictive measures.

As one who has lived many years in Central Europe under all sorts of prohibitions, restrictions, and controls, I have always admired and loved the supposedly indomitable spirit of freedom in this great country. It is a traumatic experience to see the lighthearted sacrifice of several freedoms with the adoption of the program of payments restrictions. I would never have thought that this wonderful country could sink so low as to impose restrictions on foreign travel.

SOME THEORETICAL EXPLANATIONS

But now I must make good on my promise to present explanations for my skepticism concerning the effectiveness of the corrective measures. The explanations are theoretical, but I hope they will not appear esoteric or specious.

I shall use as illustration the restriction of direct investment, which is intended to save $1 billion a year.

There are two extreme positions concerning the effectiveness of such a corrective measure. At one end is the opinion that a reduction of a financial transfer, say by $1 billion, will leave all other items in the payments balance unchanged and merely reduce the financing item, that is, reduce the loss of gold or the increase in liquid foreign liabilities.

At the opposite end is the opinion that a reduction in financial transfers by $1 billion will reduce the export surplus by the same amount and hence will leave the deficit, and the need to finance it unchanged.

I propose to regard the first theory as naive and the second as over-sophisticated; both are wrong. The truth lies in the middle, and whether it comes closer to the naive or to the over-sophisticated theory will depend on circumstances. What kind of circumstances control the outcome can be briefly indicated,—still with reference to the same illustration, the reduction in direct investment abroad.

If American firms that have for several years been making direct investments abroad are now barred from doing so unless they can raise new capital in foreign markets, it is possible that the increased demand in the foreign capital markets leads to a backflow of foreign capital from the United States. It may be short-term capital or it may be long-term capital that returns to Europe. To repeat the example used before, American firms issuing new securities in a European market may find foreign buyers who secure the needed funds by selling in the New York stock market some of the American shares they have been holding. The incentive for such a switch from old to new securities is clear: newly issued securities have to be offered at slightly reduced prices. To the extent that this way of financing is used, the restrictive measure by the United States will be ineffective.

Let us assume that the American firms reduce direct investment in Europe but make, within the limits stipulated by the new mandatory restrictions, some investments in Canada which they might not have made otherwise. The addition to the investible funds available in Canada may make it possible for Canadians to engage in the purchase of European securities. This would again constitute substitution of another form of capital flow from the United States to Europe.

Let us assume next that direct investment abroad is in fact reduced by the full $1 billion and that there is no replacement by any other funds going from the United States to Europe. Investment in Europe in preceding years has unquestionably contributed to effective demand and, directly or indirectly via third countries, to purchases of goods and services from the United States. The amount so used may have been relatively small; if so, the feedback from the reduction in investment, resulting in a reduction of American exports, may be small too. But it will surely be greater than zero.

The next repercussion to be considered is connected with the use the American firms make of the funds which they, but for the restriction, would have invested in Europe. If they use any of these funds for increased investment in the United States, this will amount to an injection of additional funds into the stream of effective demand. Some fraction of any addition to effective demand is likely to show up as an increased demand for imports. The fraction may be small, but not zero.

To the extent that the domestic market, because of the increase in effective demand, becomes more attractive than foreign markets, American firms will be less eager to seek foreign outlets and will divert some of their production from export to domestic sales. It is unlikely that the amounts involved would be very large, but it is just as unlikely that they would be zero.

We have seen that increases in our financial transfers to foreign countries have for many years failed to produce equal increases in our export surplus. The same conditions that can explain the incomplete adjustment of the trade balance to increased financial transfers can explain also why reductions in our financial transfers are unlikely to be matched by equal reductions in our export surplus. On the other hand, just as our increased financial transfers have increased our export surplus significantly, so reductions in financial transfers can be expected to reduce our export surplus.

CONCLUSIONS REGARDING THE PAYMENTS DEFICIT

I shall not be so bold as to present my conclusion in the form of a numerical forecast. It is not possible to predict a result determined by so many unknown variables. At this point we do not even know whether the Congress will pass the proposed surcharge on the income tax. This one factor alone can make a difference of about $1 billion in the payments deficit. That is to say, if we get the surtax, and thereby reduce the spending power of individuals and corporations, imports will be smaller and exports larger than if no tax increase is imposed.

But there are too many other factors in the picture to permit anyone to come up with a reliable forecast. Nobody knows, for example, what will happen concerning movements of foreign capital. This item can change either way and in very substantial amounts.

None the less, I believe that conclusions of a qualitative sort can and should be drawn. The two conclusions on which I feel pretty sure are the negative and regrettable ones concerning the effects of the restrictive program. There will not be an improvement of the payments balance by $2.5 billion, as the Administration seems to hope. And whatever improvement will be achieved by the program, it will be only temporary and will not contribute to the adjustment process, will not bring us closer to a solution of our problem.

The widely believed excuse that our military expenditures abroad, chiefly those connected with the war in Viet-Nam, are too large to permit balance in our payments to be achieved, is not justified. Our total financial transfers, inclusive of military expenditures, have been between 2.3 and 1.5 per cent of our GNP. This is a modest drain on our resources. There is no reason why a nation should be unable to accomplish a real transfer of such magnitude.

Adjustment of the balance of goods and services to make the real transfer match a financial transfer of around two per cent of GNP is not an impossible task, provided the adjustment process is allowed to work. I agree that we must not try to do it by depressing domestic incomes and prices. I am afraid that we must not expect our major trading partners to help us sufficiently by means of inflations of their income and price levels. But I see no reason other than superstition and timidity why we should not try to achieve the required relative reduction of our income and price level through adjustments of foreign-exchange rates. The rate adjustment that would achieve the needed adjustment of the trade balance is quite modest and should be negotiable.

BRITAIN: WILL THE BUNGLE WORK?

The Economist

Was it really all planned a fortnight before, or was it done in a panic-stricken last-minute rush? Probably half and half. Some ministers diligently spent the weekend putting out a cover story, giving the best rationalisation of events. Other accounts raise questions about the whole operation. But it can be accepted, on balance, that about the beginning of November Mr. Wilson and Mr. Callaghan were tentatively converted to the probable inevitability of devaluation, although they then spent the next two weeks expensively and timorously hedging their bets. Their friends will say they had three reasons for their initial half-decision.

One was that a fearful confidence flight out of sterling had been in progress since midsummer, with only occasional pauses for breath. A second reason is that a majority of academic economic opinion and a swelling section of the press were in favour of devaluation, and were saying so increasingly openly. But the third and worst blow was that at the end of October Mr. Callaghan's advisers presented him with figures that suggested a British balance of payments deficit lasting well into 1968. There were going to be no cheering figures to wave in the faces of the speculators—and the pro-devaluers—for long, grinding months to come.

The Chancellor therefore reported to the Prime Minister that the rate probably could not be held. Once he had made this report, the amount of the probable devaluation was fixed pragmatically rather than scientifically. It was felt that any devaluation below 10 per cent would be regarded by the speculators as too small; while anything above 15 per cent would invite some retaliatory devaluations by other countries as well as causing grave annoyance round the world, not

From "Britain: Will the Bungle Work," *The Economist*, November 25, 1967, pp. 868–73.

less in Washington. A nice round figure near to the top of the range was to devalue to $2.40 to the £1, thus incidentally allowing the American penny to look the British penny in the face for the first time. This depreciation of the pound amounted to 14.3 per cent in terms of dollar value, while the arithmetical equivalent increase in U.S. dollar prices in terms of sterling is 16⅔ per cent (i.e. a British exporter who sells something in America for $280 and used to get £100 for it, will find that at the $2.40 rate he gets £116⅔ instead).

THE EXTRAORDINARY HAGGLE

There followed a remarkable two weeks during which the British Government hawked its tentative half-decision round the world. In a series of bilateral and multilateral discussions, most of the leading overseas nations were asked: how would you react if we were forced to devalue? This pilgrimage ran the enormous risk that there might be extensive leaks, and a surge of informed speculation against the pound. In the event, to do foreign governments credit, there were no extensive leaks; whether there was any really informed speculation probably depends on what one means by "informed."

Three reasons could be adduced for the British Government's blabbermouth act. One is the portentous argument that "a great international reserve currency like sterling could not be devalued unilaterally, but only after extensive international discussions," the more closely one examines what this fine-sounding excuse for a full two-week delay is supposed to mean in the particular circumstances of November, 1967, the more dubious it looks.

The second reason was that it was still considered important to find out what was the top rate of devaluation that would be unlikely to invite retaliatory devaluations from abroad. There does not seem to be much ground for supposing that the British Government ever seriously considered forcing the pace. The President of the Board of Trade told the Commons on Tuesday that "it would not have been right to think in terms of a large devaluation of 30 per cent or so." When probing into informed quarters this week, it seemed right to test out the argument that a devaluation of 30 percent might have given Britain a 30 per cent advantage over countries (such as West Germany) which would have been strong enough to maintain their parities even then, plus the argument that if a lot of other currencies (including the dollar) had then come down by 15 per cent, that would merely have meant that world liquidity would have been increased by a useful and nearly-worldwide rise in the price of gold. The united official response to any such suggestion is a shocked: "We certainly would not have wanted to spread unnecessary inflation and confusion round the world."

But there does seem at some time in early November to have been a contingency discussion in Whitehall of the possibility of resorting to a floating rate for sterling (not on intellectually-argued economic grounds, but because it was thought this might be the only way of finding out in practice what differential on the rate foreign countries would allow to us). And the vague threat of a bigger devaluation than 15 per cent may also have played some part in arranging the total loan to Britain of around $3 billion (a standby of $1.4 billion from the International Monetary Fund, the rest from foreign central banks) with which the 14.3 per cent devaluation is now to be supported. It may also have been at this stage that, in order to smooth the way with foreign creditors, the Government decided, probably unwisely, to dilute the effectiveness of the 14.3 per cent devaluation by agreeing to remove the existing export rebate after next April 1st (see below). The reminder that this rebate exists has prompted the French to say that, instead, it must be removed now.

However, the third, and almost certainly the most important reason, for this questioning of foreign countries about their possible reaction to devaluation, was that up to last week only a half-decision had been made. Up to a fairly late stage the Chancellor more than half-hoped that the answer to his question might be: "Devaluation of sterling would be such a blow to the world monetary system that we will offer you a loan of £3 billion or thereabouts, without strings, for three to five years, in order to stave it off." In that event, Mr. Callaghan and Mr. Wilson would have chosen to struggle on at the old $2.80 rate. Moreover, it is highly probable that during the past week they changed their private definition of the sort of loan that would have sufficed to persuade them to try to stick fast at $2.80. Mr. Callaghan must have been shocked at the first intimations of how unpopular any "loans-with-strings" would be among Labour backbenchers. It is this changing mood that makes it so difficult to adjudicate between those who say that "this was a devaluation planned more than a fortnight before," and those who say that "Wilson was forced to devalue because foreigners had lost patience with lending him money." To some extent the argument here may be over a distinction without a difference.

THE BOTCHED RUN-UP

One of the charges that Mr. Callaghan is naturally most determined to refute is that the Government handled the last 72 hours before D-day, last Saturday, with gross incompetence. He has produced foreign bankers to swear that he handled it well. That is, of course, very easy. The gravamen of the charge against Mr. Callaghan is that he put the convenience of foreign banking authorities above the national interest of Britain with unnecessary punctiliousness.

On Wednesday night, on the eve of Thursday's cabinet meeting which was likely to seal the decision of devaluation, the Treasury must have been fearful that rumours of devaluation would mount. Instead, the Treasury was given an uncovenanted benefit when the BBC phoned to seek confirmation of a remarkably detailed and wrongheaded rumour about an imminent loan being granted to save the pound; the source of the rumour was Paris (possibly not far from the source of the BBC's other non-scoop some weeks before, announcing a hardening of General de Gaulle's arteries). The Treasury said "no comment" to the rumour, but it may well have said it by no means discouragingly; any false rumour of a loan seemed much better for sterling than the expected true rumour of devaluation at that time.

Nevertheless, when the cabinet met on Thursday, it was impressed by Labour backbenchers' outcry at the BBC report, which they interpreted to mean a loan with quite a few strings; this may have encouraged the cabinet's unanimous decision to accept devaluation. The Government puts the blame on what happened next on the fact that that afternoon the Speaker agreed to call a question by a Labour backbencher about the possibility of a foreign rescue operation. Mr. Callaghan's reply was a mixture of honest evasion and misleading innuendo. He said that he "hoped that some of the speculators get their fingers burned," at a time when the cabinet had already determined that all speculators against sterling would get a nice gain of 16⅔ per cent. But, to do credit to his integrity if not to his nous, there was more evasion than deception.

When he sat down, it seemed obvious that the exchange markets could not sensibly be allowed to remain open on Friday unless a loan was announced before the start of business on that day. Otherwise it was certain that a credibility chasm about the Government's ability to maintain $2.80 would open up; and the Bank of England would spend Friday pouring the nation's remaining gold and dollar reserves down the drain.

Even in the light of Mr. Callaghan's punctiliousness, it passes understanding why the Government did not then advance devaluation by 48 hours. It would have been quite possible to have found a time around or after midnight on Thursday when both the European and North American markets would be closed, and to declare that the Friday (instead of the next Monday) would be a bank holiday. It is true that a handful of exchange dealers in Japan and Australasia might have had a nasty moment as the newsflash reached them that sterling had been devalued by 14.3 per cent while they were in mid-pencil flourish, but this would have been a small price to save Britain from losing 14.3 per cent on all of the £300 million or whatever it was that flowed from the Bank of England on that day. While the life blood was thus flowing out, and 24 hours after his own cabinet had unitedly decided on devaluation, Lord Chalfont (who admittedly is a minister outside the cabinet) stood up in Paris to say that "there is no plan to alter the exchange rate." The most charitable interpretation of this is that Lord Chalfont meant that his colleagues were engaged in changing the rate without a plan, but in a blind panic rush.

Does this sad story of extreme kindness to foreign susceptibility in the handling of the operation mean that the amount of the devaluation has probably also been pitched too low? Here there is one ground for comfort. The best judgment one can make is that the amount of the devaluation probably was fairly well in line with what was recommended by economists in the government machine. The place where the Government's political weakness is likely to have done more damage is in providing an inadequate dose of internal deflation to back the devaluation up.

British export prices will not, of course, gain a full 14.3 per cent competitive advantage as a result of last Saturday's move. There are four main reasons for this:

(1) Export costs will be increased by the rise in the sterling price of the imported raw materials going into them; the best estimate is that there will be an average rise in export costs of between 3 and 4 per cent on this account.

(2) The Government has decided to dilute the devaluation by abolishing the previous rebate of certain indirect taxes to exporters. It says that this export rebate is no longer needed; and that some foreign countries regarded it as an illegal subsidy to British exports, which the Government would be wise to abolish so as to avoid treading on delicate corns at a time when protectionism (especially against dumped or subsidised exports) is increasing in many countries, not least the United States. The removal of the rebate will add to average export costs by just under 2 per cent.

(3) In most parts of the country, though not in the development areas, the Government is also discontinuing the subsidy to manufacturers from the system of premium rebates under the Selective Employment Tax. In such a way are great schemes of the past brushed aside. The SET will now become a payroll tax on workers employed in service industries, a nil tax on most workers employed in manufacturing, and a wage subsidy on the employment of workers in manufacturing only in high unemployment regions. For the long term, this should make SET look a more logical tax. For the short term, however, it will involve a rise in the production costs of most manufacturers; it is estimated that the average addition to export costs may be around ½ per cent.

(4) For purely political reasons, the Government has announced that it will raise corporation tax by 2½ per cent (to 42½ per cent) in the next budget. This will certainly be treated as an addition to total industrial costs, including export costs, although there is admittedly room for debate by how much.

When these four factors are added together, they may amount to a dilution of the 14.3 per cent devaluation by something like 7 per cent. If so, the comparative price advantage gained by the average British exporter from the devaluation might be somewhere around 7½ per cent.

Past experience has suggested (admittedly on somewhat shaky evidence) that a 1 per cent drop in British export prices can lead to something rather under a 2 per cent increase in Britain's volume of exports. In economic jargon, British exports are believed to have a price elasticity of demand equal to something just under 2. Apply this to Britain's new potential average price advantage of perhaps around 7½ per cent, and there may be some grounds for hoping that Britain's volume of exports could be raised by devaluation by something rather under 15 per cent. Admittedly, this is probably nearer to the upper limit of an intelligent guesstimate, and it would take place only after a time lag. Perhaps it would be better to write down one's hopes, and suggest a figure of 10 to 15 per cent.

Simultaneously, economic analysts believe that a 1 per cent rise in British import prices tends to reduce Britain's volume of imports by about ½ per cent; (in technical jargon, the elasticity of demand for British markets is believed to be about ½). Although the sterling prices of many imports from countries that have not devalued will rise by the full 16⅔ per cent, the average rise should be less than this: because some imports come from countries like New Zealand that devalued with us, while others are of commodities whose prices might be partly sensitive to a drop in British demand. A reasonable guess is that the average rise in import prices caused by devaluation might be about 10 or 12 per cent, after a time lag; if so, devaluation could lead eventually to the volume of British imports being some 5 or 6 per cent lower than it otherwise would have been. As an additional import-saver, the Government plainly intends to be generous to British farmers in order to encourage more domestic production of food.

Even the lowest of these projections—a rise in export volume by around 10 per cent and a fall in import volume of around 5 per cent—should bring about a basic improvement in Britain's balance of payments by rather over £800 million a year. On the figures so far, therefore, the Government might even be erring on the cautious side when it reaches its own calculation of an improvement of some £750 million. About £250 million of this would be required to meet the deterioration in Britain's terms of trade arising from the fact that import prices will rise by more than export prices do. The remaining £500 million is the figure which Mr. Callaghan referred to when he said in his devaluation statement that "we need an improvement in our balance of payments of at least £500 million a year, and the Government intends to ensure that this is achieved."

It should be emphasized that nobody is expecting to see this improvement straightaway; indeed in the first half of 1968—because the effect of the adverse terms of trade is likely to show up before the improvement in export volume—the Treasury is resigned to the probability that the balance of payments may actually be worse than it otherwise would have been. The $3 billion credit from the IMF and the central bankers is presumably intended to be ready for use in this period if necessary. But from the second half of 1968 on, the Government hopes that the basic improvement in the balance of payments will get steadily under way, and by 1969 it expects a substantial surplus.

Two points should be made about this arithmetic:

(1) If Britain could really attain a basic £500 million a year improvement in its balance of payments, many of its problems would be solved. Indeed, since the country is probably only running a "normal" deficit of perhaps £200 million a year now, some people would say that a £500 million improvement would put us in the bad neighbour, nearly-permanent-surplus country class. But this present £200 million a year deficit is being run when Britain is in a state of some recession; a £500 million a year basic improvement might enable us to balance our books even in the stockpiling phase of an entry-into-boom year. Perhaps, Mr. Wilson may be dreaming, during an entry-into-boom pre-election year of 1969–70? If in periods when no excessive stockpiling was taking place, a £500 million basic improvement drove us into an uncomfortably large balance of payments surplus—well, some surplus will be needed so that we can repay our debts, and it might also at last become possible to remove our draconian restrictions on private foreign investment.

(2) But this basic improvement of £500 million will depend wholly on the assumption that average costs in Britain's export industries will not rise by more than the amounts suggested above. If, in addition to these amounts, there is a burst of wage inflation, then, for every 1 per cent by which British wages per unit of output rise by more than competing countries' wages, we must expect to lose up to 2 per cent of the needed rise in British exports. And this leads to consideration of the most worrying point of all. Mr. Callaghan told the House last July that devaluation would require a new incomes freeze in conditions when prices would be rising. The Government has funked imposing this, and has thereby put its whole rescue operation in danger.

INFLATION AT HOME?

Mr. Wilson imposed a compulsory wages freeze for six months in July, 1966—at a time when his other measures did not include devaluation, so that the whole sacrifice was demanded to no effect. He has deemed it politically impossible to repeat the dose now, at a time when it really would hold out hopes of a fundamental cure. This is a dereliction of duty. Commentators will have to wait and see how firmly the policy of the nil norm is enforced in the public sector's own wage negotiations before they can be sure how big a dereliction it is.

The Treasury is probably now fearful that dangers may arise not only on the side of cost inflation, but of demand inflation as well. The devaluation has occurred at a time when the prospect ahead already seemed to promise growth in the next twelve months at above officialdom's cautious target rate of 3 per cent per annum (or around £1,000 million per annum in terms of real resources). Now, on top of this, there is to be imposed the extra £750 million of new export demand and import-substitution demand required to improve the balance of payments by £500 million, and to wipe out the £250 million deterioration in the terms of trade (all figures in terms of annual rates). The original devaluation programme probably also assumed that there would be a thoroughly desirable increase of £100-£200 million a year of private fixed investment, spurred on by these new opportunities in the export and import substitution fields. Sadly, the Government's foolish increase in corporation tax and abandonment of the export rebate, plus the abolition of the manufacturers' premium rebates on SET, are likely to have wiped out that hope.

But there still remains the £750 million to bridge. The package of internal measures in this crisis has been more politically-motivated, and therefore more derisory, than in any previous crisis. It may be argued that this is because the battered Labour party is in direr political straits of unpopularity than was the governing party in any previous crisis. But that is no excuse. Throughout his Chancellorship, Mr. Callaghan has generally shown considerable political courage, often in misguided causes. Now, as that Chancellorship nears its end, his (or more probably Mr. Wilson's) nerve has tragically failed, just when courage could at last have paid off in terms of real and major national advantage.

Apart from the measures to curb industrial investment, the only deflationary moves which the Government has regarded as politically possible are:

(1) An increase in Bank rate to 8 per cent. This has been accepted

because everybody assumes that it will not last for long; foreigners probably will not allow it to.

(2) A demand to commercial banks that they should "limit bank advances except, of course, to priority borrowers, especially exporters." If the aim is to keep a rigid ceiling on bank advances, this could be quite a tough squeeze—but, inevitably, an incredibly blunt and untidy one.

(3) An increase in the hire purchase regulations on the sale of cars at home, so that buyers are forced back to a minimum deposit of 33⅓ per cent and a maximum repayment period of 27 months. Mr. Wilson devoutly hopes that this discriminatory control will not cause as much unemployment in the motor industry as it did last time, because now devaluation has at last given car makers an extra and positive incentive to sell more abroad.

(4) The usual promise that "defence expenditure will be reduced by over £100 million next year," and that "other public expenditure, including nationalised industries' capital expenditure, will be reduced by £100 million." These are ostensible cuts in planned increases that the authorities concerned say would otherwise have taken place. Details of some of them have already been announced. Those inclined to believe this sort of cut may do so.

The Government's own estimate (or pretended hope) seems to be that all these measures together will cut back demand by an annual rate of something over £250 million (with the credit squeeze working more strongly at the beginning of the period, and the supposed cuts in government expenditure working more towards the end of it). The other £400 to £500 million a year, needed for the £750 million, is then apparently expected to come from the cut in demand that should arise automatically from a 2½ to 3 per cent rise in the cost of living as a result of the rise in import prices. Indeed, the Chancellor on Monday seemed to be putting a greater weight even than £500 million on to this factor. He said that, without devaluation, he had expected that personal consumption (which was over £24 billion last year) should have risen by about 3 per cent in 1968; but, chiefly because of the rise in prices following on devaluation, he now believed that the "bulk of the increase in personal consumption that would have taken place would be transferred" to strengthening the balance of payments instead. Is this to be believed?

WILL CONSUMPTION BE RESTRAINED?

One returns to Mr. Callaghan's original formula for a post-devaluation programme: that there should be an incomes freeze while prices are rising. There is some reason to doubt whether officialdom may not be overestimating the speed or automaticity with which a 10 to 12 per cent rise in import prices will work itself through to even a 2½ or 3 per cent rise in the cost of living. Eleven months after the last devaluation, in August, 1950, British import prices were some 22 per cent higher than they had been a year before, but the old retail price index was only 2 per cent higher. This was in the period when the Crippsian wage freeze was in force, but the old policy of artificially keeping down the index of food prices was not (because a ceiling had been put upon food subsidies in April, 1949).

If the Government were really relying on the rise in prices to check consumption, it should now actively be encouraging price rises, on replacement cost principles of accounting. Liquor shops with a stock of French wine should be urged to put up their prices immediately. Otherwise there may be a run on this and other imported products in the next few months, while stocks at the old pre-devaluation prices last. Then, when stocks are denuded, the shops—who will not want to have empty shelves—may stock up with more imports again, thus actually causing a temporary rise in foreign expenditure instead of the expected fall. But it hardly needs to be emphasized that Labour ministers certainly have not been urging retailers to move quickly to put up their prices in this way. On the contrary, every politician from the Prime Minister down has been uttering dire admonitions that nobody should raise prices unless his recorded import costs make this absolutely essential.

This attitude of the Government, combined with its decision to continue with only a voluntary incomes policy, could lead to the worst possible results. One fears a situation in which (a) retail prices do not rise following devaluation by as much as the Government is expecting; but (b), because the Government is expecting that bigger rise, it is soft-hearted in its wages policy even in the public sector; and then (c) the rise in wages does indeed push prices up by more than 2½ to 3 per cent, but in a cost-induced inflation with wages in the lead. In that event, consumption will not be reduced; in some circumstances, it could actually rise by more than it would have done without devaluation. *The Economist* does not believe that this would necessarily mean that the opportunity for improvement in the balance of payments would be wholly lost. Probably there is more room for expansion in the economy than the target 3 per cent per annum to which the Treasury cautiously sticks. But it is certain that this continuation of cost inflation and consumption boom would cut tragically severely into the advantages that devaluation could otherwise achieve.

If there is a consumption boom of this kind, unemployment may well come down below a seasonally-adjusted figure of 1.8 per cent a year from now (compared with this month's 2.5 per cent, announced on Thursday). Labour's political popularity may well recover. Some part of the stock exchange's first bullish reception of the news this week may even prove to have been justified. But investors should note that they could have an additional hurdle to surmount. If demand inflation has risen by next April, this now very-politically-motivated Labour Government may decide to meet the situation by swingeing new taxes directed wholly against the so-called rich. If all these things happen, life for the ordinary man at $2.40 may still be better than the last four years of life at $2.80. But the entirely possible achievement of making the next seven years the period of the British economic miracle will have been missed.

B. Who Should Adjust?

PRACTICAL ASPECTS OF THE PROBLEM
OF BALANCE-OF-PAYMENTS ADJUSTMENT

Otmar Emminger

Deutsche Bundesbank

I. SOME INTRODUCTORY REMARKS

A. The Role of Exchange-Rate Policy

I assume that for all practical purposes variations of exchange rates will in the future, as at present, be used only in exceptional cases as a method of balance-of-payments adjustment among the major industrial countries. I would not, however, rule out that in the future we may witness not only occasional adjustments of single exchange rates which are grossly out of line but also the transition of a single country to a flexible (or a more flexible) exchange rate for quite some length of time. Nevertheless, I consider it unlikely that in practice exchange-rate variations will be used in a more generalized and permanent way as an instrument of adjustment among industrial countries. It should be understood that this working assumption regarding exchange-rate policy is based on the assumption of a relatively stable development of the U.S. economy as the dominant economy of the Western world. Should the U.S. economy continue on a strongly inflationary path for any length of time (or should it inadvertently fall into a prolonged deflationary depression), then a number of other countries may have to revise their ideas on the appropriate exchange-rate policy.

I recognize that it may be one of the most important and difficult practical problems to decide, in light of all the relevant national and international considerations, in what circumstances and at what point

From Otmar Emminger, "Practical Aspects of the Problem of Balance-of-Payments Adjustment," *Journal of Political Economy*, Vol. 75, No. 4, Part II (August 1967), 512–22. Reprinted by permission of the University of Chicago Press. Copyright 1967 by the University of Chicago.

exchange-rate adjustment should be used in preference to other methods of adjustment. I do not want to go here into this very complex matter (which does not easily lend itself to theoretical generalizations). In what follows I shall confine myself to problems of adjustment within the framework of a system of fixed exchange rates, as it has evolved in actual practice out of the Bretton Woods principles. I shall place special emphasis on problems which we have encountered in practical attempts at some international co-ordination of economic policies and in discussions on rules of the game or a code of good behavior.

B. International Versus Interregional Balance-of-Payments Problems

From a practical point of view, it is not difficult to see some major differences between international and interregional payments problems. One of them is, of course, the greater easiness of financing an imbalance between regions of a country as compared to financing imbalances between different countries. Of far greater importance, however, is the fact that there exist national monetary and fiscal policies, national wage and cost developments, and other significant national economic characteristics which usually have a pervasive effect on all regions of a country. The existence of diverse national policies may lead to divergencies in the development of demand and cost levels between various countries to an extent which would hardly be conceivable between the regions of a single country.[1] Thus, it is difficult to visualize acute payments problems (apart from slow long-term changes) arising between regions of the same country out of short-term discrepancies in demand and cost developments. Moreover, once an imbalance between regions begins to arise, the "automatic" processes of monetary adjustment usually begin to work at an early stage, without being impeded by an offsetting national monetary and financial policy. This does not, of course, exclude the possibility that an interregional imbalance may occasionally be cushioned for some time by short-term credit movements or other kinds of financing operations. Where international and interregional adjustment problems seem to show a rather similar character is in the case of imbalances arising out of "structural" shifts in demand, production, etc. But even here there usually exist special equilibrating forces between regions inside a country (impact of fiscal and budgetary policies, unemployment assistance, special regional aid and development programs), whereas in the international sphere autonomous monetary and financial policies often work against an adjustment to such slow structural changes as well as to shorter-run disturbances.

This rather sketchy juxtaposition of international and interregional adjustment problems serves to bring out the fact that if balance-of-payments adjustment becomes a major problem in practice, this is very often due to the existence of national financial and other economic policies which are directed to various policy goals. Among these, balance-of-payments equilibrium does not always enjoy the highest priority. One of the difficulties of adjustment between various countries lies precisely in the existence of differences between national priorities, for example, differing emphasis on price stability, full employment, growth, external balance, etc. Another arises out of institutional differences: one country relying, for demand management, mainly on monetary policy, and here again especially on interest-rate policy; another relying more on budgetary policies, licensing of building, capital market controls, etc. These differences may have particularly distorting effects on capital flows between these countries, which will no longer be primarily based on genuine differences in the supply and demand of capital and in profitability, but will be largely influenced by institutional differences and by national preferences for diverse monetary, fiscal, and other policy instruments.

II. PROBLEMS OF DIAGNOSIS

A. Balance-of-Payments Aims

Whether there is an imbalance and how large it is must, of course, be judged against some recognized aim of balance-of-payments policy. It is true that "equilibrium" does not always consist in "zero" movements in official reserves (gross or net, as the case may be). There may be justifiable or even desirable surpluses or deficits, and there may be a useful redistribution of reserves (witness the U.S. deficit from 1950 to 1956!). I do not believe, however, that *in practice* it is normally very difficult to detect and recognize an undesirable and disturbing imbalance as such, although there may be doubts about its portent and duration and still more doubts about how best to cope with it.

Nor do I believe that the problem of recognizing an unwanted deficit is particularly difficult *in the case of the United States,* because of its unique role as a reserve center and as an international financial intermediary. It is true that sometimes one could be in doubt whether in the American case the correct measure of balance or imbalance should be the official reserve transactions or the overall liquidity balance. But I do not believe that it would really be difficult, in practice, to decide whether there still is a U.S. deficit that needs adjustment. It may be true that sometimes confidence factors enter the evaluation, as was once suggested by a U.S. Treasury spokesman.[2] It is not likely, however, that these confidence factors are largely determined by a wrong concept of international financial relationships on the part of the outside world, especially on the part of the Europeans, and that, therefore, the U.S. deficit could be "cured" simply by better educating and informing these outside observers, as has been claimed by some eminent American economists, such as Despres, Kindleberger, and Salant.

A real practical problem when assessing a given balance-of-payments situation is, however, to evaluate how far certain elements in the picture are volatile or likely to be of a more permanent nature. A correct evaluation of this kind may be of decisive importance for practical balance-of-payments policy (cf. also section II, D).

B. *Averting Versus Curing Imbalances*

From a practical point of view, a major task of a good adjustment policy would seem to be to prevent large-scale imbalances, especially deficits, from arising, rather than to deal with those that have already "raised their ugly head." This is essential for two reasons: first, because the longer the unbalancing factors have been in existence the more havoc they will have wrought (for example, on the cost level of the deficit country), and the more painful it will be to eradicate them. Second, in a world with a general bias toward creeping inflation, every major deficit, even if it can still be brought under control by ordinary demand policies, has a tendency to add fuel to the inflationary tendencies in the world at large.

C. *Early Diagnosis*

Early detection and early correct diagnosis of emerging imbalances are, therefore, particularly important. It is for this reason that Working

Party 3 of the Organization for Economic Co-operation and Development (OECD) has recently proposed the institution of an "early-warning system." It goes without saying that it will not be easy to agree on a system of concrete statistical indicators for emerging imbalances, which would serve as "warning signals" applicable to a number of countries.

Sometimes the deficits are concealed, at least for the superficial observer, by short-term money movements. Thus, the huge United Kingdom basic deficit of 1964 hardly showed up in official reserve movements before September, 1964, because in the preceding eight months it was nearly covered by increases in foreign sterling balances and by capital inflows from the Euro-dollar market. In a similar way, the large Italian deficit of 1962–63 did not immediately show up in the official reserves as it was at first financed by the Italian commercial banks having resource on a large scale to the Euro-dollar market, until the Italian Central Bank stopped these inflows in August, 1963. These short-term money movements not only hid the seriousness of the underlying imbalance from public (and political!) awareness, but also prevented the "automatic" liquidity effect of the deficit from making itself fully felt. Similarly, the large current account deficit of Germany in 1965 was to a large extent offset by sizable short- and medium-term capital inflows; and these inflows, very much to the despair of the German Central Bank, at the same time largely offset the restrictive effect of German monetary policy, thus contributing to the slowness of the domestic monetary adjustment. Such experiences raise the question whether the existence of a very large pool of volatile international capital like the Euro-dollar market is really an advantage, or, to put it the other way around, whether under present circumstances full freedom of capital inflows of a financial nature (especially of short-term bank money) is always compatible with an efficacious national monetary policy and adjustment process (cf. section III, C).

D. Correct Diagnosis and the Timing of Remedial Action

In the three practical cases mentioned, the authorities knew, of course, from the outset that behind the rather reassuring official reserve figures a large basic deficit had been emerging. In the United Kingdom and in Italy the authorities were taking what the Bank of Italy repeatedly called a "calculated risk." The United Kingdom authorities publicly declared in the spring of 1964 that the deterioration of the current account balance was an inevitable consequence of the much-desired investment boom which would in the longer run increase the competitiveness of British exports; that the disquieting increase in imports probably represented a temporary "hump" due to restocking; and, therefore, it was entirely proper to deal with the problem by financing the deficit out of reserves and existing international credit facilities without any real demand adjustment. This miscalculation ushered in the biggest and longest of all sterling crises since World War II. In Italy the authorities, up to August, 1963, were loath to break the investment boom too suddenly and took the "calculated risk" of financing the wage explosion of 1962–63 in order to avoid large-scale unemployment. In the Italian case, in contrast to the British experience, the adjustment policies, speeded up in early 1964 by a threatening foreign exchange crisis and by pressures from Italy's partners in the EEC, worked nearly with lightning speed, the balance of payments turning into a surplus again from April, 1964, onward, with Italy very soon becoming the major surplus country in the world. In the German case, the authorities clearly saw the disadvantages of the offsetting capital inflows, and they took those measures against them that were at their disposal. But they refrained from instituting a system of direct controls against these capital inflows (in the—later justified—hope that the restrictive monetary effects of the external deficit would nevertheless "bite" in the end).

E. Diagnosing the Causes and Nature of the Imbalance

The above-mentioned cases show that sometimes there may be doubts about the nature or at least about the seriousness of the emerging imbalance. In the majority of cases, however, we have quite simple and straightforward cases of *overexpansion of national demand* exercising its effect on the balance on current account. It has been a common feature of such cases of excess demand to find their main expression in a sudden expansion of imports. In such straightforward cases the remedy is usually as simple: to eliminate the overexpanded demand by appropriate monetary and financial demand policies. In such cases there is no conflict between the requirements of internal and external equilibrium.

Overexpansion of demand, however, usually acts also on the domestic wage level, although sometimes with a time lag. While excessive demand is usually reversible, excessive wages usually are not, or only at great difficulty and over some length of time (for example, by a wage stop leading to a decrease in wage costs per unit of output). Occasionally a cost inflation is not the result of a prior demand inflation; as the Italian case of 1962–64 shows, a "wage explosion" can come about for (political or other) reasons which are, at least in part, independent of the demand inflation. Such an "independent" cost inflation, if financed by the authorities, contributes in its turn to demand inflation. In all such cases, one of the most important practical problems consists in evaluating whether the cost level of the country concerned has already been pushed up so high as to definitely impair the competitive position of that country and make it impossible to restore external equilibrium under conditions of full employment by "simple" demand policies. Such a situation would call for a different remedy. Thus, a correct diagnosis of the cause and nature of the imbalance may be quite important for the cure.

F. Diagnostical Difficulties in Cases of Simultaneous Demand and Cost Inflation

An imbalance due to, or at least accompanied by, a cost inflation no longer presents a "pure" or "simple" case. Here we usually run into a conflict between the requirements of external balance and of domestic policy goals. While it is relatively easy to state the case theoretically, it is often extremely difficult to assess in practice whether the cost push has damaged the competitiveness of the country concerned beyond repair. In the Italian case mentioned, the wage explosion of 1962–64 pushed up the wage costs per unit of output in manufacturing by more than 30 per cent from the end of 1961 to the end of 1964. A number of foreign observers began, at the beginning of 1964, to doubt whether Italy could regain both external and domestic equilibrium without devaluation. This went so far that at that time all the German travel agencies advised their clients who intended to make a trip to Italy not to exchange more money into Italian lire than was absolutely necessary for the next few days—in expectation of the coming devaluation. Now the same country seems to be on its way back to near-full employment, with a sizable external margin to spare, and still on the old exchange-rate parity.[3] In the case of the United Kingdom, it has also been im-portant for the authorities to evaluate correctly whether the continuing deficit on current account has been due to a reversible overexpansion of demand or to a definite and irreversible loss of competitive power. In some cases, the only way to find a convincing answer seems to be a pragmatic policy of trial and error: to repress the excessive demand and stop the cost push, and then to see what happens to the balance of payments. As a change in the exchange rate would provide durable adjustment only in conditions of full control over the domestic demand and cost level anyway, nothing is lost if one first tries to establish this control on the basis of the old parity as a practical test of the nature and extent of the disequilibrium. This seems to be the practical justifi-cation for the present anti-inflationary British policy.

G. Disagreement on Causes of U.S. Deficit

These practical examples show that in cases where both demand and cost disparities are at stake a correct evaluation, and therefore also a correct cure, may not be easy to arrive at. We get into even more seri-ous trouble where structural reasons of all sorts—large disequilibrating capital movements, etc.—are involved. The classical case in this respect is, of course, the obstinate U.S. deficit. Although this has existed for so many years, there does not yet exist a generally agreed diagnosis of the nature of the disequilibrium between the United States on the one hand and Continental Europe on the other, at least not for the period 1958–65.[4] On the European side, during all this time, the United States was criticized for its easy-money policy, "artificially low" interest rates, and even for its "inflation"; the complaint about "imported infla-tion"—imported from the United States, that is—has been a common slogan in Europe. On the U.S. side, the Europeans were criticized for their underdeveloped and fragmented capital markets on which most of the disequilibrating capital movements were blamed; furthermore, the Europeans were also blamed for their one-sided reliance on mone-tary restriction, and for their alleged unwillingness to play their proper role as surplus countries. Without going into any details here, it may be summarily said that practically every part of the arguments on both sides could easily be shown to be either factually wrong or, if not wrong, to be beside the point.

During all these diagnostical *dialogues des sourds* (dialogues of the deaf), real adjustment went on to an astonishing degree. While in the United States in the period 1958–65 labor costs per unit of output in manufacturing fell by about 3–4 per cent, they rose in the same period in the EEC countries by more than 25 per cent on an average; in addition, during this period two European surplus countries, viz., Germany and the Netherlands, appreciated their currencies by 5 per cent. This long-drawn-out adjustment in the world economy also clearly illustrates that the burden of adjustment lay very one-sidedly on the shoulders of the European surplus countries. There was no significant deflation on the U.S. side, but a large—and in the end intolerable—measure of inflation on the side of the European surplus countries. The argument occasionally brought forward by Americans that this "imported" inflation could have been avoided by the European side neutralizing or "sterilizing" the inflows of foreign exchange or of American capital, thus running a "compensated surplus" without inflation over an extended period, is hardly worthwhile discussing before a group of eminent economists. It overlooks two things: first, the direct effect of a foreign-induced surplus on current account on demand in the surplus country which cannot be so easily neutralized as the pure liquidity effect; second, the well-proven fact that the more surplus countries tried to withstand the imported inflation, the greater became the demand and cost disparities and, not least, the disparities in the interest rate levels.

H. Inflationary Bias of Present Adjustment Process

It may, from all the experiences in the postwar period, be safely said that our present international system has a clear inflationary bias and a clear bias to the disadvantage of surplus countries. To quote the IMF (Annual Report for 1964, p. 4): "The existing rigidities of price systems and cost structures make it difficult for price reductions in deficit countries to play a major role in the adjustment of payments positions, and, with prices remaining stable in the United States, much of the adjustment in relative costs and prices has occurred through increases in the

surplus countries." The fund, by the way, noted this asymmetry with
approval and sympathy. (IMF Annual Report for 1964, p. 4: "The
international monetary system has been able to meet the challenges to
which it has been exposed.") It may safely be said, also, that nearly
every sizable deficit problem of one of the larger countries will, in the
end, be solved in practice through a further turn in the overall inflationary spiral in the world economy. This explains why the sufferers
from this process—and they have been for a long time mainly Continental European countries—show such a strong interest in some rules
on agreements that might diminish the number and size of imbalances
in the world economy.

III. POSSIBLE REMEDIES

A. Main Practical Problems

While it is true that sometimes the appropriate remedies for an imbalance are not directly related to the primary cause and nature of the
imbalance, the cases mentioned in section II, F and G, show quite
clearly that at other times a correct diagnosis of the causes and nature
of a deficit may be essential for finding the correct remedies. The main
practical problems in finding, and applying, the appropriate remedies
for disequilibria seem to me to lie in the following fields:

1. Determining whether the correct remedy is pure financing (temporary deficit), directly influencing some items in the foreign balance
(by controls, fiscal measures, etc.), or effecting a real adjustment of
demand/supply and cost relationships.

2. Applying the right mix of policies for real adjustment.

3. Dealing with disequilibrating capital movements.

4. Determining the respective responsibilities of surplus and deficit
countries. As to (1), some of the difficulties of judgment involved are
illustrated by the above-mentioned cases of the Italian, British, and
American deficit positions.

Working Party 3 of the OECD has recently published a report on
"The Balance of Payments Adjustment Process." This report contains
a list of agreed "prescriptions for general economic policy," which are
to serve as a guide or a set of presumptions against which national adjustment policies shall be appraised as to their appropriateness.

B. Policy Mix

In a recent report by some representatives to the Joint Economic Committee of Congress on "Free World Economic Cooperation," it was said that "the most urgent adjustment need is for guidelines establishing the appropriate mix of domestic fiscal and monetary policies." To this, many people would probably add also the appropriate admixture of incomes policies.

From my experience I believe that the right policy mix, especially the right mix of monetary and fiscal policies, can be very important. When there is an overexpansion of demand, it may be extremely important even for the evolution of the domestic economy whether the necessary restraints are imposed by monetary policy alone, or by budgetary and fiscal policies, or by a combination of both. In the recent past, in nearly all countries, there has been a (justified) complaint that the burden of restraining demand lay too one-sidedly on the shoulders of monetary policy and that this was having distorting effects on the economy and, in particular, on the financial markets. In all the major cases of internal and external disequilibrium in recent years, international organizations have made detailed recommendations, especially on the appropriate combination of fiscal and monetary policies, usually combined with a counsel of perfection on incomes policies (that is, the cases of Italy, Germany, the United Kingdom, and the United States).

I do not, however, believe that it would be appropriate or even feasible to expect monetary policy to be mainly (or even entirely) responsive to a country's external position, and fiscal policy to be mainly or exclusively geared to the needs of the domestic economy. Nor do I believe that by a very judicious mixture of both adjustment would become painless.[5]

The most important obstacle to applying the correct policy mix is, of course, politics. Moreover, in nearly all countries institutions are not well adapted to a flexible fiscal policy, and as regards incomes policies workable institutions exist hardly anywhere. For these reasons, some of the well-meant and well-thought-out international recommendations on the proper policy mix for adjustment often sound hollow or, as already mentioned, like counsels of perfection.

C. Capital Movements

As already mentioned, the one-sided application of monetary adjustment measures, and especially the reliance on interest-rate policies, may lead to capital movements whose motivation has nothing to do with real and lasting differences in capital productivity and profitability as between the participating countries. Very often, it is mere differences in attitudes vis-à-vis monetary policy, or differences in financial institutions and traditions, that lead to capital movements that are either disequilibrating or that tend to defeat the intended effects of monetary policy.

The latter is particularly true of *short-term money flows*. With the existence of a vast reservoir of volatile capital funds—the volume of the Euro-currency market is estimated at between ten and twelve billion dollars—a restrictive monetary policy in a small- or medium-sized country will often be defeated by large inflows of money. Even if such inflows may be "equilibrating" in the technical sense, insofar as they cover an existing deficit in the balance of payments, they may be detrimental because they may prevent a restrictive monetary policy from having the desired effects. (This has, for instance, been the experience of Germany and other European countries over the last two years.) Thus, while they may equilibrate the balance of payments in a statistical sense, they may at the same time prevent a more basic adjustment in the balance of payments from coming about. In such cases the question will arise: What is more important, the freedom of short-term money flows (which in the recipient country will have to be sterilized anyway), or the efficacy of a stabilizing monetary policy?

Other big practical problems are: (*a*) What segment of the balance of payments should bear the main burden of adjustment? Should capital movements be "untouchable" even if this would mean a very painful and costly adjustment of the current account items and consequently of the whole domestic demand and cost level? Or should capital movements be the adjustable part of the total balance of payments? (*b*) Should the adjustment measures be limited to financial incentives? In what circumstances would a direct interference with capital flows be justified?

The problems mentioned under (a) are particularly complicated by the fact that certain adjustment policies may have contradictory effects on the trade and the capital sectors. Thus, in a deficit country a restraint of demand may well serve to improve the current account, but may at the same time create additional incentives for an outflow of capital to more promising parts of the world. Conversely, the long-lasting monetary expansion in a number of European countries which was the inevitable effect of their surpluses created, at least for a period, a general climate of promising development and high profit expectations that increased the attractiveness of Europe for capital imports from America and, thus, partly defeated the equilibrating effects on the monetary expansion on the current account sector of the external balance.

I am convinced that there is no general, all-embracing answer to all these questions, but that every case has to be judged in the light of its circumstances. Perhaps we may one day arrive at a set of agreed criteria for evaluating these single cases. It is, however, significant that the problems of how to deal with international capital flows in the framework of balance-of-payments adjustment and in relation to the efficacy of national monetary policies come up again and again in the various bodies of the EEC; and it has, up to now, not been possible to find a common view on them even within this rather closely knit and homogeneous organization of countries.

D. *Responsibilities of Surplus and Deficit Countries*

One cannot always ask a country to take over the entire responsibility for adjustment, even if it is quite clearly the source of the disequilibrium. The correction of important imbalances is in the interest of deficit and surplus countries alike.

In most of the simple or "straightforward" cases, where there is imbalance because in a country the general level of demand is too high or too low, there can be no doubt about the responsibility.

More difficult is the apportioning of respective responsibilities when, as a consequence of demand inflation or otherwise, an intractable cost disparity has arisen. Here adjustment may be impossible without inflation and deflation, respectively. In more extreme cases, exchange rate adjustment may be the best solution. But not all countries are in the same position in this respect. In the case of the reserve currency countries, a change in parities (or the transition to a fluctuating rate) is justifiably held to have such important repercussions on the whole international system, and in particular on the present reserve system, that it could be envisaged only *in extremis*. Some people, especially in the United States, have drawn the conclusion from this, that whenever a clear case of exchange-rate adjustment between the United States and outside countries arises, it should be the latter that do the adjusting. While this conclusion may be partly tenable in a case where one or two of these outside countries are themselves in an extreme position that lends itself clearly to exchange-rate adjustment, it becomes a much more difficult proposition once the disequilibrium is a more pervasive one. Moreover, it must not be overlooked that the unpleasant domestic effects of an exchange-rate adjustment, particularly of an upward revaluation, may be much more severe in a small country where the foreign sector is much larger in relation to national income than in a huge, largely self-sufficient country like the United States.

The problem will usually be even more difficult when the imbalance is due to capital movements not directly related to demand or cost disparities, or is due to other structural shifts. These "complex" cases present the real difficulties, not only for diagnosis and cure but also for the apportionment of responsibilities between surplus and deficit countries. It has been an unpleasant experience that in all the major complicated cases, each side has expected the other to assume the main burden of the responsibility for adjustment.

Perhaps two principles could help to find solutions. First, those countries that can contribute to adjustment by a relaxation of controls and interferences and, generally, by a larger flow of goods and funds should do everything in their power to favor international adjustment. Second, those countries should be held primarily responsible for adjustment that are furthest away also from domestic equilibrium and that are most out of line in relation to international cost levels.

Finally, the problem of surplus versus deficit countries is often put as being one of expansion and inflation versus contraction and unemployment. On this reasoning, there is often a bias against recommending a deflationary contraction of the economy. But in the world in which we live, the problem is usually quite different. What is usually asked from a deficit country is not to deflate but to eliminate inflation —no more than that. Thus, when the United Kingdom in 1964 had its biggest deficit ever—$2.4 billion for the current and long-term capital account—the recommendations given by the IMF and Working Party 3 (Group of Ten) asked no more than that the British authorities pursue a policy that would keep nominal wage increases within the overall increase in productivity; thus, not deflation but merely a return to stability was expected. Had the United Kingdom been able, for just two years, to live up to this recommendation of cost stability (instead of letting the wage cost per unit of output go up by 6–7 per cent in one year), it would certainly have been able to wipe out its huge deficit.

It is difficult for the surplus countries to accept the burden of adjustment, if the deficit countries are not even able to maintain reasonable cost and price stability in their economies. For the surplus countries this means a continuous adjustment to an upward floating balloon.

E. Final Remark

One final remark: Has the adjustment *mechanism* "virtually broken down" in the present international economy? Not at all. In cases where a serious attempt was made to eliminate a big external deficit by restraining domestic demand, the adjustment mechanism nearly always worked with astonishing speed and vigor; witness the cases of Italy (1964), Japan (1964–65), Germany (1965–66). In the Italian and Japanese cases the shift from deficit back into surplus was even overdone. Where adjustment has failed up to now (September, 1966)— namely in the case of the United States and of Great Britain—either no attempt at all or only a half-hearted and belated attempt has been made at demand management policies. Thus, the "mechanism" as such has not broken down. It simply has not always been used—for good or bad reasons.

NOTES

1. While there may be large structural divergencies in the economic development of various regions of a country, it has repeatedly been shown that, for example, wage developments have a surprisingly uniform pattern over the whole territory of a country over the short term and may show large discrepancies internationally.
2. Undersecretary of the Treasury Joseph W. Barr, in a speech on September 21, 1965: "Our feeling in the Treasury is that equilibrium cannot be defined solely in terms of a figure; it is importantly a matter of confidence. . . . But while we may not be able to define in precise numerical terms what equilibrium is, we can say that it does not exist when the U.S. is continually losing gold."
3. A closer inspection would have shown that from 1961 to 1964 Italy seems only to have lost that extra margin of cost competitiveness that it had accumulated

from 1957 to 1961. The dangerous effect on its balance of payments was due more to the suddenness than to the extent of the wage increases.

4. Of late, there seems to be some convergence of view, as hardly anybody would, or does, deny that the renewed deterioration of the U.S. current account balance since 1965 has something to do with the re-emergence of domestic inflation in the United States.

5. In the report quoted above, it is claimed, *inter alia:* "By adopting flexible fiscal policies countries should be able to correct external imbalances without reducing domestic output or inflating the price level. Ideally, interest rates should be partially responsive to a country's external position. The domestic effects of rates determined in this light should be offset by changes in fiscal policy."

COMMENTS ON ADJUSTMENT RESPONSIBILITIES

Richard N. Cooper

Professor of Economics,
Yale University

Emminger points out that the cure for international imbalance must typically be related to its cause or diagnosis. He gives the example of overexpansion of domestic demand, which can lead both to an excess demand reflected in abnormally high imports and, with time to a deterioration in the cost-competitiveness of the country's products at home and in world markets. There is a crucial difference between a deficit which can be eliminated simply by reducing domestic expenditures and one where costs have gotten so far out of line that some internal or external change in the country's price level will ultimately be required.

While Emminger is right in some sense, and his illustration is apt, I would prefer to formulate this question differently. In logic the cause is irrelevant to the proper remedy. The appropriate cure for international imbalance should be related not to the cause of the imbalance but to deviations from other policy targets (in the sense in which Tinbergen has used this term). Very often the "cause" of an imbalance will be reflected in deviations from other policy targets, and, hence, in these cases the cause should affect the cure. But there will be many cases in which the cause and the appropriate cure are unrelated. Here a choice must be made among national objectives. Policies to restore overall imbalance should be selected on the basis of a national (and international) cost-benefit calculation, not on the basis of the cause.

From Richard N. Cooper, "Comment," *Journal of Political Economy*, Vol. 75, No. 4, Part II (August 1967), 541–43. Reprinted by permission of The University of Chicago Press. Copyright 1967 by the University of Chicago.

One of the key practical problems of an effective adjustment process is how to get surplus countries to adjust. I only half-facetiously suggest that this is even more difficult than getting reserve currency countries to adjust. Under the gold standard system adjustment was symmetrical. Countries in deficit experienced a deflation of monetary demand, but countries in surplus had an automatic inflation of monetary demand. These days that process has been largely broken on both sides (although in the past few years some surplus countries have acquiesced in some inflation). Deficit countries can ultimately be forced to adjust, since they will run out of reserves and financing can be withheld from them. No such sanction exists for surplus countries. France, for example, had a surplus for the seven years 1959–65, a surplus roughly twice as large in terms of GNP as the U.S. deficit. Germany's surplus lasted more than a decade, although it became more moderate in 1961–65, and in 1965 Germany even ran a deficit. Italy had a truly enormous surplus for the three years 1964–66, a surplus due in large part to deficient demand in the domestic economy. Stimulation of demand would not only reduce idle resources there but would also work toward external balance. Yet Italy received far less pressure to reduce this large surplus from its Common Market partners and others than it received to reduce its deficit in 1963 or than the United Kingdom and the United States received to reduce their deficits. This is true in spite of the fact that the surplus of Italy, relative to its trade and to its domestic economy, was far larger than the deficits of either Britain or the United States; and it exceeded the large British deficit of 1964 in absolute size.

Ideally, responsibility for adjustment between deficit and surplus countries should be divided according to some world welfare criteria, but we have no such criteria. Indeed, there has been no serious explicit discussion of them in official circles. I might make some partial remarks on that question, however, particularly in light of Emminger's assertion that during the last five or six years the burden of adjustment has fallen very one-sidedly on the surplus countries. This assertion raises both a factual question and an analytical one. Many private U.S. firms and government agencies would certainly be surprised to learn that they have borne very little burden as a result of the U.S. balance-of-payments program. But at a more general level, the United States did take deflationary measures in the severe budget of 1959, largely as a result of balance-of-payments considerations. The Kennedy administration was basically out of sympathy with that approach, but it nonetheless refrained from reflating as rapidly as might have been possible. Balance-of-payments considerations—and public attitudes toward "gold losses"—played a major role in the caution with which the administration moved toward more aggressive economic expansion. As a result, the United States lost more than $150 billion worth of output during this period, a loss that exceeds by 50 per cent the entire annual output of Germany, which is the second largest economy in the non-Communist world.

The analytical question concerns what exactly we mean by "burden of adjustment." Many Europeans feel very strongly about inflation; and inflation is politically important for that reason alone. But that is not the same as saying inflation was or is a great "burden" in economic terms. The burden of creeping inflation is yet to be demonstrated in analytical terms,[1] and indeed there are those who even go so far as to argue that moderate inflation is beneficial, not detrimental. Even if we leave that argument to one side, it is particularly questionable whether recent inflation in Europe has been a great burden, since much of the upward adjustment in costs there has not been reflected in higher prices.[2] Past savings have not been arbitrarily appropriated to any great extent through inflation. Rather, inflation has shifted the distribution of income. This obviously represents a cost to some segments of society, but it is a benefit to others; and without some explicit judgment about who should get what it is difficult to say whether European countries have been made worse off or better off as a result of their experience during the last five years. In contrast to inflation, unemployment imposes a heavy cost on some segments of society with no corresponding benefits to others. Whatever economic cost one might attribute to European inflation, it certainly cannot come close to the lost output in the United States.

NOTES

1. Tibor and Anne Scitovsky have examined the possible costs of creeping inflation in the United States and conclude it is very small compared with the costs of underemployment.
   ("Inflation versus Unemployment: An Examination of Their Effects," in Joseph Conrad et al. Inflation, Growth, and Employment, Englewood Cliffs, N.J.: Prentice-Hall, Inc., for the Commission on Money and Credit, 1964.)
2. I dismiss the steady but moderate increases in consumer price indexes for this purpose. These indexes do not reflect improvements in quality and they contain

a heavy component of wages, so they naturally increase as real economic growth proceeds, leading to higher factor incomes. Japan offers the outstanding illustration, with its steady improvement in international cost competitiveness accompanied by increases in the "cost of living" of more than 5 per cent per annum since 1960. European commodity prices have risen far less than the rise in unit labor costs, and in some cases have fallen.

PART IV

Reform of the System: Our Policy Choices

INTRODUCTION

That the operation of the international monetary system in recent years has been unsatisfactory or, at least, is capable of considerable improvement, is argued by most observers in both surplus and deficit countries. But how should the system be improved? The multiplicity of suggestions has been almost overwhelming. As typical of the major points of view, we consider four broad types of possible reform:[1]

1. Patching up the present adjustable peg system by such measures as the provision of a new international reserve asset.
2. Creation of an international dollar standard
3. Return to a gold standard
4. Initiation of exchange rate flexibility

In our Conclusion, these alternatives are evaluated further in light of their effects in reducing or eliminating the liquidity, confidence, and adjustment problems discussed in the previous sections of this volume.

Two major steps toward evolutionary reform of our international monetary system were undertaken in 1967 and 1968. They were the closing of the London gold pool, discussed by Edward M. Bernstein in "The Gold Crisis and the New Gold Standard," and the establishment of a plan for creation of Special Drawing Rights (SDR's), outlined by Martin Barrett and Margaret L. Greene in "Special Drawing Rights: A Major Step in the Evolution of the World's Monetary System." The two steps are related, because the gold pool countries, simultaneously with the closing of the pool, declared that they no longer found it necessary to buy gold: they were satisfied with the existing stock of monetary gold because of the prospective new reserve asset, Special Drawing Rights.

To meet the official confidence problem that would still remain because of the existence of multiple reserve assets, Bernstein proposes that central banks agree to hold the bulk of their reserves in a Reserve Settlement Account at the IMF.

Emile Despres, in his "Proposal for an International Dollar Standard," argues that the dollar should be considered the primary reserve asset. Gold is desirable because of its convertibility into dollars at a fixed price, and not vice-versa. The demand for gold is artificially high as a result of United States policy of unrestrictedly buying and selling gold at $35 an ounce from foreign official agencies.

Despres proposes that while the U.S. continue its willingness to *sell* gold unrestrictedly, it should impose limitations on the amount it would *buy*. The price of gold in either transaction would remain at $35 an ounce. He suggests reciprocal credit arrangements between the United States and other countries to substitute for the redundant amounts of gold under his quota buying scheme. Specific details of the proposal are omitted in the reading selection, and may be found in the original source.

The purpose of Despres' plan is to reduce the demand for gold in favor of the dollar, and thus establish a full fledged "dollar standard." Walter S. Salant in his "Commentary on the Despres Proposal" examines whether the announcement effect of the plan might lead perversely to an increase in the demand for gold. He suggests that a perverse reaction would not persist under a firm change in the U.S. policy.[2]

Salant discusses some of the measures that would enhance the probability of success of Despres' plan. Since the plan involves unilateral action on the part of the United States, Salant argues that it should be resorted to only if international co-operation fails to reform the international monetary system.

The position of France has been that far from establishing a dollar standard, the world should return to the gold standard. President de Gaulle declared his views in a famous press conference in 1965. The relevant excerpt of his statement is presented in the reading "Return to the Gold Standard."

Jacques Rueff, in the reading "Increase the Price of Gold," supports de Gaulle's position. Rueff points out that a substantial increase in the price of gold (in terms of the dollar and other currencies) is a prerequisite to the establishment of a gold standard. Only with such a price increase could the United States pay off all its outstanding dollar liabilities.

To many economists, the major disadvantage of a gold price increase is that it would signal a reversal in the trend toward diminution of the role of gold for monetary purposes. Why expend valuable resources in digging up and reburying gold when international reserves could be created by fiat at almost zero cost and in predetermined amounts? To the cold-hearted economist, the answer is that to do so is irrational. However, few of us are always rational, and to many there is still a mystique about gold. Some of the popular myths that contribute to the mystique of gold are critically analyzed by Robert Warren Stevens in "Mankind's Addiction to Gold."

The classic case for allowing the price of foreign exchange to move to clear the foreign exchange market, and thus keep balance of payments equilibrium, is presented by Milton Friedman in "Free-Market Determination of Exchange Rates." Friedman discusses the two polar cases of exchange rate adjustment: discrete adjustments in the level at which the exchange rate is pegged (such as the British devaluation), and complete absence of government intervention in the foreign exchange and gold markets, i.e., allowing the relative prices of national currencies to be freely determined by market forces. In the latter case there would be no need for national governments to hold international reserves; for the exchange rate would always adjust to bring balance of payments equilibrium. Friedman concludes that this is the better of the two methods discussed.

Between these extremes there are a number of possible forms of limited flexibility, and these are discussed by James E. Meade in "The Various Forms of Exchange-Rate Flexibility."

Is a flexible exchange rate really a policy alternative for the United States? It is often argued that an effective devaluation under the adjustable peg is not an option open to the United States, because other countries would be sure to follow suit. The corollary to such behavior is that, under a flexible rate system, other countries would not allow the dollar to depreciate relative to their own currencies. The possibility of such reactions does limit the ability of the U.S. to initiate unilaterally a system of flexible rates. Nevertheless, breaking the link between gold and the dollar would give the United States considerable additional policy freedom. This is considered by Leland B. Yeager in

"Unilateral Action on International Monetary Policy." If other countries did continue to peg their currencies to the dollar, then we would be on the dollar standard envisioned by Despres. If not, there would be exchange rate flexibility. (Of course, it is possible that some foreign governments would react in the first manner while others would follow the second option.) Yeager also considers the question of what would happen if U.S. gold did run out. He finds the possibilities to be far less frightening than the predictions of a world-wide depression like that of the 1930's.[3]

These plans are considered further in the Conclusion to this volume.

NOTES

1. For further discussion of plans for reform, see [19], [44], [47], and [57].
2. The change in gold policy proposed by Despres is quite different from that taken in the closing of the London gold pool. The fact that the private market price of gold rose above $35 an ounce after the closing of the gold pool does not indicate a presumption that official demonetization of gold would lead to a similar result.
3. It is true that in the 1930's there was a world-wide depression and there were exchange crises, but the primary chain of causation did not run from the latter to the former.

A. Patching Up the Adjustable Peg System

SPECIAL DRAWING RIGHTS: A MAJOR STEP IN THE EVOLUTION OF THE WORLD'S MONETARY SYSTEM

Martin Barrett and Margaret L. Greene

Economists, Foreign Research Division,
Federal Reserve Bank of New York

A major benchmark in the evolution of the international monetary system was reached in September 1967 when the members of the International Monetary Fund (IMF) agreed on a proposal for establishing a new reserve facility to meet the possible need for a supplement to existing international reserve assets. This supplement is designed to assure an adequate supply of international liquidity for a growing world economy if, as is expected, the growth of more traditional reserve assets—gold and foreign exchange—should prove inadequate. The plan provides a means for regularly creating special drawing rights (SDR's) in the Fund, which the participating countries would accept as reserves and could use in international settlements. Although the plan contains certain provisions to ensure the attractiveness of SDR's, their value as a reserve asset rests fundamentally on the obligation of participants to accept them in exchange for a convertible currency. To be sure, the proposal places some restraints on the ability of participating countries to use these assets and limits their obligation to accept them. But, because in general SDR's could be used automatically for the settlement of international payments, they fulfill the essential function of any reserve asset.

This new facility to some extent represents a logical extension of the Fund's current operations, but it departs from the Fund's ordinary procedures in several important respects. First, SDR's will be more

From Martin Barrett and Margaret L. Greene, "Special Drawing Rights: A Major Step in the Evolution of the World's Monetary System," Federal Reserve Bank of New York *Monthly Review*, Vol. 50, No. 1 (January 1968), 10–13.

readily available than the credit that the IMF now provides through drawings in the credit trenches.[1] Any participating country will be able to use SDR's whenever it has a balance-of-payments or reserve need to do so. Its exercise of this right will not be subject to consultation or prior challenge nor contingent on the adoption of prescribed policies designed to restore balance-of-payments equilibrium. Second, the SDR's are intended to provide a permanent addition to international reserves, whereas most current IMF transactions give rise to only a temporary increase. Third, the SDR's will be distributed to all participants in proportion to their IMF quotas. On the other hand, reserves that arise as a by-product of the Fund's credit operations normally add, in the first instance, to the total reserves of the borrowing country alone and only indirectly to the reserves of other countries. Finally, the use of SDR's does not entail repayment according to a fixed schedule, as does the use of the Fund's ordinary resources, although SDR balances must be partially reconstituted following large and prolonged use. In short, the SDR's are intended to provide systematic and regular additions to international liquidity, and to be readily available to any member of the Fund which elects to participate in the project.

The plan takes the form of draft amendments to the Fund's Articles of Agreement. These draft amendments will be submitted to all the members of the IMF for ratification—a process that could be completed late in 1968 or early in 1969. However, for reasons discussed more fully below, an affirmative vote for adoption of the amendment does not automatically lead to activation of the mechanism, and just when the plan will be implemented is not known.

THE PLAN IN OUTLINE

Allocation of Special Drawing Rights

The general criterion [according to which SDR's should be provided] is that there must be a widely recognized need to supplement existing international reserve assets. Indeed, the procedure for the introduction of SDR's is clearly designed to ensure that there is broad support for any decision on reserve creation. Thus, the managing director of the IMF, after having satisfied himself that there is a need to supplement monetary reserves, will undertake whatever consultations may be necessary to determine whether or not there is sufficient support among the participants for the creation of SDR's in the amount he proposes. After the concurrence of the Fund's executive directors, the proposal must then be approved by the board of governors of the Fund by an 85 per cent majority of the voting power of the participants. The Common Market countries, with almost 17 per cent of the voting power in the IMF, could thus veto the creation of SDR's if they vote as a unit, as could the United States with 22 per cent of the voting power.

Since the SDR's are intended to assure the adequate long-term growth of total reserves, the amount created will not ordinarily vary from year to year, nor will it be influenced by the reserve needs of individual countries. Instead, the amount to be issued will be for a "basic" period of several years—during which predetermined allocations are to be made at specified intervals. Initially, the basic period will be five years, but the IMF may decide that any future basic period will be of a different duration. The proposal does not indicate the amount of SDR's to be issued; that will be decided on the basis of a collective judgment of global reserve needs, which will depend in part on the growth of other forms of reserve assets. If it were decided to create $1 billion to $2 billion annually in the initial basic period, for example, total reserves would expand in the first year by 1.4 per cent to 2.8 per cent—considerably less than the 3.6 per cent average annual increase in total reserves from 1960 to 1964 and not significantly greater than the 2.3 per cent growth during 1965 and 1966. All members of the IMF will be able to participate in the "special drawing account" through which all the operations relating to SDR's will be carried out, and allocations will be made to all participants in proportion to their IMF quotas. Thus, the United States would receive roughly 25 per cent, or between $250 million and $500 million a year, if $1 billion to $2 billion of SDR's were issued annually.

If unexpected developments make it desirable to change the rate at which SDR's should be issued, it will be possible, under the same consultation procedure, to increase or decrease this rate for the rest of a basic period or to adopt a new basic period with a different rate of creation. Such changes will ordinarily require an 85 per cent majority vote. However, a decision to reduce the rate of issue for the remainder of a current basic period can be taken by a simply majority of the voting power of the participating countries.

Use of Special Drawing Rights

A participating country will be entitled to use SDR's to acquire an equivalent amount of convertible currencies to finance a balance-of-payments deficit. The user of SDR's will acquire currencies, not out of resources held by the Fund, but directly from other participants or through the intermediation of the Fund. Convertible currencies are expected to be purchased from countries with strong balance-of-payments and reserve positions, thereby following the Fund's existing criteria for the selection of currencies to be used in its lending operations. However, a reserve center may also use SDR's to purchase balances of its own currency held by another country—provided the latter agrees—by transferring SDR's directly to that country. Whether the transfers are arranged directly between participants or indirectly through the Fund, the countries that use SDR's will have their SDR holdings in the special drawing account reduced and those countries that receive them will correspondingly have their SDR holdings increased by an equal amount.

SDR's may not be used for the sole purpose of changing the composition of a country's reserves. In other words, a country cannot use SDR's simply to build up its foreign currency balances or gold holdings. Although the use of SDR's will not be subject to prior challenge, the IMF may make representations to any country that has failed to observe this principle and may direct transfers of SDR's to that country to restore its SDR holdings. Nevertheless, over time a participant could find the share of its reserves held in SDR's falling if it were to use SDR's when in deficit and receive other reserves when in surplus. Such changes in the composition of reserves, however, will generally be avoided through the guidance of transfers of SDR's by the IMF.

Reconstitution Provision

Participating countries that use SDR's may incur an obligation to restore (or "reconstitute") their position to some extent, depending on the amount and duration of their use. The reconstitution provision in the plan specifies that a member's average use of SDR's over a basic period is not to exceed 70 per cent of its average cumulative allocation. Translated in terms of holdings, this obligation means that over any basic period a country's average holdings should be at least 30 per cent of its average allocation over the same period. If at any given time holdings of SDR's fall below this 30 per cent average level, it will be necessary to reconstitute and hold them for a sufficient time to establish the minimum average ratio.

The reconstitution provision is designed to prevent any tendency toward financing large and persistent payments deficits by exclusive reliance on SDR's. In fact, the reconstitution provision includes the principle that "participants will pay due regard to the desirability of pursuing over time a balanced relationship between their holdings of special drawing rights and other reserves." However, the reconstitution provision does not prevent a country from using all its SDR's when its balance-of-payments difficulties are temporary in nature. If the balance-of-payments difficulties that give rise to the use of SDR's are in fact short-lived, then a country which had utilized all its allocation of SDR's in the early part of a basic period could reconstitute its average holdings simply by minimizing the use of its allocation or accumulating SDR's in the latter part of the period. Otherwise, a participating country would have to acquire them either directly from other participants or through the intermediation of the IMF in exchange for some of its other reserve assets. If a country began using SDR's toward the end of the period, holdings of its allocation at the beginning of the period might enable it to satisfy any reconstitution requirement.

The reconstitution provision may, in effect, impose a repayment obligation on part of a country's use of SDR's, but it does not seriously compromise the quality of the SDR's as a reserve asset. That portion of SDR's which is not required to be reconstituted (70 per cent of the cumulative allocations) is as absolutely at the disposal of a participating country to meet balance-of-payments deficits as any asset can be. Moreover, the reconstitution provision is less onerous than the repayment (repurchase) provisions currently applicable to drawings on the IMF. Such drawings must be completely liquidated within three to five years either directly through repayments by the debtor country to the IMF or indirectly by other members' drawings on the IMF of the debtor's currency.[2]

Acceptance Obligations

Every participating country is obligated to provide currency in exchange for SDR's freely and to keep those it receives (so long as it does not have need to use them) until its total holdings are equal to three times the amount of its cumulative allocations. That is, if a country's initial allocation were $100 million and it used none of its SDR's, its acceptance obligation would be $200 million. If the country had transferred all its initial allocation to other countries, its acceptance obligation would be $300 million. A country could, of course, accept and hold SDR's in excess of this amount, and the plan gives surplus countries some incentive to do so. The SDR's will carry a gold-value guarantee. Moreover, holdings of SDR's will earn a moderate rate of interest, although the yield will presumably be less than that on United States Treasury bills.

The limitation on holding countries' obligations to retain SDR's would appear to reduce the facility's usability as a reserve asset, since it is essential that a country have absolute assurance that it will be able to use its SDR's to acquire convertible currencies to meet all or part of its payments deficit. In the long run, however, this limitation seems unlikely to be serious. If, after the plan has been in operation for a number of basic periods, the amount of SDR's outstanding becomes quite large, a country with a balance-of-payments deficit is almost certain to find some surplus country which holds less than its obligatory limit of SDR's. Moreover, the reconstitution provision, which encourages persistent deficit countries to use other reserves in addition to SDR's, will help to avoid excessive transfers of SDR's. Finally, transfers of SDR's may be made not only to participants with a strong balance of payments but also to countries with a strong reserve position even when they have a moderate payments deficit.

For these reasons, the margin between the amounts of SDR's created and the acceptance obligations will probably be large enough to assure any participant that its holdings are fully usable. If, for example, a proposal were made to create $1 billion of SDR's annually, the United States, with about 25 per cent of IMF quotas, would receive $1,250 million over a five-year period and would not reach its acceptance limit in the fifth year until it held $3,750 million of SDR's, or 75 per cent of the SDR's outstanding. The Common Market countries as a group, with about 17 per cent of IMF quotas, would not reach their acceptance limits until they held about $2,550 million of SDR's— slightly more than half the total issue. If either the United States or the Common Market countries as a group were to have temporary deficits which were settled with the maximum transfer of SDR's, the acceptance limits would be large enough to accommodate a transfer in either direction.

SOME UNRESOLVED ISSUES..

The plan appears to provide a workable mechanism for the creation of a supplement to existing reserve assets. But smooth operation of the mechanism depends not only on the provisions, guarantees, and limits contained in the proposal but also on the degree to which various countries, in particular the surplus countries, will support the plan and accept SDR's as a reserve asset.

The question immediately arises as to when the plan will be activated. The adoption of the proposal, which requires an 80 per cent majority of the voting power of IMF members, seems assured, but activation of the plan requires an 85 per cent vote. Thus, an affirmative vote for the adoption of the amendment would not necessarily be sufficient to assure activation, and the Common Market countries as a group could veto any proposal to issue SDR's.

Ratification of the plan may be delayed, if creation of SDR's becomes linked to overall reform of the present provisions of the Bretton Woods Agreement. Some Common Market countries seek modification in the voting provisions of the Fund in order to require an 85 per cent vote for approval of quota increases. In effect, this reform would give the Common Market countries the same veto power on regular IMF operations that the United States now enjoys. An alternative and in many ways preferable course by which the Common Market countries could obtain a decisive voice in the IMF would be by increasing their subscription to the Fund to the point where they have just over 20 per cent of the total voting power.

Assuming that the plan is ratified by the IMF members, its activation might nevertheless be delayed until there is substantial reduction in the United States balance-of-payments deficit. The position of the French government, as stated by Michel Debré, Minister of Economy and Finance, is "that the mechanism cannot come into play until the balance-of-payments deficits affecting the countries whose currencies are designated as 'reserve currency' have disappeared." This is an extreme view which has not been taken by other countries. Moreover, as President Johnson indicated in his statement on the new United States balance-of-payments program, movement toward balance will, by curbing the flow of dollars into international reserves, limit the growth of existing reserve assets: "It will therefore be vital to speed up plans for the creation of new reserves."

Even if the plan were promptly implemented, the need to restore balance-of-payments equilibrium in this country would in no way be reduced. The amount of SDR's the United States would obtain each year is small, compared with the size of our recent deficits, and the plan does not prevent countries from converting their existing dollar holdings into gold. Consequently, continued balance-of-payments deficits would still pose a threat to our gold reserves. If the dollar is to continue to function as the principal trading and reserve currency, the United States must substantially strengthen its payments position. Changes in the workings of the world monetary system will not relieve this country of this task.

NOTES

1. At present, a member of the Fund may purchase (or "draw") the currencies of other members by depositing with the IMF an equivalent amount of its own currency. The normal quantitative limitations on the use of the Fund's resources depend on the size of the member's quota (which equals the member's subscription in gold and in its own currency to the Fund's resources). Drawings are virtually automatic in the "gold tranche"—i.e., as long as the total amount drawn does not exceed the 25 per cent of the borrowing country's quota normally subscribed in gold. But a country can make additional drawings, in the "credit tranches", only after it has agreed to take measures to correct its balance of payments.

2. Only up to the point where the Fund's holdings of a member's currency fall short of 75 per cent of the quota—as may happen when that currency is used for other countries' drawings—can that member draw from the IMF without incurring a repayment obligation.

THE GOLD CRISIS AND
THE NEW GOLD STANDARD

Edward M. Bernstein

President,
EMB (Ltd.), Research Economists

I. FURTHER EVOLUTION OF THE GOLD STANDARD

Crisis and Progress

1967-1968

The international monetary system established at Bretton Woods in 1944 has been under almost constant pressure during the past twelve months. The difficulties had their immediate origin in the inability of the United Kingdom to restore its balance of payments without a change in the parity of sterling. The difficulties were intensified by the large and persistent deficit in the U.S. balance of payments. The devaluation of sterling on November 18, 1967, was followed by massive speculation in gold in the London gold market—the gold crisis. The seven countries in the gold pool undertook to contain this speculation by providing gold out of their reserves at the ceiling price of $35.20 an ounce. Repeated statements of the gold pool could not remove doubts of their willingness and ability to continue to supply gold from their reserves on the large scale and for the indefinite period that would have been necessary to quench the speculative demand. The gold speculation gathered momentum, and after having supplied about $3 billion to the London market from mid-November to mid-March, the central bank governors representing the gold pool decided to terminate their intervention in the London gold market and other gold

From Edward M. Bernstein, "The Gold Crisis and the New Gold Standard," *Quarterly Review and Investment Survey.* New York: Model, Roland & Co., Inc., First Half, 1968, pp. 1–12.

markets. The London gold market was closed on March 15, 1968, not to be reopened until April 1. This, in brief, is the chronicle of the gold crisis which has at last come to an end.

In the midst of these uncertainties, far-reaching measures were taken to assure the continued strength and stability of the world economy. The devaluation of sterling, although it had unfortunate short-run consequences, has made it possible to restore the U.K. balance of payments. The prospects for the rehabilitation of sterling have been much improved by the new budget which will help to eliminate excess demand, stabilize prices and costs, and free the real resources necessary for a payments surplus. In the United States, new measures to limit U.S. foreign direct investment and to reduce outstanding bank credits to foreigners were put into effect on January 1, 1968. These emergency measures are an essential part of a comprehensive program to secure a substantial reduction in the U.S. payments deficit this year. The possibility of slowing down the fighting in Vietnam, as a consequence of the initiative of President Johnson, provides additional hope that the strain on U.S. resources, which is the basic cause of the payments deficit, will be gradually relieved. The most important step that the United States can take now to strengthen the dollar is to reduce the budget deficit by raising taxes as requested by the Administration.

The leading industrial countries and the International Monetary Fund have agreed on major steps that will provide a strong foundation for a new gold standard. The most important of these measures is the proposal for creating a new reserve asset, Special Drawing Rights (SDRs), to supplement gold and foreign exchange. At a meeting in Stockholm, March 29–30, 1968, the Group of Ten gave their approval (with France dissenting) for the immediate presentation of such an amendment to the Fund charter. In the meantime, at a meeting in Washington, March 16–17, 1968, the central bank governors representing the gold pool agreed on a new gold policy isolating private gold markets from the international monetary system. In essence, the monetary gold stock will remain at its present level. Thus, the growth of monetary reserves in the future will have to come entirely from the issue of SDRs.

Despite the crisis through which the international monetary system has passed, it has been a year of progress. The great industrial countries have accepted greater responsibility for maintaining an orderly international monetary system. They have made it possible to have an adequate growth of monetary reserves in the future through the creation of a new reserve asset, SDRs. The logical corollary to SDRs is the policy of isolating private gold markets from the international monetary system. Together, these measures have accelerated the evolution of a new gold standard better suited to the needs of the world economy.

Co-operation on a New Gold Standard

The gold crisis revealed the extent to which the stability of the international monetary system could be disturbed by the vagaries of gold speculators. In the United States, the Gold Reserve Act of 1934 recognized the danger of permitting domestic hoarders to deplete the gold reserves of the monetary system. The danger is even greater that, in a period of temporary weakness of a major currency, the Bretton Woods system of fixed parities could be undermined by speculative raids on the gold reserves of the international monetary system in the hope of forcing a change in the monetary price of gold. To prevent this, the gold pool terminated its intervention in the London market and adopted a new policy that will protect the international monetary system from gold speculation. At a meeting in Washington on March 16–17, 1968, the governors of the central banks of the United States, the United Kingdom, Belgium, Germany, Italy, the Netherlands, and Switzerland (representing the gold pool) stated the new policy, as follows: (OLIGOPOLY !)

The Governors believe that henceforth officially held gold should be used only to effect transfers among monetary authorities, and, therefore, they decided no longer to supply gold to the London gold market or any other gold market. Moreover, as the existing stock of monetary gold is sufficient in view of the prospective establishment of the facility for Special Drawing Rights, they no longer feel it necessary to buy gold from the market. Finally, they agreed that henceforth they will not sell gold to monetary authorities to replace gold sold in private markets.

This new policy will freeze the stock of monetary gold at about the present level; that is, the gold reserves of all countries outside the Communist group and the gold holdings of the IMF, the BIS, and the European Fund. The new gold policy will assure a solid foundation of $40 billion of gold to serve as the principal reserve in the new gold standard that is now evolving. With the monetary gold stock frozen at about the present level, the necessary growth of monetary reserves for an expanding world economy will have to be met in another way. The great industrial countries (the Group of Ten) and the IMF decided that the best way to assure an adequate but not excessive growth of monetary reserves is through the creation of a new reserve asset.

A plan for SDRs was submitted to the annual meeting of the Board of Governors of the IMF at Rio de Janeiro in September 1967. In accordance with a resolution of the Board of Governors, the Executive Directors of the IMF prepared an amendment to the Fund charter which will authorize the issue of SDRs and their allocation among the 107 member countries. The amendment will also change the voting requirements for some of the decisions of the IMF in order to give greater voice to the European surplus countries and to make sure that drawings on the IMF in excess of a country's net creditor position (the gold tranche) will be treated as reserve credit and submitted to appropriate tests for reserve credit.

The ministers and central bank governors of the Group of Ten met in Stockholm on March 29–30, 1968, to consider a tentative draft of the amendment to the Fund charter. They reaffirmed their determination to co-operate in the maintenance of exchange stability and orderly exchange arrangements based on the present $35 official price of gold and they agreed that the plan to establish SDRs will make a very substantial contribution to the strengthening of the international monetary system. In the next few days, the final text of the amendment will be mailed to the governors of the IMF for their approval. When this approval is given by correspondence, the amendment will be submitted to member countries for ratification. The ratification may be completed in 10 to 12 months. Some further time will be necessary before a decision is taken to activate the new reserve facility. The French delegation did not associate itself with the parts of the Stockholm communiqué on the maintenance of the present price of gold and the agreement on SDRs and changes in the rules and practices of the IMF.

The French Government stated that it wants fundamental changes in the international monetary system. In the opinion of the French Government, the recent difficulties have their origin in the gold exchange standard; that is, the use of dollars and sterling as reserves. The privileged position of dollars and sterling as reserve currencies, in the French view, tends to encourage persistent deficits in the payments of the United States and the United Kingdom. The French propose, therefore, that the monetary price of gold be raised substantially, doubled or more, and that dollars and sterling no longer be used as reserves, so that monetary reserves hereafter would consist exclusively of gold valued at the higher price. Facilities for reserve credit would be available through the IMF, but under rigorous conditions.

The French position has no support in the Group of Ten. An international monetary system cannot be based on gold if the price of gold is to be responsive to the same market influences as other metals. The very essence of the gold standard is that the monetary price of gold should remain a fixed reference point for the value of currencies. As for dollars and sterling, it is not possible to reverse the historical process by which large amounts of these currencies came to be held as reserves. Nevertheless, it is not desirable to have any further growth in the foreign exchange component of monetary reserves. Thus, with the stock of monetary gold frozen and foreign exchange reserves fixed at about the present level, the only source of further growth of international monetary reserves would be SDRs. This would greatly simplify the problem of assuring an adequate growth of aggregate monetary reserves.

The plan for the new reserve facility contains a provision under which a member of the IMF may refuse an allocation of SDRs (opting out). When the plan is ratified and activated, it will be possible for France to decide to opt out of an issue of SDRs. It is doubtful whether it would be in the interest of France to refuse an allocation of SDRs in order to insist on gold settlements exclusively when all other great trading countries will be using SDRs and foreign exchange, as well as gold, to settle their payments surpluses and deficits. While it would be unfortunate if France were to dissociate itself from the operations of the new reserve facility (SDRs), the international monetary system could function reasonably well despite its abstention.

While France did not associate itself with some parts of the Stockholm communiqué, it did subscribe to Paragraph 6 in which the ministers and governors of the Group of Ten and Switzerland said that "they intend to strengthen the close co-operation between governments as well as between central banks to stabilize world monetary conditions." The common interest in the successful functioning of the international monetary system far outweighs any temporary advantage that could be achieved in a clash of national policies. That is why France will undoubtedly decide to play its full part in the new gold standard.

The basic principles of this new gold standard are clear. The Bretton Woods system of fixed parities will continue unchanged, with the par values of all currencies defined in terms of gold at the present official price of $35 an ounce. The private markets for gold will be isolated from the monetary gold stock. The amount of gold and foreign exchange reserves will remain fixed at about their present level, and the growth of monetary reserves will take place through the issue of SDRs. Currencies will remain convertible, as they now are, with gold, foreign exchange, and SDRs all used together in balance-of-payments settlements. Such a gold standard is a natural evolution of the international monetary system in response to the needs of the world economy. Some of the problems that could arise because of a difference between the monetary price and the private market price of gold or because of a preference by some countries for gold rather than SDRs and dollars are discussed below.

II. PRIVATE GOLD MARKETS UNDER
THE NEW GOLD STANDARD

Premium Gold Prices and the Gold Standard

Under the classical gold standard as it existed prior to 1914, national currencies were redeemable in gold coin. As people were free to use gold coin for any purpose—to export it, hoard it, or melt it—there was complete equivalence of gold and money at the mint price. Such an equivalence is not essential under a modern gold standard. It is true that except for a brief period, the price of gold in the leading private markets was about $35 an ounce from November 1953 to March 1968. But this 15-year stability in private gold markets was exceptional. From 1940 to 1953, the price of gold in private markets was always at a premium—sometimes at a very high premium. Furthermore, from 1961 to 1968, the price of gold in private markets was kept close to $35 an ounce only by large-scale intervention of the gold pool.

On October 20, 1960, a brief burst of speculation in gold was touched off by rumors, during the U.S. presidential campaign, of a possible change in U.S. gold policy. As a consequence, the price of gold in the London market rose to $40.60 an ounce and then quickly subsided. Some central banks regarded the premium price for gold as a serious reflection on the stability of currencies and therefore a strong encouragement to gold speculation. In February 1961, the gold pool was formed by the central banks of eight countries (France was in the pool until June 1967) to keep the price in the London market at not more than $35.20 an ounce. While sales of the gold pool did not ordinarily exceed purchases, except for brief periods, the gold pool had to support the market almost steadily during the past two years. On March 15, 1968, the London gold market was closed and the remaining members of the gold pool agreed to isolate the private market entirely from the monetary gold stock. This, in effect, means a two-price system —a fixed monetary price of $35 an ounce and a fluctuating price in private gold markets.

There are some who hold the view that a two-price system for gold is inherently unstable. They fear that some central banks will sell gold from their reserves at premium prices. They even see a possibility that some central banks will act as arbitrageurs, selling gold for dollars at premium prices and using the proceeds to buy gold from the U.S. Treasury at $35 an ounce. These fears are unfounded. A two-price system for gold is not a novelty. It existed all through World War II and for eight years after the war. The London market was not reopened (March 1954) until the premium on gold had been eliminated several months before.

It may be helpful to analyze the factors that determine gold prices in private markets. There is a steady demand for gold for industrial purposes and for hoarding in those areas in which gold is a customary form of investment for savings. In addition, there is a highly volatile speculative demand for gold that reflects the state of confidence in currencies. Until the formation of the gold pool, changes in the speculative demand for gold were manifested mainly in higher or lower prices, subject to the limitation that the price could not fall much below the monetary value of $35 an ounce. As would be expected, the price of gold (in U.S. dollars) was close to the postwar peak in July and August 1949, just before the devaluation of sterling and other European currencies. At that time, American smelting companies quoted an export price of about $50 an ounce, FOB New York, for foreign gold sold by them on consignment. Once the European currencies were devalued, the dollar price of gold for export to private markets began to fall and by April 1950 it was down to $38 an ounce, FOB New York. Except for a brief period at the start of the Korean war, prices continued to fall and by November 1953 the premium in private gold markets, except in the Far East, had virtually disappeared. Prices fell and remained at $35 an ounce from 1953 to 1960 because of the greater confidence in currencies, particularly the European currencies.

After the establishment of the gold pool in February 1961, changes in the private demand for gold were manifested only in larger or smaller quantities of gold absorbed by hoarders and speculators. The principal factor affecting changes in the demand for gold was still confidence in currencies, although after 1960 it was confidence in dollars and sterling that was of primary importance. The private absorption of gold rose to a higher plateau averaging over $1 billion a year from 1960 to 1964. The large U.K. payments deficit brought another rise in the private absorption of gold to an average of about $1.6 billion in 1965 and 1966. In the last quarter of 1967 and the first quarter of 1968, speculation was on such a scale that about $3 billion must have gone into private uses and holdings in 1967 and a similar amount may go into private hands this year. Some of the gold sold in the London market from mid-November 1967 to mid-March 1968 probably went to central banks. By far the larger part went into speculative holdings which are now enormous.

Isolation of Private Gold Markets

Premium prices for gold in private markets would disrupt orderly exchange arrangements and deplete the gold reserves of the international monetary system if central banks were permitted to sell gold at premium prices. In the early postwar period, a number of countries did sell gold at premium prices in private markets. This was in violation of the IMF rule that monetary authorities should not engage in gold transactions that depart from the official price of $35 an ounce by more than the prescribed margin. In June 1947, the IMF issued a formal statement deprecating premium transactions in gold in these terms:

A primary purpose of the Fund is world exchange stability and it is the considered opinion of the Fund that exchange stability may be undermined by continued and increasing external purchases and sales of gold at prices which directly or indirectly produce exchange transactions at depreciated rates. From information at its disposal, the Fund believes that unless discouraged this practice is likely to become extensive, which would fundamentally disturb the exchange relationships among the members of the Fund. Moreover, these transactions involve a loss to monetary reserves, since much of the gold goes into private hoards rather than central holdings. For these reasons, the Fund strongly deprecates international transactions in gold at premium prices and recommends that all of its members take effective action to prevent such transactions in gold with other countries or with the nationals of other countries.

After the 1949 devaluations and the remarkable improvement in the European payments position, the price of gold in private markets fell considerably, so that there was much less inducement to undertake sales at premium prices. In September 1951, the IMF terminated its supervision of the gold transactions of its members but reiterated the principle that sales of gold at premium prices are contrary to the obligations of members under the charter of the IMF. The new statement said:

Despite the improvement in the payments position of many members, sound gold and exchange policy of members continues to require that to the maximum extent practicable, gold should be held in official reserves rather than go into private hoards. . . . Accordingly, while the Fund reaffirms its belief in the economic principles involved and urges the members to support them, the Fund leaves to its members the practical operating decisions involved in their implementation, subject to the provisions of Article IV, Section 2 [on gold transactions based on par values] and other relevant articles [of the IMF charter].

The action taken by the gold pool on March 17, 1968, is in harmony with the principles of the IMF. The members of the gold pool decided not to sell gold to private markets, regardless of price. This includes domestic as well as foreign gold markets, and it applies to the sale of monetary gold for use in the arts and industry as well as sales for hoarding and speculating. The gold pool added a new sanction to make this policy effective. If any country sells gold to the private market, it will not be able to replace it by buying gold from the seven countries in the gold pool. The withdrawal of the gold pool from the London market has greatly strengthened the international monetary system. That is why the IMF endorsed this action in the following statement:

During their meeting in Washington over the past two days, the active members of the gold pool have decided to stop supplying gold from monetary reserves to the London gold market or any other gold market. This decision is readily understandable as a means of conserving the stock of monetary gold which has recently been subject to heavy drains through such operations in the London market. The decision, of course, involves no departure from the obligation of these countries to maintain the par values of their currencies established with the International Monetary Fund.

"Countries adhering to the Articles of Agreement of the Fund undertake to collaborate with the Fund to promote exchange stability and to maintain orderly exchange arrangements with each other. It is most important that monetary authorities of all member countries should continue to conduct gold transactions consistently with this undertaking, and that they should cooperate fully to conserve the stock of monetary gold. Such action will be an important contribution to the functioning of the international monetary system.

The members of the gold pool also stated that as the existing stock of monetary gold is sufficient, in view of the prospective establishment of the new reserve facility (SDRs), they no longer feel it necessary to buy gold from the market. It will, in fact, be generally helpful to isolate the private market for gold from the monetary stock of gold. Sudden decreases or increases in the monetary stock of gold, because of official sales to speculators or purchases from speculators, cannot be conducive to the orderly growth of monetary reserves at a regular rate. The logic of the new gold standard is that the growth of monetary reserves should come exclusively from the issue of SDRs.

III. GOLD, DOLLARS, AND SPECIAL DRAWING RIGHTS

Equivalence of All Reserve Assets

The new gold standard will have as monetary reserves an unchanging amount of gold, about $40 billion, a fixed fiduciary issue of about $24 billion of foreign exchange (mainly dollars and sterling), and a steadily increasing proportion of SDRs. With only SDRs being added to reserves, growing at a rate of about $2 billion a year in the initial 5-year period, it will be possible to have an assured growth of aggregate monetary reserves at a trend rate suited to an expanding world economy. There is a danger, however, that a traditional preference for gold as reserves, perhaps intensified by higher prices in private gold markets, could disrupt the smooth functioning of the new gold standard.

An international monetary system based on multiple reserve assets cannot operate effectively unless the different reserve assets are equally attractive to hold and to use. Otherwise, there is a danger that central banks will hoard the preferred reserve asset (gold) and use the other reserve assets (dollars and SDRs) in international settlements. If such an attitude should emerge, transfers of SDRs would not have the disciplinary effect in inducing balance-of-payments adjustments that is essential for the proper functioning of the international monetary system. On the other hand, transfers of gold, after using up less preferred reserve assets, could have the effect of signaling an impending reserve crisis. The only way to avoid such disruptive behavior is to require countries to use all of their reserve assets indiscriminately in international settlements.

This problem has been in the forefront of all discussions on the creation of a new reserve asset. One method of avoiding a disruptive preference for gold would be to link gold and the new reserve asset at a fixed ratio in all settlements—say, $1 of gold and $1 of the new reserve asset. Such a composite gold standard could work reasonably well among a limited number of countries such as the Group of Ten. It could not be applied effectively when all of the 107 members of the IMF hold and use the new reserve asset, as many of the members have a major part of their reserves in dollars and sterling. The basic principles for the indiscriminate use of all reserve assets were stated by a distinguished French expert in November 1965, when the Frnch Ministry of Finance was urging the adoption of a new reserve asset in the form of the CRU (the collective reserve unit). The two principles can be summarized as follows:

(a) Each deficit country should use its different reserve assets for settling its deficit in precisely the same proportions as it holds these reserves—gold, dollars or sterling, and the new reserve asset (SDRs).

(b) Each surplus country should acquire the different reserve assets for settling its surplus in the average ratios of gold, dollars or sterling, and the new reserve asset (SDRs) used by all deficit countries, so that all surplus countries would acquire the different reserve assets in the same ratios.

Despite their simplicity, these principles would not be easy to apply equitably. A country that has a deficit in Year I and offsets it by an equivalent surplus in Year II should have no change in the composition of its reserves. This would not be true with the application of the principles stated above. Thus, a deficit country having a high proportion of gold and a small proportion of dollars and SDRs would settle its deficit with a large proportion of gold. The following year, when the same country has an equivalent surplus, it would receive the different reserve assets in the ratios in which they are used by all deficit countries. This could involve a much smaller proportion of gold than it paid out in the previous year. Similarly, countries that have a surplus in the earlier years, when the amount of SDRs outstanding is small, would normally receive a larger part of their settlement in gold. Countries that have a surplus in the later years, when the amount of SDRs outstanding is large, would normally receive a smaller part of their settlement in gold. These fortuitous changes in the composition of a country's reserves could be avoided by having settlements adjusted to a cumulative surplus and deficit basis.

Settlements in the SDR Plan

The outline of the plan for Special Drawing Rights, as given in the Rio resolution, recognizes that countries do not in fact regard all reserve assets as equally attractive and it therefore requires participating countries to use and hold SDRs and other reserve assets on an equitable basis. The provision that participating countries will not be required to hold SDRs in excess of three times their cumulative allocations (i.e., net acquisition of twice their allocations) recognizes that there will be a preference for gold and possibly other reserve assets instead of SDRs, at least in the earlier years of the operation of the plan. A number of specific provisions of the plan are designed to make sure that participating countries use other reserve assets along with SDRs in an appropriate manner.

The outline of the plan for Special Drawing Rights states that except under the guidance of the IMF, "a participant will be expected to use its SDRs only for balance-of-payments needs or in the light of developments in its total reserves and not for the sole purpose of changing the composition of its reserves." Without such a provision, countries would be able to use their SDRs, directly or indirectly, to acquire dollars and then use the dollars for conversion into gold. They could do this, for example, by paying out SDRs when they have a deficit and by acquiring dollars (and gold) when they have a surplus. The right to use SDRs, as well as gold, to maintain the convertibility of the dollar is an important safeguard against such practices.

To prevent one-sided use of SDRs in the settlement of deficits, participating countries will be required to reconstitute their position in SDRs in accordance with rules and regulations that will be prescribed by the IMF. At the end of the first five years of the operation of the plan, the average net use of SDRs by a participant is not to exceed 70 per cent of its average net cumulative allocations during this period. If a participating country has used a larger average proportion of SDRs, it can be required to reconstitute its holdings of SDRs by transfers of other reserves for SDRs under the guidance of the IMF. Participating countries will have to "pay due regard to the desirability of pursuing over time a balanced relationship between their holdings of SDRs and other reserves," presumably by using them together in appropriate ratios in balance-of-payments settlements.

The principal means that the IMF will have to assure the use of all reserve assets in appropriate ratios for balance-of-payments settlements is through the selection of the countries to which SDRs will be offered in exchange for a currency that is convertible in fact. Normally, currencies will be acquired for SDRs from countries that have a strong payments and reserve position. It would be possible, however, for the IMF to guide SDRs to a country with a strong reserve position, even if it has a moderate payments deficit, provided it had surpluses in the past. In selecting countries to which SDRs should be transferred, the "primary criterion will be to seek to approach over time equality among the participants [with a cumulative balance-of-payments surplus or a strong reserve position] . . . in the ratios of their holdings of SDRs, or such holdings in excess of net cumulative allocations thereof, to total reserves."

These two tests are not the same. By one test, equality in the ratios of holdings of SDRs to total reserves, all countries in a strong reserve position would harmonize the composition of their reserves, or at least the ratio of SDRs (whether allocated or earned) to their other reserves. By the other test, all countries with a cumulative surplus would apparently acquire SDRs in excess of their cumulative allocations in the same proportion to their total reserves. It would probably be better to require all surplus countries to acquire the same proportion of

SDRs and other reserve assets in settlement of their cumulative balance-of-payments surpluses. This would result in the *pro rata* accumulation of all reserve assets by surplus countries in the ratios in which they are used by deficit countries.

Whatever the precise criteria the IMF will ultimately apply on the use and holding of SDRs, it will be difficult to assure appropriate use of all reserve assets, so as to avoid a disruptive preference for gold over dollars and SDRs. The changes that would occur in the composition of the reserves of surplus and deficit countries through international settlements could not, in the first instance, be in accord with the criteria of the IMF, except under the most fortuitous circumstances. The attempt to establish the appropriate composition of reserves through guided transfers would require endless shuffling of SDRs and other reserve assets among surplus and deficit countries. Such guided transfers would underline the strong preference of central banks for some reserve assets; that is, gold.

Reserve Settlement Account

The transfer of reserves by deficit countries and their acquisition by surplus countries must be based on principles that define the appropriate use of all reserve assets in international settlements. It is unnecessary, however, to establish an elaborate system of guidance, adjustment, or reconstitution for this purpose. The objectives could be achieved very simply if the participating countries were to place all of their reserve assets in a single account with the IMF. When this account is drawn down by deficit countries, it would involve the proportionate use of their different reserve assets *pro rata* on a cumulative basis. And when this account is built up by surplus countries, it would involve the acquisition of different reserve assets in the same proportions by all surplus countries on a cumulative basis.

The countries participating in the plan would deposit their gold, dollars and other foreign exchange reserves, and SDRs (at each successive allocation) in a Reserve Settlement Account in the IMF. The deposits would be denominated in a Reserve Unit (RU) equal to one U.S. dollar with a guaranteed gold value. A country depositing $500 million of gold, $200 million of U.S. dollars, and $100 million of SDRs (in successive allocations) would receive a deposit credit of 800 million RUs. And a country depositing $200 million of gold, $500 million of

U.S. dollars, and $100 million of SDRs would also receive a deposit credit of 800 million RUs. Thus, in setting up the Reserve Settlement Account, no distinction would be made between the different reserve assets that members deposit.

The gold deposited by a participating country with the Reserve Settlement Account in return for RUs would not have to be transferred physically from its present place of safekeeping. Instead, it would be earmarked in the name of the Reserve Settlement Account. This would not only save the cost of physical movement of the gold, but it would have the additional convenience of retaining the gold at centers convenient to the depositing country which, in fact, would have a reversionary right to the gold.

The dollars, sterling, and other foreign exchange deposited with the Reserve Settlement Account would have to be transferred to the account, although a country would retain a reversionary right to the foreign exchange it deposited. In general, a member would deposit all of its foreign exchange reserves, except agreed working balances. In order to avoid a growth of foreign exchange reserves outside the Reserve Settlement Account, members would not be permitted to accumulate excessive working balances. Thus, further acquisition of dollars or sterling by a member would have to be presented for conversion in Reserve Units. In effect, the present amount of foreign exchange reserves would become a fixed fiduciary issue that could not be increased in the future. Provision could be made, however, for retirement of some of the dollars and sterling from time to time and their replacement with special issues of SDRs when the United States or the United Kingdom has a large surplus in its balance of payments. The foreign exchange deposited in the Reserve Settlement Account would be guaranteed in terms of gold and invested in special securities paying a moderate rate of interest—say, 3 per cent a year.

Similarly, when the new plan is activated and SDRs are issued, the successive allocations to members will be made by crediting them with an equivalent deposit in the Reserve Settlement Account. The growth of aggregate monetary reserves at a steady but moderate rate hereafter would come from the regular issues of SDRs. This is so because there would be no further increase in the monetary gold stock and the amount of foreign exchange reserves would be fixed when the Reserve Settlement Account is established.

A deficit country requiring a currency for intervention in the exchange market would acquire it by converting RUs into that currency. And a surplus country acquiring a currency through intervention in the exchange market would have that currency converted into RUs. In practice, only RUs would be used in international settlements. The drawing down of its RU account by a deficit country would thus involve the *pro rata* use of its reserve assets (gold, dollars or sterling, and SDRs) in the proportions in which they were deposited by that country in the Reserve Settlement Account. Similarly, the building up of its RU account by a surplus country would involve the acquisition of a claim on gold, dollars or sterling, and SDRs in the proportions that they compose of the deposits of the deficit countries, so that all surplus countries would acquire the same proportion of these different reserve assets. Furthermore, settlements in RUs would involve automatic adjustments on a cumulative basis.

Advantages of a Reserve Settlement Account

A Reserve Settlement Account would facilitate the functioning of the international monetary system with its multiple reserve assets. It would concentrate the gold reserves of all participating countries, thus assuring the isolation of the monetary gold stock from private gold markets. The deposit of dollars and sterling in the Reserve Settlement Account would prevent the continued accumulation of reserves in this form, obviate the risk of massive conversion of these currencies into gold in a time of crisis, and facilitate their gradual liquidation and replacement by SDRs under appropriate conditions. The present foreign exchange reserves would thus become a fixed fiduciary issue in the international monetary system. The assets held by the Reserve Settlement Account would be either gold or gold-guaranteed (foreign exchange and SDRs). The Reserve Settlement Account would earn interest on its foreign exchange holdings and on SDRs. It would, therefore, be in a position to pay interest to participating countries on their imputed holdings of foreign exchange and SDRs.

The operations of a Reserve Settlement Account would be in complete harmony with the principles stated in the outline of the plan for Special Drawing Rights. It would assure the use of all reserve assets in international settlements in a manner equitable to all countries, whether they have a surplus or deficit. The Reserve Settlement Account would obviate the need for guidance, adjustments, and reconstitution of holdings in the administration of the Special Drawing Account. With such a system, no participating country would have any reason for limiting its acquisition of SDRs to any multiple of its cumulation allocations. Thus, the SDRs would, in fact, be a reserve asset without qualifications of any kind as to their use in international settlements—on precisely the same basis as gold, dollars, and sterling. This is of basic importance in an international monetary system in which the growth of reserves in the future will come exclusively from new issues of SDRs. For this reason, the establishment of a Reserve Settlement Account is an essential step in the evolution of the new gold standard.

B. An International Dollar Standard

PROPOSAL FOR AN INTERNATIONAL DOLLAR STANDARD

Emile Despres

Professor of Economics,
Stanford University

A proposal for strengthening the international monetary system which was originally circulated in the spring of 1965 is outlined below. Its adoption—and, perhaps, merely its serious consideration—would bring to an end the state of nagging semi-crisis in the international economy which has persisted since 1959, and it would reverse the present growth of mercantilist restrictionism.

The central postulate underlying this proposal is that the dollar is not only "as good as gold" but is, fundamentally, much better than gold. In the present day world, gold derives its desirability as a monetary asset from the fact of its unlimited convertibility into dollars at a fixed price. The dollar is not merely a national currency; it is, indeed, the predominant international currency. It is widely used for commercial settlements not only in trade with the United States but in trade between foreign countries. It is the principal unit of account in international lending and borrowing, both long-term and short-term, even when both borrower and lender are foreign entities. Free world central banks and monetary authorities, other than those of the sterling area and the French community, settle their deficits and surpluses, in the first instance, by taking in or paying out dollar balances.

Except by special arrangements, gold is no longer used directly in settlements between foreign countries. Although foreign countries

From Statement by Emile Despres, in *New Approach to United States International Economic Policy*, Hearings before the Subcommittee on International Exchange and Payments of the Joint Economic Committee, 89th Cong., 2d sess., 1966 (Washington, D.C.: U. S. Government Printing Office, 1966), pp. 39–42.

may elect to exchange dollars for gold or gold for dollars, the dollar is the medium of payment and gold simply a potential source of, or use for, dollars. The United States is the only country which stands ready to buy gold on demand or sell gold to foreign central banks and monetary authorities. Although other countries have defined the legal parity of their monetary units in terms of gold, all IMF members except the United States have taken advantage of the option provided under the Articles of Agreement of the International Monetary Fund to set the upper and lower support limits in terms of dollars. Since so large a part of the free world's international obligations—commercial and financial—is denominated in dollars, it is, in the last analysis, dollars and not gold which are desired for international settlements. The evolution of credit money over the past four or five centuries has proceeded to a point where gold has become a dollar substitute, rather than the dollar a gold substitute.

Whatever may have been the case in the past, the desire for gold as a monetary asset is today contrived and artificial. It rests upon the confident assumption that the United States government will always stand ready to supply dollars in exchange for gold without limit and at a price not less favorable to gold holders than 35 dollars an ounce. Certainly the anxiety which the U.S. government has shown in the face of go̶ ̶̶sses has done nothing to weaken the confidence with which this ̶̶̶ion is held. Nevertheless, the United States, although committed to defending the dollar, has no comparable commitment to the ̶se of gold.

 ̶s that the United States, as the world's financial ̶ ̶ ̶problem and not a balance-of-payments problem ̶blem arises from an inflated demand for gold, ̶ present United States gold policy. The present state ̶s of the international monetary system can be corrected by bringing about a genuine change in prevailing asset preferences, reducing the desire for gold and increasing the desire for dollars. Such a shift in asset preferences can be brought about by United States action alone and not by international negotiation to create some supplementary reserve asset. Within the context of prevailing asset preferences, any international agreement would be too limited in scope and too rigid in its operation to permit the needed re-establishment and development of an unrestricted, integrated, international capital market based upon the United States. By distributing liquidity on a symmetrical formula which does not take account of the special banking problems of the financial center, it would give reserves to countries that do not need them without appreciably easing the positions of those who do.

The present inflated demand for gold rests upon persistent belief in the possibility of dollar devaluation and the confident expectation that, in any event, gold can always be converted into dollars without limit at no less than $35 an ounce. A change in asset preferences can be effected only by changing these expectations. Only in this way will the actual demand for dollar assets be brought into line with the underlying character of the dollar's international role.

Despite repeated official statements of the U.S.'s determination to defend the dollar and the steps which have been taken for this defense, belief in the possibility of dollar devaluation underlies the bulk of the private speculative demand for gold and probably exerts some influence upon the decisions of central banks and monetary authorities with respect to the composition of their reserves. So long as we stand ready to convert gold into dollars without limit at $35 per ounce, the holding of gold becomes a safe potential source of dollars, risking little more than the interest foregone. The desirability of gold as a monetary reserve asset depends upon the fact that the conversion of gold into dollars is universally taken for granted. If convertibility of gold into dollars were convincingly limited, gold not eligible for purchase by the United States woud lose its usefulness as an international monetary asset. International settlements between foreign countries are largely carried out in dollars, not in gold, and it is scarcely conceivable that foreign central banks and monetary authorities would agree to use in settlements among each other an asset not freely exchangeable for dollars.

The kinds of steps which, in my judgment, the United States should take to alter prevailing asset preferences are given below:

1) The present 25 per cent gold reserve requirement against Federal Reserve notes should be repealed and it should be made more explicitly clear than at present that all the monetary gold which the United States holds would be used if necessary in defense of the dollar. Gold should be treated not as a last line of defense to be conserved and husbanded but as a readily available reserve to be employed alongside swap credits and forward exchange operations and IMF drawings and other newly developed financial devices. Although we have reiterated

our determination not to devalue, continuation of the existing reserve requirements against Federal Reserve notes together with U.S. zealousness to avoid gold losses whenever possible has created a widespread impression that in the face of persistent gold losses, the U.S. would resort to devaluation long before its 13 billion dollars of monetary gold had been exhausted.

2) In addition, the United States should announce a new policy with respect to the purchase of gold. While continuing to stand ready to sell gold without limit at the statutory price of $35 an ounce, the U.S. should impose strict limitation upon the amount of gold which it stands ready to buy at this price and should substitute firm credit lines for the monetary gold rendered redundant by quota limitations on U.S. purchases. This proposal involves no change in the price at which we would stand ready to buy gold. However, it would end the unlimited convertibility of gold into dollars, and it would substitute credit for the monetary gold made redundant by the quota limitations.

The steps outlined above surely would result in a marked shift in asset preferences from gold to dollars and would remove the elements of weakness which impair the effective operation of the existing system by preventing the United States from performing its appropriate banking function. A dollar reserve system would be established free of the critical weaknesses of the existing system.

The adoption or even serious consideration [of the proposal] in the U.S. official quarters would require a radical change in prevailing official doctrine regarding the dollar's relationship to gold and the applicability to a world financial center of traditional notions of balance-of-payments equilibrium. So long as present doctrines are adhered to and so long as solutions are sought by attempting to negotiate multilateral agreements for supplementary reserve assets which do not give recognition to the inherent asymmetry between the position of a financial center and that of its clients, there is little reason to expect much improvement in the condition of contained crisis which has prevailed during the sixties.

COMMENTARY ON THE DESPRES PROPOSAL

Walter S. Salant

Senior Staff Economist,
Brookings Institution

Despite its undoubted merits the Despres plan raises a number of questions, economic, legal, and political.

A major criticism of the Despres plan is that there is no certainty that the change in U.S. gold-buying policy would shift asset preferences of foreign monetary authorities and private citizens from gold to dollars, and that the demand for gold might in fact rise, instead of falling, as Professor Despres assumes.

It should be noted that Professor Despres, being fully aware that the change in U.S. gold-buying policy might be ineffective if made when the United States is losing gold, proposes some preparatory steps which, in his opinion, would suffice to overcome this problem. First, he proposes that we make clear that we welcome continued use of the dollar as a reserve currency by countries that propose to hold a reasonably stable fraction of their reserves in this form. Second, he proposes that we invite the monetary authorities of other countries to convert promptly into gold any portion of dollar reserves which exceed the amounts they desire to hold. Third, he suggests exempting from control the flow of U.S. capital to the sterling area and to countries which hold the major portion of their reserves in dollars, except to the extent that controls are necessary to prevent capital from leaking through these countries to others. Finally, he would exempt all these "dollar-

From Walter S. Salant, Letter to Hon. Jacob K. Javits, July 19, 1965, published in *Guidelines for International Monetary Reform*, Hearings before the Subcommittee on International Exchange and Payments of the Joint Economic Committee, 89th Cong., first sess., 1965 (Washington, D.C.: U.S. Government Printing Office, 1965), pp. 562–70.

bloc" countries from the interest equalization tax. These inducements would increase the willingness, and in fact stimulate the desire, of many countries—including the United Kingdom, a major holder of gold—to hold a portion of their reserves in dollar balances.

I think this program of preparatory steps could be strengthened by several additions. One would be to eliminate the statutory requirement of gold reserves against Federal Reserve notes. This would tend to reduce fears about the adequacy of U.S. gold reserves. Another would be for the U.S. Treasury to purchase at least $3 billion of foreign exchange of continental European countries, paying for it with gold. This would substitute a single large and controlled gold loss for a series of uncontrolled losses which might otherwise occur after the United States invites other countries to convert unwanted dollar holdings into gold. Finally, I would seek to arrange in advance with the United Kingdom and Canada to convert some of their present gold holdings into dollars to provide an offset to gold losses that we could expect when others act on our invitation to convert dollars into gold.

These preparatory steps would greatly reduce the net gold losses that would result from the invitation to convert dollars into gold and they would greatly increase the probability, if not assure, that the new gold-buying policy would change reserve asset preferences in favor of the dollar.

In terminating the gold drain quickly, such steps, in Professor Despres' opinion, would advance the date of the effect which he predicts would in any case occur eventually. But some critics have questioned that the demand for gold relative to dollars would ever fall. They regard this demand as entirely irrational and unpredictable. As one economist has said, when the sheep get in a panic, you cannot tell which way they will run. These critics apparently believe that if the demand for gold increased in the first stage of the policy, the initial speculative effects would give rise to further developments that would sustain the rise, so that the first speculative reaction would be self-justifying. Presumably they have in mind the possibility that an announcement such as Professor Despres proposes, instead of having the effect he intends and expects, might have the opposite effect, causing great uncertainty in the rest of the world about what the United States would actually do and perhaps leading some people to conclude that in the end the United States would actually go back to buying gold at a price above $35 an ounce.

My opinion on this point is that, provided one assumes that the United States embarks on the policy with firm determination to live with its decision, the criticism that the eventual effects of the Despres plan on the demand for gold at $35 an ounce are unpredictable is quite incorrect. It either assumes that U.S. policy will vacillate in the face of initial confusion or of initial gold losses, or else it throws economic analysis completely to the winds. Considering first the eventual effect, even if speculative factors and the psychology of hoarders, official and private, are unpredictable, persistence in the policy would make fundamental factors prevail in the end. When a holder owning approximately one-third of the world's monetary stock and perhaps one-quarter of the world's total gold stock limits its previously unlimited willingness to buy gold while continuing its unlimited willingness to sell, the price of gold must fall sooner or later. So long as the U.S. Government embarked on this policy with clear and confident purpose, there would be nothing to cause an offsetting increase in the non-speculative demand of others for gold at $35 an ounce. Any initial increase in demand would eventually be satisfied by U.S. sales. The speculative component of the demand would then diminish, leaving the market more than saturated at $35 an ounce. The proposition that "anything could happen" might be true for a brief period when people in the gold market are figuring out the effects of the new policy, but it is not credible for any longer period. To conclude that anything could happen when U.S. policy is firm, one must forsake economic analysis and assume that we have nothing more rational to rely on than tea leaves.

If we consider the effects over a fraction of a year, conceivably this temporary period of confusion could last that long. But if one gives major speculators credit for ability to recognize fundamental factors, it might well be measurable in days, or even in hours. On the assumption of firm U.S. policy, the speculative demand for gold would probably fall rapidly. Presumably, under this policy, the United States would also stop participating in purchases of the London gold pool; announcement of this would probably have considerable effect in changing the odds facing a speculator. The change in speculative demand would cause substantial dishoarding of gold. That this is an important element in the total private demand is clearly indicated by the close relationship between indicators of changes in the demand for gold, such as the price on the London gold market and losses by the gold pool, and widespread fears and rumors about the stability in the value of the dollar and the British pound. The private absorption of gold has also varied, according to such estimates as exist, with such speculative fears and rumors. These fluctuations cannot seriously be attributed to fluctuations in industrial use, let alone in hoarding by peasants, literate or illiterate.

All this assumes, as I have noted, that the policy is firmly embarked on by the United States. Of course, if speculators think the United States will change its mind, and might even switch to a policy of buying and selling gold at a price above $35 an ounce, it is true that anything could happen. The policy should not even be referred to as an alternative in the course of negotiations unless there is a serious intention of carrying it out.

It is argued that the articles of agreement of the International Monetary Fund make it possible for other countries to force gold on the United States via the Fund. This argument is based on a combination of two requirements of the articles. One requirement is that the Fund must take gold from some members, either in exchange for their currencies on the initiative of the member (art. V, sec. 2), or, in the case of countries holding gold in their reserves, as payment when they repurchase their own currencies (art. V, sec. 7). The other requires the United States to accept gold from the Fund if the Fund deems it appropriate to replenish its holdings of dollars and to pay for them in gold (art. VII, sec. 2(ii)). The first element of the argument is correct, but the second requires the Fund initiative. ("The Fund may, *if it deems such action appropriate* to replenish its holdings of any member's currency * * * require the member to sell its currency to the Fund for gold.") The Fund could not force gold upon the United States because the U.S. vote plus the vote of other countries in the dollar bloc who would support the revised system would prevent such a decision.

The first link in the argument does raise a question whether the Fund would become a dump for gold ineligible for U.S. purchases. Professor Despres recognizes this problem, although I do not know if the solution of it that he has in mind is wholly satisfactory. Presumably the United States would seek to make agreements with other countries under which they would agree not to finance their purchase of foreign currencies from the Fund by payment of gold. The difficulty that might not be solved by an agreement between the United States and another member arises from section 7(b) of article V, which requires members to repurchase their currencies from the Fund under specified conditions and requires that these repurchases be paid for in specified ways, which depend partly on the composition of these reserves at the end of the year, and of the changes in them during the years. As a result, goldholders are required to pay the Fund for some portion of their repurchases with gold.

My own chief doubts about the Despres plan arise from the fact that the proposal involves a unilateral action by the United States which would greatly increase its financial power—or rather make its financial power correspond more closely with its real economic power—and that the unilateral action might increase the existing divisions among the major Western countries, to the detriment of such cooperation as now exists. I should think it preferable first to seek improvements in the monetary system by more cooperative means, reserving the Despres plan for adoption in case we could not get what we want—or what we should want. I would feel safer in trying to obtain needed reforms by agreement than in risking some of the hazards of a unilateral decision which would have to be regarded as irreversible if it were to work. I think it premature now to assume or conclude that cooperative efforts will fail. If a persistent effort along such lines fails, however, I would regard the Despres plan as the soundest and most attractive unilateral plan for solving the problem.

C. Return to the Gold Standard

RETURN TO THE GOLD STANDARD

Charles de Gaulle

President of France

The gold exchange standard no longer corresponds to present realities and, in consequence, entails heavier and heavier inconveniences.

Let us note that the conditions that gave birth to the gold exchange standard have been deeply modified. The currencies of Western European states have been restored to such an extent that the total of their gold reserves equals that of the Americans and would even surpass it if these states decided to convert their dollar holdings into gold. The kind of transcending value attributed to the dollar has lost its initial foundation, which was possession by America of the greatest part of the world's gold.

We consider it is necessary that international trade should rest, as before the two World Wars, on an undisputable monetary basis bearing the mark of no particular country.

What basis? Indeed, there can be no other criterion, no other standard, than gold—gold that never changes, that can be shaped into ingots, bars, coins, that has no nationality and that is eternally and universally accepted as the inalterable fiduciary value par excellence.

In international trade, the supreme law, the golden rule—it is indeed an apt term, which should be put back into full effect—is the obligation to establish equilibrium from one monetary zone to the other, through real and effective movements of the precious metals in the balance of payments resulting from their trade.

Indeed, the end of the gold exchange standard without upheavals and the restoration of the gold standard, as well as complementary and provisional measures that are essential, particularly the organization of

From "On the Gold Standard," Excerpts from Remarks by President de Gaulle, *The New York Times,* February 5, 1965, p. 12.

international credit on this new basis—all this should be examined carefully by the states, and particularly by those states that have special responsibilities because of their economic and financial might.

The appropriate framework for these studies and negotiations is already in existence. The International Monetary Fund, which has been created to ensure the solidarity of currencies, to ensure it as far as it can be done, is certainly a very suitable place for such negotiations. The Club of Ten—which, as you know, is composed, besides the United States and England, on the one hand of France, Germany, Italy, Belgium and the Netherlands, on the other hand of Japan, Sweden and Canada—can prepare the necessary proposals and, finally, it would be the task of the six states that appear to be on the way to achieving an Economic Community in Western Europe, to draft between them and to expound to others the solid system that would conform to common sense and correspond to the renascent economic and financial power of our old continent.

France is ready to contribute actively to this great reform, which must take place in the interest of the whole world.

INCREASE THE PRICE OF GOLD

Jacques Rueff

Chancellor, Institut de France,
Economic Adviser to President de Gaulle

To state my approach positively, I am in profound agreement with my dear friend Triffin about the diagnosis of the crisis. I think he has the great merit of having been one of the first to state the diagnosis. I did it in 1932—because I was much older than he—when the situation was the same. He had the great merit to do it later on.

As for the remedies, I do not believe that those put forth very logically by Mr. Triffin and by Mr. Bernstein will ever be applied. It is for that reason that I propose another approach. What I have in mind would need to be achieved through an international convention embracing the Group of Ten plus some other countries.

The countries would agree, first, not to increase, from a certain date onward, their reserve balances in dollars and sterling, this clause in no way interfering with the holding of working balances in these currencies. I put sterling and dollars together, though the case of sterling is somewhat different from that of the dollar. The fundamental need and objective is to create a situation in which the deficit country will lose what the surplus country gains.

In this connection I shall use an illustration which I have sometimes employed in the past. If I were to discover a tailor who would agree to return to me the amount of my bill on the very day I pay him, I would be much less cautious about ordering new suits, and my own balance of payments would be in deficit. That is the only secret of the deficit in the U.S. balance of payments: the United States has a deficit because

From Jacques Rueff, "The Rueff Approach," in *Monetary Reform and the Price of Gold,* ed. Randall Hinshaw (Baltimore: The Johns Hopkins Press, 1967), pp. 39–46.

the dollars it has used to settle the deficit have been returned to that country through the gold-exchange standard. The point is fundamental —all the rest is trivial.

To restore an effective payments system, something will have to be done about the existing dollar and sterling balances held as reserves. In the case of the dollar balances, you know the figures: Foreign countries at present have close to $14 billion in official dollar holdings, while the United States has about $13 billion in gold, almost $11 billion of which is immobilized as a cover for note circulation. The reserve requirement against notes could, of course, be changed, and I would not object to that. But if foreign central banks were to seek to convert any substantial part of their dollar holdings into gold, they would gravely disturb the situation and create the necessity for a U.S. embargo on gold.

I do not need to say that this is not simply a matter of French ill will. As you know, in 1965 the French demand accounted for only about half of the total gold outflow from the United States. After all, nobody can expect creditors to remain quiet when they see a deterioration of U.S. solvency. I do not mean a lack of wealth; the United States is by far the most powerful economy and by far the richest country in the world. This is a matter of monetary solvency, and you cannot expect central bankers who have dollars and who feel a responsibility toward their depositors to remain sitting idly, waiting silently for the day when their dollar holdings may no longer be convertible into gold.

Thus, if you want to restore an effective system of payments, you must get rid of the great part of the dollar and sterling balances. So the second point of the convention would be to increase simultaneously, and in the same proportion, the price at which central banks purchase and sell gold. The amount of the increase would be decided by common agreement, but one can foresee that, since the price level in the United States has doubled since 1934—when the gold price was fixed at its present level by President Roosevelt—the new gold price should be approximately doubled. Because of the great improvement since 1934 in techniques for extracting gold, a smaller increase might be acceptable, provided the price were set at a proper level in relation to the cost of production.

As a third point, the United States and Great Britain would agree to devote a part of the increase in the nominal value of their respective gold stocks to the immediate repayment in gold of the dollar and sterling balances in the hands of central banks. I consider that the greater part of the dollar balances ought in this way to be repaid. The situation regarding the sterling balances is different, because much of the sterling is in the hands of Commonwealth countries, with which there are reliable "gentlemen's agreements"; therefore, I would not insist that all of the sterling balances be repaid, but would leave to the British government the question of deciding the proper amount.

If the price of gold were approximately doubled, the official dollar balances could be paid off in gold without affecting the dollar value of the remaining U.S. gold holdings. The $13 billion of U.S. gold would be worth $26 billion at the new price and, of this, the United States could use about half to repay the central banks, while retaining the same cash position in terms of dollars. Thus the change in the gold price would involve no risk of deflation or inflation for the United States.

For Britain, the situation would be quite different. Britain has about $2 billion in gold. If the gold price were doubled, that would mean $4 billion. This would be only enough to repay a third of the $12 billion in outstanding sterling balances, even if the entire British gold stock were used for that purpose. But these $12 billion in sterling balances, as I said before, are really profoundly different in character from the dollar balances, and I repeat that it should be for the British government to decide what it thinks necessary to repay.

Nevertheless, if we are to re-establish an efficient international monetary system, it is essential that the British government be in a position to repay those sterling balances that it deems necessary to repay; and this brings me to the fourth point in the convention. Apart from the key-currency countries, there would be important countries which have gold and which have no balances to repay. If the price of gold were doubled, the nominal value of their gold stocks would be correspondingly increased. Therefore, I propose that these countries offer Britain a twenty- or twenty-five-year loan equal to the amount of the sterling balances which were not already consolidated *de jure* or *de facto,* thus enabling the British government to repay these balances. This is not an extraordinary proposal; between the two wars, we often did things of this kind. When I was at the Treasury in France, we offered large loans to Great Britain, and, in the reverse direction, Britain on various occasions made available important resources to us. This is in the best tradition of treasury operations, and I am convinced that the credit of Britain is such that there would be no difficulty whatever in working out such a loan.

The loan, however, would absorb only a part of the nominal surplus resulting from the increase in the price of gold. I propose that some of the remaining surplus be devoted, by common agreement, to aid to developing countries in the form of loans. The loans could be made through existing insitutions, or by using the surplus to provide capital for a new institution, or by simple transfer to the developing countries. This is a matter which should be discussed in common by those directly concerned.

Finally, the remaining surplus ought to be devoted, again by common agreement, to the repayment of debts—especially debts to central banks.

If all these things were done, international settlement in gold could be restored without any danger of insolvency among the deficit countries. To be realistic, however, we must concede that such a plan will not be put into operation so long as it goes against the grain of public opinion in the United States. It is very important, therefore, to meet this objection.

As I see it from the outside, public opinion in the United States is inclined to object to a change in the price of gold for a number of distinct reasons. It has been argued that such a step would be incompatible with monetary stability; that it would be reactionary, retrograde, inequitable; that it would be contrary to American and British interests; that it would be unduly favorable to gold-producing countries such as South Africa and the Soviet Union; and finally—the main argument—that it would be an outrage to the honor of the United States. I learned of this last argument at a meeting in New York, when my old friend Bill Martin said, "After all, and above everything, it is a matter of the honor of the United States." If this were true, I really would never propose a plan of this kind. I have not forgotten our debts to the United States and Great Britain—not just in the financial meaning of the word, but in the political and existential meaning—and I would not make a proposal injurious to the United States. Therefore, I will try to meet these objections.

First, there is the argument that an increase in the price of gold would be dangerous to monetary stability. Is it really possible to consider as reasonable a policy which would maintain one price alone— the price of gold—at the level chosen in 1934 by President Roosevelt, when the commodity price level in the United States was only half as high as it is now? Imagine what you would think of such a policy if it were applied to wheat or steel. The need for gold is approximately proportional to the general level of prices. Is it reasonable to maintain artificially the value of the existing gold stock and of the yearly production of gold at half of what it would be if gold were restored to its normal place in the hierarchy of prices? To maintain the price of gold at its 1934 level is to impose a very dangerous handicap on the international monetary system through an artificial limitation on the value of existing stocks of gold and of current production.

It is true that, under normal conditions, absence of change in the price of the monetary standard is the basis of the mechanism through which it can maintain the stability of the commodity price level over long periods. Thus in 1914 the index of prices in the United States was approximately the same as in 1820, despite an immense increase in production and despite the temporary upheaval of the Civil War. But to maintain the stability of the commodity price level, the monetary mechanism must operate continuously. Twice in the past half century, it has ceased to function—during World War I, when the U.S. price level increased by 50 per cent, and during World War II, when the price level more than doubled. After such a change, there are only two choices for the country wishing to restore freedom of international payments—either a reduction of commodity prices, restoring them to the level of the monetary parity, or an increase in the price of gold to a level corresponding to the change in the general level of prices. The first method—a reduction in the price level—is the remedy which Britain tried to apply in 1925. The result was more than a million unemployed, and the policy finally had to be abandoned. But at that time the problem was only an adjustment of 10 per cent. Imagine the disaster which would result in the United States from a policy aiming at a 50 per cent reduction in the price level! That is why I argue that the price of gold should be changed. Such a change would be once and for all, provided there is no new world war and provided there is no re-establishment of the gold-exchange standard regime. Contrary to the view that a change in the price of gold would be dangerous to monetary stability, the situation is just the reverse: a change in the price of gold is necessary for the achievement and maintenance of monetary stability.

Second, let us consider the argument that a change in the price of gold would be reactionary and retrograde. Those who oppose the suppression of the gold-exchange standard see in this step a return to the monetary system of our grandfathers. But this is a great mistake. It is not a question of re-establishing the gold standard, because the gold standard exists now, as I have said. President Roosevelt did not destroy, but re-established, the gold standard through an increase in the price of gold. Similarly, a change in the price of gold now would not be a return to the past, but a correction of a mistake which was sowing the seeds of a great world depression.

Third, a word about the argument that a change in the price of gold would be inequitable. The maintenance of the gold price at its 1934 level offers to anybody producing a certain weight of wheat or steel, or any product whose price has doubled since 1934, a weight of gold which is double what he would have received then in exchange for his product. Is it fair, equitable, or just, when gold is scarce and when the world is trying to limit the demand for gold, to offer such an inducement to obtain gold for what one produces?

Fourth, we come to the argument that a change in the price of gold would be contrary to American interests. The last time I was in the United States, I paid a visit to an important American senator, who said to me, "I know very well what the policy of your country is; you want to take all our gold; then you will double the price and make an enormous profit at our expense." I told him, "My dear friend, it is just the reverse. Our advice is to double the price of gold while you still have it, and to give us only half the amount we are entitled to ask you against our dollar balance." It is not a French position I am defending; it is a position in the interest of the whole world, for the sole purpose of re-establishing an effective international monetary system.

Fifth, let us take a look at the argument that a change in the price of gold would be unduly favorable to certain gold-producing countries, such as Russia and South Africa. Consider first the case of Russia. All the information I have appears to show that the cost of producing gold in Russia is very high and that Russia would prefer to pay for its imports, not in gold, but in goods. But suppose that change in the price of gold were to make it easier for Russia to include gold among its exports. What is so bad about selling what we produce in exchange for Russian gold as well as for Russian wheat, steel, and coal? With respect to South Africa, the people who are opposed to an increase in the price of gold because they do not want to aid South African production are the same people who fear that the present system is leading to deflation. But you cannot have an increase in gold production and refuse to pay the price.

We come finally to the last point—the argument of my friend Bill Martin that changing the price of gold would impair the honor of the United States. But why? The dollar balances have no gold clause attached to them. No court in the world—and I have been a judge for ten years on the Court of the European Community—has ever ruled that the gold clause would apply where it has not been expressly stipulated. To behave as if a gold clause existed where it does not exist is to make a free gift to the holders of dollar balances at the expense of the debtor country, the United States. These holders cannot claim to have a moral, implicit right to a gold clause, as is proved by the fact that some of them have expressly obtained a gold guarantee. One must not confuse the two kinds of claims; either there is a gold clause or there is not. If there is not, there is no moral right to repayment at a fixed value in gold.

The honor of a debtor nation lies in its ability to continue repaying its debts. I am sorry to say that, in the present circumstances, nobody can imagine that the United States, in the absence of a new policy, will be able to repay the dollar balances unless it issues a fully inconvertible guarantee. Would it be less of a reflection on the honor of the United States to change the status of the dollar and to repay in a currency inconvertible into gold? It would seem to me much more honorable to apply an article which has been written into the charter of the International Monetary Fund—an article designed for exactly the situation in which we are today.

In conclusion, I am absolutely convinced that the price of gold will be changed, because there is no other practical solution which is economically sound and morally acceptable that has a chance, politically, of being accepted. The only question which is fundamental is—when? If the change is made à froid, before a crisis, the world will have been saved the horror of a new depression. If it is not, then what shall we have? Import quotas in the United States, exchange control, and finally, I am sorry to say, an embargo on gold. This will be a disastrous conclusion to all that has been accomplished in the past ten years and to all the efforts which are now being made toward the liberalization of trade. It will be an immense setback in civilization that must be avoided at any cost; and that is the reason we must find somewhere enough statesmanship so that an effective and practical remedy will be applied before it is too late.

MANKIND'S ADDICTION TO GOLD

Robert Warren Stevens

Associate Professor of International Business,
Indiana University

There is a mystique about gold deeply rooted in the human psyche; but there is no longer any rational argument for tying money to gold. Gold is an artifact handed down to us from earlier periods of history, and it has become so deeply lodged in the collective human consciousness, that to some people it will seem improper, even immoral, for others to discuss it. The fact must be stated, however: The use of gold for monetary purposes is an anachronism in the modern world, capable of causing terrible damage because it is so utterly inappropriate to the conditions of modern life.

In early, relatively primitive societies, the use of gold for coins made great sense. As the textbooks still point out, it was scarce and malleable, and goldsmiths were available in commercial centers who would assay one's coins for a modest fee. Later, as mercantilist writers pointed out, it made sense for hostile nation-states to accumulate gold as a state treasure. It was more useful than paper money for paying bribes to one's enemies and it would probably be an acceptable form of payment if tribute or ransom were required. Today, I suppose a quasi-rational argument for gold would be that it might be one of the few commodities that would almost certainly be valuable in a post-nuclear holocaust world.

As David Hume pointed out, gold could also be made somewhat

From Statement by Robert Warren Stevens, in *Contingency Planning for U.S. International Monetary Policy,* Statements by Private Economists submitted to the Subcommittee on International Exchange and Payments of the Joint Economic Committee, 89th Cong., 2d sess., 1966 (Washington, D.C.: U.S. Government Printing Office, 1966), pp. 111–15.

useful in the world of the classical economists. If correctly handled by the sovereign (note the new condition) it would make possible a world of laissez faire, internationally as well as domestically. We may recall Hume's exposition of the classical specie flow argument: As gold would flow into or out of relatively isolated nation-states which had few reliable communications with other nation-states, no central banks, few national statistics, and no reliable systems of national accounting, it could be watched as a fairly reliable indicator of whether the balance of payments was in surplus or deficit. As Hume also added: If the sovereign (note the "if") would leave the gold alone to do its monetary work, price levels in the various isolated nation-states would rise and/or fall in such a manner that no form of explicit cooperation with other nation-states would be necessary. Therefore, laissez faire policies toward the domestic economy and toward international trade could both safely be followed.

So much for history; let us now ask, why do people like gold today?

1. *Does tying money to gold prevent its overissue?* Certainly not. Clearly, declaring a gold parity for a national currency has not prevented a number of countries which are members of the IMF from overissuing their currencies and experiencing very strong price inflations.

The pseudoclaim by believers in gold that it can prevent overissue of a currency is false for two reasons which are well known:

(*a*) No government in the modern world will accept a 1-to-1 ratio between its gold stock and its domestic money supply, nor will any government accept for long any fixed ratio between the two.

(*b*) Governments in the modern world are clearly not averse to raising the price of gold—i.e., increasing the number of units of their domestic money per unit weight of gold—when it pleases them to do so. Most European countries did this in 1949 and France has done it twice since then.

If the stock of gold really did restrain governments from overissuing their currency, neither of these things could happen. The claim that gold does so is false. Instead, governments decide how much money they wish to issue for other reasons; this often results in price inflation, and after a while governments bow to mankind's addiction for gold by raising its price too. Under these circumstances, owners of gold have an effective guarantee that the price of their commodity can go only one way—up.

2. *Does gold, nevertheless, provide a healthy discipline to government treasuries and finance ministries?* Certainly not. This kind of "discipline" was a serious domestic problem for many countries in the 19th century. Financial institutions operate on the principle of fractional reserves and when banks were required to convert their bank notes or deposits into gold, there were frequent occasions when they could not meet this obligation and therefore were forced to close their doors. The fear that a bank might be unable to convert its obligations into gold could cause a "run" on the bank; the failure of banks at times of economic recession intensified the recessions by reducing the supply of money and undermining confidence.

Gradually this destructive form of "discipline" was removed from domestic economies by the creation of central banks such as the Federal Reserve banks in the United States. These central banks, besides supervising commercial banks and insisting upon sound banking practices, serve as "lenders of last resort" to commercial banks, enabling them to honor their obligations to the public although they still operate on the basis of only fractional reserves. In the United States we also removed the threat that gold could ever again impose this kind of "discipline" upon our domestic economy by removing the obligation of our financial institutions to pay gold to their domestic creditors.

In international finance, it is precisely this kind of "discipline" which provides the threat to the security of the United States today. It is a "discipline" similar to that provided by a hydrogen bomb: one watches one's step or else the instrument of "discipline" gets out of hand causing a general collapse.

Even worse, it is the hegemony of gold in the field of international finance which, by instilling the fear that one may have to endure this type of discipline, forces mercantilist-type policies upon national governments. It also requires that balances of payments be defined in mercantilist ways. Messrs. Despres, Kindleberger, and Salant will never succeed in their commendable effort to persuade governments to adopt less restrictive balance-of-payments definitions as long as gold tyrannizes over the minds of men.

3. *Does not gold provide a satisfactory form of financing international payments?* No. Money should be a tool of economic life, not a master of the destiny of nations as gold is today. Finance, the textbooks rightly say, should be the handmaiden of productive economic activi-

ties, not their master. Moreover, a money supply—internationally as well as domestically—should be flexible so that it can increase and decrease in response to the needs of commerce and industry. Gold, on the contrary, is about as flexible a monetary medium as the stone currency of Yap Island.

It is quite legitimate for central bank managers to wish to accumulate internationally acceptable assets in order to be able to finance their international payments, but these assets should be the obligations of an international authority; there is no reason why they should be gold.

4. *Is not gold a desirable asset to serve as a store of value?* No. It is a far less satisfactory store of value than almost all other assets because it is sterile. Real estate is equally tangible and may earn its owner a high return; works of art may appreciate far more than gold; diamonds will always be coveted by people and may be displayed as ornaments which bars of gold cannot be. None of these assets, when privately hoarded, threatens disruption to stable world order.

Official agencies, too, should be able to hold whatever they like so long as their holding of it does not threaten the security of the rest of us. Interest-earning obligations of a revitalized IMF would provide an ideal instrumentality for them.

5. *Is not gold a good weapon for the private citizen to use against the state?* Yes. Gold is basically a weapon which is coveted for this very purpose in many parts of the world. It is a symbol of mistrust, even lawlessness. Its owners expect its possession to place them above the law, in the sense that sooner or later governments will have to knuckle under and raise the price of the asset they have cornered. Its owners usually advocate deflationary policies—even the destruction of credit —but they do not expect these policies to be followed in today's world. Therefore they accumulate gold in the hope that they can force such policies onto governments or, if not, force them to increase the price of gold.

Gold is a weapon—similar to pistols in the Old West on the personal level, similar to nuclear weapons today on the international level. Its owners believe the world is basically anarchic and they expect to protect themselves by holding gold.

The main difference between the political effects of gold and nuclear weapons in the world today is that the U.S. Government believes that it will be free to make independent decisions about invoking the "discipline" of nuclear weapons in the future, while the peripheral countries in the gold-exchange standard know that, in time, they will be able to invoke the "discipline" of gold against a cornered U.S. government.

The longrun truth may be that the world will not be able to find genuine financial stability until it has rooted gold itself out of the dominant position it now holds. Today gold has become a weapon which, held in the periphery of the world monetary system, is a means of speculating against the U.S. dollar. Its holders have no fear that gold will ever be worth fewer dollars, but they confidently expect it to become worth more dollars—someday. That day will come whenever the U.S. Government can be forced to raise its price.

Today the U.S. Government is in the ridiculous position of firmly supporting the official price of gold so that its hoarders can capitalize on the future misfortunes of the U.S. Government. The stark financial fact of today's world is that there is no substitute for cooperation in international monetary matters—except gold.

D. Flexible Exchange Rates

FREE-MARKET DETERMINATION OF EXCHANGE RATES

Milton Friedman

Paul S. Russel Distinguished Service
Professor of Economics,
University of Chicago

Discussions of U.S. policy with respect to international payments tend to be dominated by our immediate balance-of-payments difficulties. I should like today to approach the question from a different, and I hope more constructive, direction. Let us begin by asking ourselves not merely how we can get out of our present difficulties but instead how we can fashion our international payments system so that it will best serve our needs for the long pull; how we can solve not merely *this* balance-of-payments problem but *the* balance-of-payments problem.

A shocking and indeed, disgraceful feature of the present situation is the extent to which our frantic search for expedients to stave off balance-of-payments pressures has led us, on the one hand, to sacrifice major national objectives; and, on the other, to give enormous power to officials of foreign governments to affect what should be purely domestic matters. Foreign payments amount to only some 5 per cent of our total national income. Yet they have become a major factor in nearly every national policy.

I believe that a system of floating exchange rates would solve the balance-of-payments problem for the United States far more effectively than our present arrangements. Such a system would use the flexibility

From Statement by Milton Friedman, in *Contingency Planning for U.S. International Monetary Policy*, Statements by Private Economists submitted to the Subcommittee on International Exchange and Payments of the Joint Economic Committee, 89th Cong., 2d sess., 1966 (Washington, D.C.: U.S. Government Printing Office, 1966), pp. 30–36.

and efficiency of the free market to harmonize our small foreign trade sector with both the rest of our massive economy and the rest of the world; it would reduce problems of foreign payments to their proper dimensions and remove them as a major consideration in governmental policy about domestic matters and as a major preoccupation in international political negotiations; it would foster our national objectives rather than be an obstacle to their attainment.

To indicate the basis for this conclusion, let us consider the national objective with which our payments system is most directly connected: the promotion of a healthy and balanced growth of world trade, carried on, so far as possible, by private individuals and private enterprises with minimum intervention by governments. This has been a major objective of our whole postwar international economic policy. Success would knit the free world more closely together, and, by fostering the international division of labor, raise standards of living throughout the world, including the United States.

Consider the consequences of effecting far-reaching reciprocal reductions in tariffs and other trade barriers with the Common Market and other countries.[1] Such reductions will expand trade in general but clearly will have different effects on different industries. The demand for the products of some will expand, for others contract. This is a phenomenon we are familiar with from our internal development. The capacity of our free enterprise system to adapt quickly and efficiently to such shifts, whether produced by changes in technology or tastes, has been a major source of our economic growth. The only additional element introduced by international trade is the fact that different currencies are involved, and this is where the payment mechanism comes in; its function is to keep this fact from being an additional source of disturbance.

An all-around lowering of tariffs would tend to increase both our expenditures and our receipts in foreign currencies. There is no way of knowing in advance which increase would tend to be the greater and hence no way of knowing whether the initial effect would be toward a surplus or deficit in our balance of payments. What is clear is that we cannot hope to succeed in the objective of expanding world trade unless we can readily adjust to either outcome.

Suppose then that the initial effect is to increase our expenditures on imports more than our receipts from exports. How could we adjust to this outcome?

One method of adjustment is to draw on reserves or borrow from abroad to finance the excess increase in imports. The obvious objection to this method is that it is only a temporary device, and hence can be relied on only when the disturbance is temporary. But that is not the major objection. Even if we had very large reserves or could borrow large amounts from abroad, so that we could continue this expedient for many years, it is a most undesirable one. We can see why if we look at physical rather than financial magnitudes.

The physical counterpart to the financial deficit is a reduction of employment in industries competing with imports that is larger than the concurrent expansion of employment in export industries. So long as the financial deficit continues, the assumed tariff reductions create employment problems. But it is no part of the aim of tariff reductions to create unemployment at home or to promote employment abroad. The aim is a balanced expansion of trade, with exports rising along with imports and thereby providing employment opportunities to off-set any reduction in employment resulting from increased imports. Hence, simply drawing on reserves or borrowing abroad is a most unsatisfactory method of adjustment.

Another method of adjustment is to lower U.S. prices relative to for-eign prices, since this would stimulate exports and discourage imports. If foreign countries are accommodating enough to engage in inflation, such a change in relative prices might require merely that the United States keep prices stable or even that it simply keep them from rising as fast as foreign prices. But there is no necessity for foreign countries to be so accommodating, and we could hardly count on their being so accommodating. The use of this technique therefore involves a will-ingness to produce a decline in U.S. prices by tight monetary policy or tight fiscal policy or both. Given time, this method of adjustment would work. But in the interim, it would exact a heavy toll. It would be difficult or impossible to force down prices appreciably without producing a recession and considerable unemployment. To eliminate in the long run the unemployment resulting from the tariff changes, we should in the short run be creating cyclical unemployment. The cure might for a time be far worse than the disease.

This second method is therefore also most unsatisfactory. Yet these two methods—drawing on reserves and forcing down prices—are the only two methods available under our present international payment arrangements, which involve fixed exchange rates between the U.S.

dollar and other currencies. Little wonder that we have so far made such disappointing progress toward the reduction of trade barriers, that our practice has differed so much from our preaching.

There is one other way and only one other way to adjust and that is by allowing (or forcing) the price of the U.S. dollar to fall in terms of other currencies. To a foreigner, U.S. goods can become cheaper in either of two ways—either because their prices in the U.S. fall in terms of dollars or because the foreigner has to give up fewer units of his own currency to acquire a dollar, which is to say, the price of the dollar falls. For example, suppose a particular U.S. car sells for $2,800 when a dollar costs 7 shillings, tuppence in British money (i.e., roughly £1 = $2.80). The price of the car is then £1,000 in British money. It is the same to an Englishman—or even a Scotsman—whether the price of the car falls to $2,500 while the price of a dollar remains 7 shillings, tuppence, or alternatively, the price of the car remains $2,800, while the price of a dollar falls to 6 shillings, 5 pence (i.e., roughly £1 = $3.11). In either case, the car costs the Englishman £900 rather than £1,000, which is what matters to him. Similarly, foreign goods can become more expensive to an American in either of two ways—either because the price in terms of foreign currency rises or because he has to give up more dollars to acquire a given amount of foreign currency.

Changes in exchange rates can therefore alter the relative price of U.S. and foreign goods in precisely the same way as can changes in internal prices in the United States and in foreign countries. And they can do so without requiring anything like the same internal adjustments. If the initial effect of the tariff reductions would be to create a deficit at the former exchange rate (or enlarge an existing deficit or reduce an existing surplus) and thereby increase unemployment, this effect can be entirely avoided by a change in exchange rates which will produce a balanced expansion in imports and exports without interfering with domestic employment, domestic prices, or domestic monetary and fiscal policy. The pig can be roasted without burning down the barn.

The situation is, of course, entirely symmetrical if the tariff changes should initially happen to expand our exports more than our imports. Under present circumstances, we would welcome such a result, and conceivably, if the matching deficit were experienced by countries currently running a surplus, they might permit it to occur without seeking to offset it. In that case, they and we would be using the first method of adjustment—changes in reserves or borrowing. But again, if we had started off from an even keel, this would be an undesirable method of adjustment. On our side, we should be sending out useful goods and receiving only foreign currencies in return. On the side of our partners, they would be using up reserves and tolerating the creation of unemployment.

The second method of adjusting to a surplus is to permit or force domestic prices to rise—which is of course what we did in part in the early postwar years when we were running large surpluses. Again, we should be forcing maladjustments on the whole economy to solve a problem arising from a small part of it—the 5 per cent accounted for by foreign trade.

Again, these two methods are the only ones available under our present international payments arrangements, and neither is satisfactory.

The final method is to permit or force exchange rates to change—in this case, a rise in the price of the dollar in terms of foreign currencies. This solution is again specifically adapted to the specific problem of the balance of payments.

Changes in exchange rates can be produced in either of two general ways. One way is by a change in an official exchange rate; an official devaluation or appreciation from one fixed level which the government is committed to support to another fixed level. This is the method used by Britain in its postwar devaluations and by Germany in 1961 when the mark was appreciated. This is also the main method contemplated by the IMF which permits member nations to change their exchange rates by 10 per cent without consultation and by a larger amount after consultation and approval by the Fund. But this method has serious disadvantages. It makes a change in rates a matter of major moment, and hence there is a tendency to postpone any change as long as possible. Difficulties cumulate and a larger change is finally needed than would have been required if it could have been made promptly. By the time the change is made, everyone is aware that a change is pending and is certain about the direction of the change. The result is to encourage a flight from a currency, if it is going to be devalued, or to a currency, if it is going to be appreciated.

There is in any event little basis for determining precisely what the new rate should be. Speculative movements increase the difficulty of judging what the new rate should be, and introduce a systematic bias, making the change needed appear larger than it actually is. The result, particularly when devaluation occurs, is generally to lead officials to "play safe" by making an even larger change than the large change needed. The country is then left after the devaluation with a maladjustment precisely the opposite of that with which it started, and is thereby encouraged to follow policies it cannot sustain in the long run.

Even if all these difficulties could be avoided, this method of changing from one fixed rate to another has the disadvantage that it is necessarily discontinuous. Even if the new exchange rates are precisely correct when first established, they will not long remain correct.

A second and much better way in which changes in exchange rates can be produced is by permitting exchange rates to float, by allowing them to be determined from day to day in the market. This is the method which the United States used from 1862 to 1879, and again, in effect, from 1917 or so to about 1925, and again from 1933 to 1934. It is the method which Britain used from 1918 to 1925 and again from 1931 to 1939, and which Canada used for most of the interwar period and again from 1950 to May 1962. Under this method, exchange rates adjust themselves continuously, and market forces determine the magnitude of each change. There is no need for any official to decide by how much the rate should rise or fall. This is the method of the free market, the method that we adopt unquestioningly in a private enterprise economy for the bulk of goods and services. It is no less available for the price of one money in terms of another.

With a floating exchange rate, it is possible for governments to intervene and try to affect the rate by buying or selling, as the British Exchange Equalization Fund did rather successfully in the 1930's, or by combining buying and selling with public announcements of intentions, as Canada did so disastrously in early 1962. On the whole, it seems to me undesirable to have government intervene, because there is a strong tendency for government agencies to try to peg the rate rather than to stabilize it, because they have no special advantage over private speculators in stabilizing it, because they can make far bigger mistakes than private speculators risking their own money, and because there is a tendency for them to cover up their mistakes by changing the rules—as the Canadian case so strikingly illustrates—rather than by reversing course. But this is an issue on which there is much difference of opinion among economists who are agreed in favoring floating rates. Clearly, it is possible to have a successful floating rate along with governmental speculation.

The great objective of tearing down trade barriers, of promoting a worldwide expansion of trade, of giving citizens of all countries, and especially the underdeveloped countries, every opportunity to sell their products in open markets under equal terms and thereby every incentive to use their resources efficiently, of giving countries an alternative through free world trade to autarchy and central planning—this great objective can, I believe, be achieved best under a regime of floating rates. All countries, and not just the United States, can proceed to liberalize boldly and confidently only if they can have reasonable assurance that the resulting trade expansion will be balanced and will not interfere with major domestic objectives. Floating exchange rates, and so far as I can see, only floating exchange rates, provide this assurance. They do so because they are an automatic mechanism for protecting the domestic economy from the possibility that liberalization will produce a serious imbalance in international payments.

Despite their advantages, floating exchange rates have a bad press. Why is this so?

One reason is because a consequence of our present system that I have been citing as a serious disadvantage is often regarded as an advantage; namely, the extent to which the small foreign trade sector dominates national policy. Those who regard this as an advantage refer to it as the discipline of the gold standard. I would have much sympathy for this view if we had a real gold standard, so the discipline was imposed by impersonal forces which in turn reflected the realities of resources, tastes, and technology. But in fact we have today only a pseudo gold standard and the so-called discipline is imposed by governmental officials of other countries who are determining their own internal monetary policies and are either being forced to dance to our tune or calling the tune for us, depending primarily on accidental political developments. This is a discipline we can well do without.

A possibly more important reason why floating exchange rates have a bad press, I believe, is a mistaken interpretation of experience with floating rates, arising out of a statistical fallacy that can be seen easily in a standard example. Arizona is clearly the worst place in the United States for a person with tuberculosis to go because the death rate from tuberculosis is higher in Arizona than in any other State. The fallacy in this case is obvious. It is less obvious in connection with exchange rates. Countries that have gotten into severe financial difficulties, for whatever reason, have had ultimately to change their exchange rates or let them change. No amount of exchange control and other restrictions on trade have enabled them to peg an exchange rate that was far out of line with economic realities. In consequence, floating rates have frequently been associated with financial and economic instability. It is easy to conclude, as many have, that floating exchange rates produce such instability.

This misreading of experience is reinforced by the general prejudice against speculation, which has led to the frequent assertion, typically on the basis of no evidence whatsoever, that speculation in exchange can be expected to be destabilizing and thereby to increase the instability in rates. Few who make this assertion even recognize that it is equivalent to asserting that speculators generally lose money.

Floating exchange rates need not be unstable exchange rates—any more than the prices of automobiles or of government bonds, of coffee or of meals need gyrate wildly just because they are free to change from day to day. The Canadian exchange rate was free to change during more than a decade, yet it varied within narrow limits. The ultimate objective is a world in which exchange rates, while free to vary, are in fact highly stable because basic economic policies and conditions are stable. Instability of exchange rates is a symptom of instability in the underlying economic structure. Elimination of this symptom by administrative pegging of exchange rates cures none of the underlying difficulties and only makes adjustment to them more painful.

The confusion between stable exchange rates and pegged exchange rates helps to explain the frequent comment that floating exchange rates would introduce an additional element of uncertainty into foreign trade and thereby discourage its expansion. They introduce no additional element of uncertainty. If a floating rate would, for example, decline, then a pegged rate would be subject to pressure that the authorities would have to meet by internal deflation or exchange control in some form. The uncertainty about the rate would simply be replaced by uncertainty about internal prices or about the availability of exchange; and the latter uncertainties, being subject to administrative rather than market control, are likely to be the more erratic and unpredictable. Moreover, the trader can far more readily and cheaply protect himself against the danger of changes in exchange rates, through hedging operations in a forward market, than he can against the danger of changes in internal prices or exchange availability. Floating rates are therefore far more favorable to private international trade than pegged rates.

Though I have discussed the problem of international payments in the context of trade liberalization, the discussion is directly applicable to the more general problem of adapting to any forces that make for balance-of-payments difficulties. Consider our present problem of a deficit in the balance of trade plus long-term capital movement. How can we adjust to it? By one of the three methods outlined: first, drawing on reserves or borrowing; second, keeping U.S. prices from rising as rapidly as foreign prices or forcing them down; third, permitting or forcing exchange rates to alter. And, this time, by one more method: by imposing additional trade barriers or their equivalent, whether in the form of higher tariffs, or smaller import quotas, or extracting from other countries tighter "voluntary" quotas on their exports, or "tieing" foreign aid, or buying higher priced domestic goods or services to meet military needs, or imposing taxes on foreign borrowing, or imposing direct controls on investments by U.S. citizens abroad, or any one of the host of other devices for interfering with the private business of private individuals that have become so familiar to us since Hjalmar Schacht perfected the modern techniques of exchange control in 1934 to strengthen the Nazis for war and to despoil a large class of his fellow citizens.

Fortunately or unfortunately, even Congress cannot repeal the laws of arithmetic. Books must balance. We must use one of these four methods. Because we have been unwilling to select the only one that is currently fully consistent with both economic and political needs—namely, floating exchange rates—we have been driven, as if by an invisible hand, to employ all the others, and even then may not escape the need for explicit changes in exchange rates.

We adopt one expedient after another, borrowing here, making swap arrangements there, changing the form of loans to make the "figures" look good. Entirely aside from the ineffectiveness of most of these measures, they are politically degrading and demeaning. We are a great and wealthy nation. We should be directing our own course, setting an example to the world, living up to our destiny. Instead, we send our officials, hat in hand, to make the rounds of foreign governments and central banks; we put foreign central banks in a position to determine whether or not we can meet our obligations and thus enable them to exert great influence on our policies; we are driven to niggling negotiations with Hong Kong and with Japan and for all I know Monaco to get them to limit "voluntarily" their exports. Is this a posture suitable for the leader of the free world?

It is not the least of the virtues of floating exchange rates that we would again become masters in our own house. We could decide important issues on the proper ground. The military could concentrate on military effectiveness and not on saving foreign exchange; recipients of foreign aid could concentrate on how to get the most out of what we give them and not on how to spend it all in the United States; Congress could decide how much to spend on foreign aid on the basis of what we get for our money and what else we could use it for and not how it will affect the gold stock; the monetary authorities could concentrate on domestic prices and employment, not on how to induce foreigners to hold dollar balances in this country; the Treasury and the tax committees of Congress could devote their attention to the equity of the tax system and its effects on our efficiency, rather than on how to use tax gimmicks to discourage imports, subsidize exports, and discriminate against outflows of capital.

A system of floating exchange rates would render the problem of making outflows equal inflows into the market where it belongs and not leave it to the clumsy and heavy hand of government. It would leave government free to concentrate on its proper functions.

NOTES

1. To simplify exposition I shall hereafter refer only to tariffs, letting these stand for the whole range of barriers to trade, including even the so-called "voluntary" limitation of exports.

THE VARIOUS FORMS
OF EXCHANGE-RATE FLEXIBILITY

James E. Meade

Professor of Political Economy,
University of Cambridge

I am one of those who favor a much greater measure of exchange-rate flexibility than is practised by the countries of the free world to-day, but life in this wicked world is a choice of evils and it may be that the evils of exchange-rate variations when one comes to look at them are worse than those of some of the other methods. I do not my-self believe this to be the case, but it is only fair to have a good look at the difficulties. Accordingly I will consider in turn each of the six main forms which, in my view, a system of exchange-rate flexibility might take and shall search for the snags in each case.

(1) The first is what has come to be known as the *Adjustable Peg* system, and is the system under which we are supposed to be living at the present time according to the rules of the International Monetary Fund. Each country fixes the value of its national currency (within very narrow upper and lower limits) in terms of some common unit (such as an ounce of gold) and undertakes to maintain the value of its national currency at this level by buying it (with gold or other foreign currencies) if it tends to fall below its par value and by selling it (for gold or other foreign currencies) if it tends to rise above its par value. But if a country's balance of payments falls into fundamental disequi-librium, then it can make a suitable adjustment in the rate at which it pegs its currency to gold—raising the price of gold in terms of its own currency if it is in deficit, and *vice versa* if it is in surplus.

From James E. Meade, "Exchange-Rate Flexibility," in *International Payments Problems* (Washington, D.C.: American Enterprise Institute for Public Policy Research, 1966), pp. 71–80.

As this system has in fact developed the stress has come to be put upon the fixity of the peg rather than upon its periodic adjustment. Certainly exchange rates have been very much less variable than many persons hoped at the initiation of the Fund. One reason for this is probably the very grave disadvantages of this method of exchange-rate adjustment. Its use builds a paradise for anti-social speculation. A country is in balance-of-payments deficit: if it is widely known that such countries are very liable to raise the pegged price of gold (and so of other currencies) in terms of their own currency, speculators have every reason to sell the currency of the deficit country and hold other currencies; the currency concerned may be depreciated, it is certain that it will not be appreciated; if the peg is changed, they gain a quick and large profit; if the peg is not changed, they lose at the very most a small margin of their money.

As the present rules of the IMF are drafted, countries must in general obtain the permission of the Fund before adjusting their pegs. If such a Fund decision were to be based upon a profound international inquiry into the alleged "fundamental disequilibrium" of the country wishing to adjust its peg, the system would become wholly unworkable. The idea of a really meaningful inquiry and discussion in an international organization of the pros and cons of altering, for example, by a large percentage the value of the dollar or sterling while all holders of dollars or sterling proceeded to take their one-way speculative option is so ridiculous as not to be capable of being taken seriously. Permission of the Fund must mean little more than overnight snap agreement with a decision which a handful of the responsible men have brooded over in extreme secrecy in the inner councils of the country concerned.

Such adjustments will tend to be rare events. In order to discourage speculation against its currency, the improbability of change will be stressed and change will appear improbable if it is in fact infrequent. If, however, as a last desperate resort a change is made, it is likely to be very large for two reasons: first, because a great deal of disequilibrium must be built up before the fatal step is admitted to be inevitable; and, second, because a new fixed peg must be chosen and —hung for a lamb, hung for a sheep—if a depreciation is undertaken it will be considered wise to err on the safe side and to choose a rate which really will insure a surplus for the depreciating country—and, therefore, incidentally a deficit for someone else.

It was not perhaps inevitable that the IMF system should have developed in this way. With a looser and in my view more useful interpretation of the phrase "fundamental disequilibrium" one can imagine a state of affairs in which a regular use was made of exchange-rate variation as an instrument of balance-of-payments control in the form of frequent small movements in the pegs—a currency being put up or down by, say, 2 per cent without any implication that it might not next month or next quarter be moved by another 2 per cent in the same direction if a greater movement seemed necessary or back to its original position if developments suggested that the former move had been unnecessary. Such a system would to some extent keep the speculators guessing; there need never build up those positions in which a huge potential one-way option is presented to operators in the foreign-exchange markets; only small movements would be expected and they might quite well be reversed. Nevertheless even in this form the system would be subject to grave disadvantages. It would still present speculators with substantial opportunities, since it would still be clear from time to time that a currency's peg might be moved in one direction but not in the other. And the system would need very close, continuous, and intimate cooperation between the representatives of the main national monetary authorities to reach agreement upon the frequent small adjustments.

(2) The present IMF system is thus one of pretty rigidly fixed rates subject from time to time to substantial and disturbing adjustment. Let us next consider a system at the other extreme, namely one of *Freely Floating Exchange Rates* in which the prices of the various currencies are determined from day to day by the free play of competition between private buyers and sellers of currencies in foreign exchange markets which are subject to no controlling intervention either by national monetary authorities or by any international institution. With such a system the national authorities would devise and use their monetary, fiscal, and wage-determining institutions in whatever way they considered to be most appropriate to achieve full employment and economic growth and to avoid instabilities and fluctuations in money incomes and prices. They would let the balance-of-payments look after itself.

Now the advocates of this system argue that the balance of payments would satisfactorily look after itself. Consider, for example, a country—such as the United States or the United Kingdom in recent years—which develops a deficit on its balance of payments. There will be an excess of domestic purchasers of foreign currencies to make payments abroad over the foreign purchasers of the domestic currency to make payments to the country in question. Foreign currencies will appreciate in terms of the currency in question. This will reduce the money price-income-cost structure of the country concerned relatively to that of other countries. All over the world, within and outside the country concerned, people will be encouraged to shift their purchases from the goods and services of other countries on to the goods and services produced by the deficit country.

It is, of course, well known to the advocates of this system that such shifts of demand which are needed to restore equilibrium will take time. Purchases will be shifted only as the new opportunities are appreciated, existing contracts run out, new plans are matured, and so on. But in the meanwhile, so it is argued, the private foreign-exchange speculator will play a useful and social role in supporting the currency of the deficit country. In the absence of the speculator the country's currency might depreciate very heavily indeed during the period when there was an excess demand for foreign currencies and before the consequential alteration in relative price-income-cost structures had had time to have its effects on imports and exports. But the speculator would realize that this period of acute difficulty was temporary; he would expect the currency to recover its value as time passed and the necessary adjustments in imports and exports were made; the speculator would, therefore, have a straightforward profit incentive to buy up the currency concerned in exchange for foreign currencies while it was extra cheap in order to make a gain on its subsequent appreciation. In short it is argued that a system of freely floating exchange rates (i) brings about long-run structural adjustments in balances of payments through appropriate changes in relative price-income-cost structures and (ii) induces private speculators to give the necessary temporary support to currencies under pressure, a support which under other systems would have to be given by the use of official reserves of gold and foreign exchange.

There is only one possible snag to this system. Could one rely upon private speculation to fulfill adequately this vital role? True, speculators buy when they expect prices to go up. But on what do they base their expectations of future prices? Is it always on a correct anticipation of what is going to happen to the basic underlying elements of long-run supply and demand? But it is never easy to tell what the future holds in store for a country's imports, exports, and international capital movements. Some speculators may base their expectations of future exchange rates mainly on what has happened recently to exchange rates; and when a currency falls in value because of some new strain on a balance of payments, they may expect a further fall simply because there has been a recent fall. Such speculation will intensify, not mitigate, the fall; the speculators' sales are added to the other pressures on the balance of payments. Then other speculators may sell the currency, although they realize that it has already fallen below its long-run value, simply because they expect this first group of less well-informed speculators to go on selling. In other words, speculation could take a form which made completely free exchange rates, subject to excessive fluctuations. And this could bring with it a further danger. An excessive depreciation of a currency could lead to a sharp rise in the price of imports. Such a price rise—particularly if as in the United Kingdom imports of food and other necessities make up a large element in the cost of living—could itself engender a rise in money wage claims and thus a rise in the domestic price-income-cost structure. And this rise in turn would justify increased pessimism about the future value of the currency.

(3) Now whether these fears be justified or not—and I would not myself be ready to assert that they are wholly imaginary—it is most unlikely that national governments would be prepared at one fell swoop to take the risk of letting the exchange rates go to fluctuate freely without any intervention. If the currency pegs were removed and exchange rates were allowed to fluctuate, the national authorities would undoubtedly insist on standing ready with their reserves of gold and foreign exchange to intervene in the exchange market from time to time. This we may call the system of *National Exchange Equalization*. The system would work in the following way. As in the case just examined currency pegs would be removed, national currencies would fluctuate in terms of each other; long-run adjustment would thus be achieved by changes in money price-income-cost structures due to alterations in the exchange rates between different domestic monies; and speculators would be free to speculate and—it would be hoped—to provide short-run support for the currency of a deficit country. But national monetary authorities would not rely wholly on private speculation. They would set up National Exchange

Equalization Funds, endowed with resources in terms of their own currencies and of gold and foreign currencies. If private speculation appeared to them to be driving down excessively the value of the national currency, they would themselves support the currency by selling foreign currencies or gold and buying the domestic currency through their own Exchange Equalization Account, and *vice versa* if private transactions seemed to be raising the short-run value of the domestic currency excessively.

This system has in my view a great deal to recommend it. But it has its own peculiar difficulties which became obvious in the late 1930's when—so far as sterling and the dollar were concerned—something like it was in operation. At that time there was a fear that a national monetary authority would use its Exchange Equalization Fund to engage in competitive exchange depreciation. For example, the U.K. authorities by selling sterling and buying dollars could depreciate unnecessarily the value of sterling in terms of the dollar, thus enabling U.K. manufacturers to undercut U.S. manufacturers even though there might be no underlying deficit on the U.K. balance of payments and no need, therefore, for such undercutting. The dangers of such action were undoubtedly much more real in the late 1930's than they would be in present conditions. Then there was mass unemployment; and national authorities were tempted to give employment to their own resources by beggar-my-neighbor international policies which stole markets from their neighbors even though their balance-of-payments position did not require such action. Nowadays there is not mass unemployment; and in any case national governments realize that they can give employment by measures which expand their own domestic markets, using measures which expand their exports and contract their imports only if they have a balance-of-payments deficit.

But even if competitive exchange depreciations are a much less real danger nowadays, it is pretty clear that the system of National Exchange Equalization must be supplemented by an extensive system of international cooperation. To put it simply, if the U.K. exchange equalization account is intervening to control the sterling-dollar rate of exchange and the U.S. exchange equalization account is intervening to control the dollar-sterling rate of exchange, it is clear that they would be well advised to coordinate their actions. But the obvious way to coordinate their actions is to agree on the rates at which they will peg their currencies and only to change the pegs from time to time in agreement; and this is, of course, in essence the present IMF system of the Adjustable Peg with which we started our discussion. In fact, it was the fear of competitive exchange depreciation engendered in the 1930's, combined with the obvious need to coordinate the action of independent National Exchange Equalization accounts, which led through the Tripartite Monetary Agreement of 1936 to the Articles of Agreement of the International Monetary Fund and the present excessively rigid exchange-rate structure.

(4) Thus National Exchange Equalization cries out for international cooperation which appears to imply the system of the Adjustable Peg, which—as we have seen—is likely to imply a rigid exchange-rate structure. A possible escape from this dilemma is through *Supranational Exchange Equalization*. Under this system national monetary authorities would renounce the use of national exchange equalization accounts; exchange rates would be allowed to vary to give long-run balance-of-payments adjustments; private speculation would be supplemented not by the operations of a number of national exchange equalization accounts but by a single Supranational Exchange Equalization authority which—like the present International Monetary Fund—would be endowed with a large fund of the various national currencies, but—unlike the present International Monetary Fund—would be empowered on its own initiative to buy and sell these currencies in otherwise uncontrolled foreign exchange markets in order to control short-run fluctuations in exchange rates.

If I am frank, I must admit that I regard this as technically the best possible solution in present circumstances. For at heart I believe that in the free world we should develop real supranational authorities. It is in my view a quite mistaken form of monetary supranationalism to start by fixing rigidly the exchange rates between national currencies as a first step towards a supranational currency. We are at a very early confederal stage in our affairs. It is the national governments which have the great taxing powers and so the instruments for controlling budgetary inflations or deflations of demand; it is the national governments which have the great central banks which control the issue of money and so interest rates; and the nations have their own different modes of wage-rate determination. It is a wise and sensible division of powers in our present confederal stage that the national governments should exercise these budgetary, monetary, and wage-fixing influences to control their own employment, growth, and price stability. This implies, I am sure, some variations in the rates of exchange between their monies. It is in the necessary Exchange Equalization between these monies that the first tentative supranational steps should be taken.

However, I am sufficiently realistic to admit that this supranational solution is politically not a starter at the present time. So reluctantly I pass on from Supranational Exchange Equalization to other possible measures.

(5) If we abandon the heroic solution of Supranational Exchange Equalization, can we do some useful but more mundane tinkering with the present excessively rigid Adjustable Peg system? I believe that we can. First of all, we could introduce *Wider Bands* within which fluctuations could take place. I have so far treated the present system of Adjustable Pegs as if each currency were precisely and exactly pegged to gold. But this is, of course, not the case. The present IMF obligation is for each member country to settle a par value for its currency in terms of gold and then not to allow the value of its currency in terms of gold to vary by more than 1 per cent above or below this par value. This means that if a country is in deficit it can allow the rate of exchange to depreciate by 1 per cent in terms of gold before having to support it from its own reserves; if it is in surplus, it can allow the exchange rate to appreciate by 1 per cent. Such small variations[1] do not allow the exchange rate to be a significant instrument of long-run adjustment; but they can exercise an important and in general beneficial effect on speculation in the exchange rates. Thus if a country is in deficit and its exchange rate has depreciated by the permitted 1 per cent, speculators (provided that there is no risk of a change in the currency's par value) will have some speculative incentive to purchase the depreciated currency; it cannot depreciate any further in gold value; it might, however, appreciate in the future by anything up to 2 per cent in gold value. This consideration will prompt speculators to support a currency when it is under pressure and thus helps the authorities to maintain the exchange rate with a smaller loss of reserves than would otherwise be necessary. This feature of a system which sets upper and lower limits to the Band within which exchange rates may fluctuate gives it an advantage over the system of National Exchange Equalization without any upper or lower limits. For a monetary authority to support its currency when it has fallen by X per cent will be much easier if speculators know that it will not fall any further than if they

realize that at any time it may be still further reduced. As against this there must, of course, be set the reduction in the range of variations which can be used as an instrument of balance-of-payments adjustment.

But there is nothing sacred about 1 per cent. Suppose that the rule of the IMF were altered so that each member country were obliged only to prevent the gold value of its currency from deviating by more than 5 per cent from its par value. Changes in exchange rates could now begin to exert some, though still a moderate, influence on basic price-income-cost structures. The most extreme permitted swing in the exchange rate between two currencies would now be 20 per cent,[2] though generally much smaller changes would be the rule. The possibility of these enlarged swings would also increase the incentive to speculators to aid the authorities in the support of a currency under pressure. For when the currency did reach its lower level there would, as before, be no possibility of a further fall in its gold value, but there would now be a possibility that its gold value might rise by anything up to 10 per cent instead of only 2 per cent.

The wider the Band within which the exchange rate can vary, the greater its power as an instrument of basic adjustment of price-income-cost structures and the greater its power to induce the support of speculators when a currency is weak and at its lower level. Why then not advocate much Wider Bands? Why not 20 per cent above or below par? Unfortunately in this wicked world one cannot have one's cake and eat it. Fluctuations within the Band raise all those problems of Freely Floating Exchange Rates or of Exchange-Equalization controls over fluctuations, of competitive exchange depreciation, and of the coordination of National Exchange-Equalization policies which we have already discussed. If the Band is kept reasonably narrow, one could without danger have a system in which exchanges were allowed to float freely without any official intervention within the permitted Band. Or, as a second-best alternative, if National Exchange Equalization were permitted within the Band one could perhaps leave the necessary cooperation between national authorities in the exchange-equalization use of their national reserves of gold and foreign exchange to be worked out by suitable *ad hoc* arrangements. Simply because the Band is limited, the dangers of anti-social speculation or of the misuse of National Exchange Equalization funds will also be limited. Permission to fluctuate by 5 per cent either side of par value combined with freely floating exchange rates or with the uncontrolled national use of national monetary reserves within those limits might well provide a better mix than at present between international restraint and freedom of national action.

(6) There is one other way in which the present IMF rules might be modified in order to give a somewhat different mix between international restraint and national freedom in exchange-rate matters. At present the rule is that a member country can alter the par value of its currency only if it is in fundamental disequilibrium and only with the permission of the IMF, except that it can make an initial 10 per cent adjustment on its own initiative. These rules might be revised in the following way. Basic adjustments to meet a fundamental disequilibrium would be hedged around with even more safeguards and would be made even more exceptional than at present. The allowance of an initial 10 per cent adjustment would be abolished; but in its place member countries would be permitted to alter the par value of their currencies by not more than $\frac{1}{6}$ per cent in any one month; moreover, they would undertake to depreciate their currencies by $\frac{1}{6}$ per cent in any one month if, but only if, they were faced with a continuing balance-of-payments deficit and to appreciate by this amount if, but only if, they were faced with a continuing surplus in their balance of payments. This system might perhaps be called that of the *Sliding Parity*. For if the right to change the parity were exercised every month, the exchange value of the currency would be changed continuously at 2 per cent per annum.

Such a system is not, of course, a panacea. But it could be used as a partial but very useful supplement to other measures to achieve long-run equilibrium. If a country were in continuing balance-of-payments deficit it could by this means lower its price-income-cost structure by anything up to 2 per cent per annum—i.e., by 10 per cent over a five-year period. If at the same time some other country were in continuing surplus, it could have raised its price-income-cost structure through exchange-rate appreciation by anything up to 10 per cent over the same five-year period. A 20 per cent adjustment in five years is by no means to be despised. But this would be the very maximum, and clearly reliance could be placed on this method only if the countries concerned had very ample reserves of gold and foreign exchange to tide them over the fairly prolonged processes of adjustment.

The system raises also important problems of exchange-rate speculation. For this reason, to operate the system the monetary authorities would have to use their short-term interest rate policies for balance-of-payments reasons. Let us take the extreme possible case. Suppose that A's currency is confidently expected to appreciate at the maximum rate of 2 per cent per annum while B's currency is confidently expected to depreciate at the maximum rate of 2 per cent per annum. B's currency would then be expected to depreciate in terms of A's currency at the rate of 4 per cent per annum. To prevent the wholesale movement of short-term funds from B to A to take the prospective 4 per cent profit on the exchange rate the short-term rate of interest would have to be maintained in B four points above the level in A—for example, at 6 per cent per annum in B and 2 per cent in A. This means that to work a system of this kind the national monetary authorities would have to cooperate in setting their short-term interest rates in the interests of preserving balance-of-payments equilibrium. They would have to rely on budgetary policies and—insofar as they can be determined independently of short-term rates—upon long-term rates but not upon short-term rates, for the control of domestic economic expansion.

If a system of this kind were adopted, it might be sensible for the monetary authorities in each country to give a gold guarantee in respect of balances of its own currency which were held as monetary reserves by other monetary authorities. This is not an essential feature of the proposal, and the decision whether or not to give such a gold guarantee could be left to each individual country. If such guarantees were given, there would develop a structure of more or less uniform short-term interest rates in all the main financial centers for such currency balances as were backed by a gold guarantee, while divergent short-term rates would appear on balances of national currencies not subject to a gold guarantee—the short-term rate being higher in those centers where the exchange rate was expected to depreciate and *vice versa.*

NOTES

1. Suppose country A is in surplus and its exchange rate is 1 per cent above parity, while country B is in deficit and its exchange rate is 1 per cent below parity. Then B's money is 2 per cent devalued in terms of A's. If later B is in surplus and A is in deficit, B's money may be 2 per cent appreciated in terms of A's money. The *maximum* swing in the exchange rate is, therefore, 4 per cent.
2. At one extreme A's currency would be 5 per cent above par with B's 5 per cent below par; at the other extreme A's would be 5 per cent below par and B's 5 per cent above.

UNILATERAL ACTION ON INTERNATIONAL
MONETARY POLICY

Leland B. Yeager

Professor of Economics,
University of Virginia

I do not suggest that a run on the U.S. gold stock would be a horrible event. It need not do any serious real damage (though it might temporarily injure U.S. prestige and lead to panicky imposition of drastic and unnecessary controls). On the contrary, exhaustion of our gold stock could even be helpful; the dreaded event would be behind us, fears about it would prove groundless and would no longer inhibit sound domestic policy, and the air would be cleared for a sensible international monetary reform giving little if any role to gold.

Once our gold ran out (if it actually did), without any catastrophe ensuing, the way would be open to healthier international monetary arrangements. Runs from dollars into gold could no longer occur because gold would no longer have a fixed-but-raisable dollar price and the dollar would no longer be backed by an exhaustible gold reserve. The exact nature of the new system would then be up to foreign countries. Any of the likely choices would be an improvement on the present system. Conceivably, foreign countries might stop pegging their currencies to the dollar or to gold or to one another. Thereby letting exchange rates fluctuate would provide an automatic balance-of-payments adjustment mechanism. Worries about such a system would turn out (I am convinced) to have been based only on defective the-

From Leland B. Yeager, "Unilateral Action on International Monetary Policy," in *Contingency Planning for U.S. International Monetary Policy*, Statements by Private Economists submitted to the Subcommittee on International Exchange and Payments of the Joint Economic Committee, 89th Cong., 2d sess., 1966 (Washington, D.C.: U.S. Government Printing Office, 1966), pp. 155–59.

orizing and on wrong interpretations of historical experience. If public opinion were not ready for free exchange rates, however, the foreign authorities would keep their currencies pegged either to gold or to the dollar. If the foreigners chose pegging on gold, the dollar would be free to fluctuate against gold and foreign currencies alike; and the exchange-rate mechanism would equilibrate the U.S. balance of payments. Today's precarious second-class relation of the dollar to gold would be gone, and keeping gold and currencies pegged to each other would be a foreign, not an American, problem.

More probably, the foreigners would let gold fluctuate and keep their currencies pegged to the dollar. (Different countries might make different choices, some adopting free rates, some a gold peg, and some the non-gold-dollar standard.) Something similar to this third possibility developed after Great Britain left the gold standard in 1931; many countries chose to keep their currencies linked with sterling rather than with gold. Such an outcome would be even more natural for the dollar nowadays; the reasons include the dominant role of the dollar in pricing and paying for goods traded internationally, the dominance of the dollar in international finance (as illustrated by the Euro-dollar market and the flotation of dollar bonds in Europe), and the use of the dollar (sometimes under another name) in many financial arrangements among foreign governments. In choosing between dollar reserves and gold reserves, foreign authorities would also have to remember that currencies (overwhelmingly dollars) and not gold are what they intervene with to keep rates stable on the foreign-exchange market; gold is suitable for their reserves only as long as it remains readily exchangeable for the currencies used in actual interventions.

Under the non-gold-dollar standard, the United States would no longer have to pursue the two sometimes conflicting goals of gold-price-and-exchange-rate stability and purchasing-power stability. Monetary and fiscal policy could concentrate on keeping the price level stable; anyway, it would have an improved chance of achieving "full employment without inflation" because this dual task, difficult enough by itself, would no longer be complicated with extraneous balance-of-payments problems. Any problems of keeping national currencies pegged to something else would fall on the foreigners who were pegging their currencies to the dollar; the United States would not be trying to peg anything. To the extent that foreigners accumulated more and more dollar reserves to be ready for bigger deficits as their international trade grew over the years, the United States would be running what present-day accounting treats as a balance-of-payments deficit. But the deficit would be self-financing and harmless because the United States would no longer be attempting the sort of pegging that makes speculative runs from the dollar into gold possible nowadays. If foreigners ever did decide to reduce their total dollar holdings, their action would necessarily entail a surplus in the basic U.S. balance of payments. No problem could arise of what to redeem foreign-held dollars in. These, like American-held dollars, would simply be spendable for U.S. goods, services, and securities.

Under the non-gold-dollar standard, the United States would enjoy the free or cheap use of foreign capital held as reserves in U.S. bank accounts or securities. The United States would reap the "seigniorage" on money-supply expansion to meet the growing combined demand for dollars for international reserve purposes as well as for the purposes of a growing home economy. Yet letting the United States enjoy this advantage would leave foreign countries no worse off than they would be holding their reserves in gold. They would even be better off in one respect insofar as a non-gold-dollar standard spared them the inflationary tendencies of a new system involving some sort of outright creation of international liquidity. They would be better off holding reserves in a currency managed to keep its purchasing power stable than holding some new international medium created and managed by criteria that would almost surely have to be vague or mutually contradictory.

If foreigners did begrudge the United States the special advantages (cheap foreign loans or seigniorage) it would enjoy under a non-gold-dollar standard, they could always adopt free exchange rates instead. Although probably the ideal system, persistent prejudices make it less likely than the non-gold-dollar standard.

If the latter is the most likely outcome—and a quite acceptable outcome—of running out of gold, why should the United States wait for that event before discontinuing both purchase and sale of gold? Well, my own preference does waver between immediate action and simply making the announcement proposed above. A few reasons, though not conclusive, do favor the announcement approach. (1) By letting the gold run out, the United States would obtain real goods and services for it; that is, foreigners could no longer obtain other goods and services for the dollars they redeemed in gold. It would not be we Americans who would be stuck with the gold upon its demonetization. (2) It would be amusing to see foreign authorities struggling to decide whether to accept the U.S. invitation to cash their dollars in for gold. They would have to realize that gold bought from the United States might not be resalable for as much as $35 an ounce if exhaustion of the U.S. gold should trigger the end of U.S. gold purchases as well as sales. Realizing what might happen, some foreign countries might even hasten to sell gold to the United States. (3) For the reasons just mentioned, the proposed announcement might postpone a run on the gold stock for a long time and thus help us muddle through with the existing system. Though hardly desirable for its own sake, muddling through would gain time for the spread of understanding. People might eventually understand the merits of a dollar standard and especially of exchange-rate flexibility and understand that the value of gold nowadays depends more on its link with the dollar than the other way around. But in the present state of opinion, a sudden immediate end to both selling and buying gold might seem like an American breach of faith. If we just let the gold eventually run out instead, our demonetizing it would appear forced by circumstances and so less blameworthy. (4) Perhaps the most important reason for muddling through is that improved understanding gained in the meanwhile would spare the world the adoption of any of the currently popular schemes for a new international fiat money, whose outright creation would probably reinforce the inflationary bias of the existing system. Any of the popular schemes would perpetuate the existing lack of any "automatic" balance-of-payments adjustment mechanism. Any such scheme would be extremely difficult to dismantle, once put into operation, and would block adoption of preferable arrangements. In the present state of general understanding about monetary matters, it is important not to rush into anything irreversible.

CONCLUSION: A FURTHER
LOOK AT THE ALTERNATIVES

REFORM UNDER THE PEGGED EXCHANGE RATE

As indicated in the readings on Patching Up the Adjustable Peg System, the closing of the gold pool and the plan for Special Drawing Rights still leave unsolved two major problems, namely, the adjustment and official confidence problems. While the closing of the gold pool does much to reduce the potential damage from private speculation, large shifts in the preferences of official institutions regarding gold, dollars, pounds, and SDR's could still lead to crises in the international monetary system.[1]

The creation of a Reserve Settlement Account such as proposed by Bernstein would give in effect a multilateral guarantee to the values of the various reserve assets vis-à-vis each other. Thus it would greatly reduce the incentives for shifts among them.[2] In the absence of such an Account, a strong case can be made for giving unilateral exchange guarantees to official holdings of the dollar and the pound, as discussed by William A Salant in Part II.[3] (It should be noted that SDR's are to be guaranteed in terms of gold, as are countries' contributions to their IMF quotas.)

Another method of curing the official confidence problem would be the creation of a truly super national central bank which could act as a lender of last resort by creating deposits on itself. In recent years this idea has been associated most closely with the name of Robert Triffin. The bases of Triffin's plan were exposited in 1960 in *Gold and the Dollar Crisis* [65]. The plan is strikingly similar to the Keynes proposal, which was rejected at the Bretton Woods Conference. Triffin suggests that there be an international central bank with the power to create credit for the benefit of national central banks. Deposits in such an organization would have a guarantee in terms of gold, be fully transferable into gold and any national currency, and would entail

216

the receipt of interest. Loans to finance balance of payments deficits would not be automatic, but would be at the discretion of the international bank. There is no formal limit to the deposit-creating powers of the Triffin bank. The only limit is really the confidence of the members in the bank, i.e., their willingness to accept the bank's "new money."

The method of altering the existing system would be the transfer of foreign exchange holdings (and gold) on the part of member countries in exchange for deposits. Triffin would give the bank the right to liquidate these foreign exchange holdings, but at a maximum rate of five per cent per annum. He suggests that reinvestment then take place in countries that are underdeveloped. He also suggests that most of the normal investment activities of the institution should take place in those countries that need the investment most, i.e., the undeveloped areas.

The objection most often raised against the Triffin Plan is that it would entail the surrender of too much national sovereignty to a super national authority. However, under any conceivable international monetary system, taking part in the world economy entails the loss of some national sovereignty, as the movement of a formerly self-sufficient woodsman to the city would involve a loss of his individual sovereignty. The loss of sovereignty implied under each of the major proposals will be considered below.

The other key characteristic of the plans for the multilateral creation of international reserves is that they do nothing to improve the adjustment mechanism under the present adjustable peg system. They are certainly not a solution to the problem of the U.S. balance of payments deficit. As Bernstein has remarked in this connection: ". . . even with a $2 billion creation, we would get a little bit under $500 million. Well, you can't even estimate the deficit of the United States within $500 million, much less solve the balance-of-payments problem with such a sum." [35, p. 100]

Of course, this is not a criticism of these plans *per se*. It is only to say that they offer a partial—not a complete—solution to the problems facing our international monetary system.

In our opinion, the Despres proposal to demonetize gold while maintaining fixed exchange rates may be characterized in the same manner. It would eliminate the confidence problem with respect to foreign dollar holdings, since the dollar would no longer be convertible into gold at the holder's discretion. However, changes in international liquidity would be tied to U.S. deficits, which could cause international liquidity to be subject to even more vagaries than tying it to gold production! While the proposal would cure the problem of the U.S. deficit from the point of view of the United States, it would not do so from the point of view of other countries. In other words, the adjustment problem would also continue to remain, though in a different form.[4]

There are two other general types of reform that have been considered. These are (1) increasing the price of gold and returning to the gold standard, and (2) instituting freely flexible exchange rates. These reforms purport to offer *complete* solutions to the problems of the international monetary system.[5]

The adjustment mechanism under the gold standard, if actually adhered to, would be far from painless, as indicated in the Introduction to Part III. Furthermore, increasing the price of gold is by no means an uncontroversial method of providing additional liquidity.

In considering the effects of a substantial increase in the price of gold, say, doubling its value as Rueff suggests, we must distinguish between the problem of the adequacy of the stock of international reserves at a given point in time and the problem of the provision of an adequate growth of reserves over time. To avoid the possibility of destabilizing speculation, the increase in the price of gold has to be a large one—large enough so that the new price would be expected to be maintained for a number of years. Thus there is considerable danger that an immediate result would be an initial problem of too much liquidity. Furthermore, it would be extremely unlikely that the most desirable price increase to adjust the existing stock of reserves would also be the best for calling forth an appropriate trend in future gold supplies.[6]

Before turning to a discussion of the pros and cons of flexible exchange rates, let us consider further the implications of the various reform proposals for national sovereignty.

It is clear that under the plans for multilateral creation of international reserve assets (such as the SDR, Bernstein, and Triffin proposals), the power to determine the rate of creation and the distribution of these assets would be vested in an international body. But would this represent a *loss* of national sovereignty by the member countries? The question is whether such proposals would involve the sacrifice of more national sovereignty than is already given up under the present system. Triffin argues rather convincingly that they would not do so. [32, pp. 129–32]

What were the sources of the growth of international liquidity under the post-war gold exchange standard—gold, dollars, increases in IMF quotas, and borrowing facilities such as the General Arrangements to Borrow. The two latter sources are subject to multilateral and bilateral negotiations, and hence necessarily involve some loss of national autonomy.

Reliance on gold might tend to minimize the national sovereignty given up to other countries.[7] But look at what it would be given up to! As Gottfried Haberler has argued, "It is unthinkable that modern countries individually or collectively would surrender sovereignty over their full employment policy, growth policy, stabilization policies to the vagaries of gold production, Russian gold sales and the whims of gold hoarders." [21, p. 8]

Nor would an international dollar standard avoid the giving up of national sovereignty for international purposes. As Robert Mundell has stated:

If the U.S. dollar were the sole international reserve asset, then there would be no gold problem, of course. The United States could follow its own monetary policy and other countries would keep their exchange rates pegged to the dollar. They would have to inflate when we do, have a depression when we have one, and so on. So that if there were no gold question, monetary policy of the world would be completely determined by the Federal Reserve System, the central bank of the United States. [34, p. 26]

Thus the dollar standard poses a dilemma. If the United States were to tailor its monetary policy purely to domestic needs, the provision of international liquidity would be haphazard. Other countries would be in scarcely a better position depending for international liquidity on the vagaries of the United States balance of payments than on gold acquisitions. Almost certainly, if fixed rates were to be maintained in these conditions, "monetary policy in New York must be set in terms of the needs of the world as a whole, and is clearly a subject for international rather than purely American concern."—C. P. Kindleberger, cited in [32, p. 131]. And to the extent that U.S. monetary policy is aimed at providing an orderly expansion of international liquidity, domestic monetary sovereignty would be sacrificed.

It should be noted that Jacques Rueff's characterization of the

United States position under the existing system as analogous to the happy customer of an unusual tailor is more applicable to a full dollar standard than to the gold exchange standard. Rueff states: "If I were to discover a tailor who would agree to return to me the amount of my bill on the very day I pay him, I would be much less cautious about ordering new suits and my own balance of payments would be in deficit." But the tailor under the present system can demand payment at any time: the non-reserve currency countries can convert their dollars into gold, and, as was indicated in the readings on The Costs and Benefits of Being World Banker in Part II, one can hardly argue that such outstanding liabilities have been of no concern to U.S. authorities. Furthermore, even under a full dollar standard, dollar holdings could always be converted into U.S. goods and services.

The distribution of sovereignty under the gold exchange standard is treated succinctly in the following statement by Robert A. Mundell:

The successful operation of the gold exchange standard requires a specific set of monetary and fiscal policy "rules of the game" in both the key currency ("inner") country and the non-reserve ("outer") countries. At the heart of the system lies the role of the size and composition of the deficit of the inner country.

The outer countries peg their currencies (directly or indirectly) to the inner country's currency (the dollar) and thus act as residual purchasers or sellers of dollars, while the inner country (the U.S.) pegs the dollar to the ultimate asset (gold), and thus acts as the residual buyer or seller of *gold*. This means that the *size* of the U.S. deficit determines the increase in reserves of the rest of the world, while its *composition* determines the change in reserves of the U.S., given the rate of increase of monetary gold holdings in the world.

When U.S. monetary policy is very expansive the outer countries have to buy up large amounts of dollars and this has direct and indirect *inflationary* consequences for the outer countries; similarly, when U.S. monetary policy is restrictive there is a scarcity of dollars and this has deflationary consequences for the rest of the world.

The outer countries' protection against an excessive or deficient flow of dollars is to alter the *composition* of the U.S. deficit and thus affect the reserve position of the U.S. When U.S. monetary policy is excessively expansive the outer countries can convert dollars into gold; this leaves the aggregate level of their own reserves unchanged, but it destroys world reserves because it reduces U.S. reserves. And similarly, when U.S. policy is unduly restrictive, the outer countries can convert gold into dollars, leaving their own reserves unchanged, but *improving* the reserve position of the U.S. The *composition* of the U.S. deficit, which is under the control of the outer countries, is the mechanism by which the outer countries, in their role as governors of the gold exchange standard system, cast their votes with respect to the appropriateness or inappropriateness of the aggregate size of the U.S. deficit.

The *vigor* with which the votes are cast, however, is circumscribed by the attachment of the inner and outer countries alike to the existing system. The outer countries can *warn* the U.S. by gold conversions, but they cannot lower the U.S. gold stock below the point at which it no longer pays the U.S. to continue running it; overly aggressive conversions would reinforce the go-it-alone forces in the U.S. represented by Professors Despres, Kindleberger and Salant. On the other hand, the U.S. freedom of action is also circumscribed in the sense that U.S. monetary policy must not be so inimical to the interests of the rest of the world that the outer countries decide, in their own protection, to opt out of the system by abandoning the dollar for gold. [34, p. 5]

For further discussion along these lines, see [53].

Even under a system of flexible exchange rates, or one under which foreign authorities peg their currencies to the dollar at their own discretion, countries would still to some extent share the consequences of others' actions.[8] In other words, the very act of taking part in international activity entails some loss of national sovereignty. As Charles P. Kindleberger has commented:

Some may regret the loss of sovereignty in the monetary and foreign exchange field. But sovereignty is being lost in various spheres—trade, defense, monetary policy, etc.—and it is as useless to weep over it as over the loss of U.S. foreign policy innocence. The household has lost the capacity to feed, clothe, protect itself, and so have the village, town, region, and state. It is sensible to expect growing interdependence of countries and in economic and political fields. It is difficult to see how independence of monetary, fiscal, payments, and other economic policy can be preserved. [36, p. 390]

IN DEFENSE OF FLEXIBLE EXCHANGE RATES

The plans for reform that have been discussed thus far involve retaining the adjustable peg system of exchange rates. An alternative proposal is simply to unpeg exchange rates (or, at least, to substantially widen the pegging points.) Exchange rate changes then could bring about balance of payments adjustment. Since rates would not be pegged, there would not be the need for international reserves which exists under the present system.

Today the vast majority of academic economists favor greater exchange rate flexibility than exists under the present system.[9] In general, those who propose completely free rates would prefer policies of limited flexibility, such as widening the points between which exchange rates are pegged, to maintenance of the present system.[10]

It is beyond the scope of this book to present a thorough discussion of the existing opinions on the technical aspects of how a system of flexible exchange rates would work in practice for a country such as the United States.[11] The key requisite for a well functioning system is that private speculation serve a stabilizing function. This means that *flexible* rates need not be *unstable* rates, as is demonstrated by the only recent experience of a major country (Canada) with flexible exchange rates.[12]

Men of "practical affairs" have lagged behind the academic world in acceptance of the idea that experimentation with greater exchange rate flexibility is desirable. Friedman considered several reasons for this. One line of objection is that exchange rate flexibility itself might be an obstacle to international transactions. Flexible rates might entail some added risk to international exchange, but experiences with flexible rates do not appear to have been unconducive to expanding international trade and investment. (See, for instance [77, Ch. 12].) One of the reasons is that, as Friedman mentions, international traders can avoid the risk of changes in exchange rates by covering their purchases or sales in the market for *forward* exchange. Such actions are similar to buying futures on commodity markets, and are quite prevalent even under the present adjustable peg system. At most, such covering would involve a slight extra cost to international transactions. And where the alternative to exchange rate adjustment is controls or deflationary domestic policies, it is not at all clear that flexible rates would have an adverse effect on international transactions.

This is a question on which it is easy to confuse ends and means. As the Joint Economic Committee has observed:

"It is one of the many ironies and inconsistencies of modern life that, to protect fixed exchange rates—the means—we have compromised freedom of capital movements and, to some extent, of trade—the ends which the fixed rates are intended to serve." [33, p. 18]

Another charge frequently levelled along this line against flexible exchange rates is that they carry an inward looking or isolationist political philosophy, while fixed rates are more neighborly and indicative of concern for the world community.[13] When we view how strongly the U.S. balance of payments position has influenced the structure of its international commitments under the existing pegged rate system, however, we may question the validity of this charge. As Friedman points out, at least under a flexible rate system the U.S. could evaluate its foreign commitments in terms of their tax rather than foreign exchange costs, and there would be no need to tie foreign aid and initiate "Buy American" legislation, nor to place discriminatory controls and taxes on international trade, travel and investment.

Furthermore, as Meade argues, if some official exchange stabilization is to be retained under a flexible rate system, it would best be done on a multilateral basis.

Another line of objection is that exchange rate flexibility would itself conflict with important national objectives. For example, there is concern over what variations in the exchange rate would do to the prestige of the dollar. But, as was pointed out in Part II, most of the benefits of being a key currency now accrue to the U.S. from the dollar's use as a vehicle or transactions currency rather than as a reserve currency, and correction of the U.S. deficit could increase its use in the former capacity. The real conflict here is with official statements that the price of the dollar in terms of gold and other currencies will not be changed.

A common "conflict of objectives" charge is that exchange rate flexibility would open the floodgates of inflation. This is really an assertion that domestic monetary and fiscal authorities are "irresponsible" and that the discipline of the balance of payments is needed to control them. One could argue that perhaps a declining exchange rate would give as much or more incentive for "responsible" domestic policies as would balance of payments deficits, but it is quite true that flexible rates are not a panacea for all a country's economic problems. In effect, they give a country greater freedom to follow the policies its authorities desire, for better or for worse. We suspect that if a country had to rely upon the discipline of the balance of payments to keep its financial house in order, then international monetary questions would be one of the lesser problems it faced.

A third type of objection to flexible rates follows from a failure to distinguish between truly fixed exchange rates and the present adjustable peg system, such that the virtues of the former are ascribed to the latter. An example of a truly fixed rate system would be that among the individual states of the United States. Such currency unification can be an important aid to efficient specialization and division of labor. Adjustments between regions would still have to take place in the face of persistent disequilibria in the areas' balances of payments, but here private capital movements are observed to play a very beneficial financing role, as perceived, for example, by James C. Ingram [29].[14] Such stabilizing movements automatically finance temporary imbalances, removing the need for unnecessary real adjustment to temporary phenomena and providing time to spread out real adjustment to a persistent disequilibrium. In the latter case, adjustment through a relative fall in the money income of the area must still be made. However, as Tibor Scitovsky [60] has pointed out, the impact of such adjustment generally is less severe, the more it takes the form of migration from the area and the less it takes the form of a decline in per capita income. Factor mobility is higher in the long than in the short run. Thus automatic, private financing allows adjustment to be eased by cushioning it over a longer period.

These considerations suggest that the higher the mobility of labor within an area, the more advantageous are fixed exchange rates, i.e., a unified currency area. By linking their monetary systems in such a manner, regions largely forgo the opportunity to follow independent financial policies, so that a depressed area (i.e., one which would have a payments deficit at full employment) would have to rely on collective action for remedy. An area in such a situation, in which there is low labor mobility and insufficient cooperation to bring about effective regional programs, generally could benefit from changes in its exchange rate.

This suggests that what is relevant is not the question of fixed versus flexible rates in principle, *but which is better for a particular political or economic unit.* In response to the pioneering contributions by Robert A. Mundell [48] and Richard E. Caves [9], there is now considerable work being done toward developing criteria for optimum currency areas, i.e., currency blocs with flexible rates between them and fixed rates within each bloc Probably the reason that the question is not put this way more often in public debate is that the United States does appear to correspond roughly to such an area.

It is the elements underlying the concept of the optimum currency area which explain why many countries would prefer to stay pegged to the dollar even if its official link to gold were removed. As discussed by Yeager, a decision by the United States to go off gold would allow other countries to make such decisions for themselves: those that felt they would reap benefits from pegging the value of their currency to the dollar would be perfectly free to do so and those that did not foresee such benefits need not.

Flexible exchange rates would eliminate the need for attempting to reach a consensus on the manner in which the responsibility for adjusting to payments imbalances should be distributed. While this question is too complex to treat adequately here, in general under flexible rates the burden of adjusting to changed circumstances is placed largely on the country from which the disturbance originated.

There are two other phenomena that probably explain much of the existing hostility to experimentation with greater flexibility. One is the prevalent tendency to prefer the known to the unknown, a tendency that affects all types of policies. On the basis of the available evidence, it appears highly probable that a flexible exchange rate would work well for the United States, but this cannot be guaranteed with certainty. There is always some risk in trying a new policy.

In addition, it is likely that such a system would work less well during its transitional period of initiation. It is hard to imagine that such a transition would have a more adverse effect on trade, with respect to either severity or time, than did the 1965 New York dock strike, for instance. However, to policy makers with a very short time horizon, such as has been evidenced in the U. S. balance of payments programs in the late 1950's and in the 1960's, such a transitional period may appear to be quite important, while the potential benefits for the freedom of trade and investment over, say, the rest of the 20th century seem much less relevant!

The second phenomenon is the conviction held by many that the solution to a problem so complex as our international financial difficulties just could not be one so simple as to let the exchange rate be freely determined by the demands and supplies in the foreign exchange market. However, many leading economists have argued exactly this.

. . . a system of floating exchange rates completely eliminates the balance of payments problem—just as in a free market there cannot be a surplus or a shortage in the sense of eager sellers unable to find buyers or eager buyers unable to find sellers. The price may fluctuate but there cannot be a deficit or a surplus threatening an exchange crisis. Floating exchange rates would put an end to the grave problems requiring repeated meetings of secretaries of the Treasury and governors of central banks to try to draw up sweeping reforms. It would put an end to the occasional crisis producing frantic scurrying of high governmental officials from capital to capital, midnight phone calls among the great central banks lining up emergency loans to support one or another currency.

Indeed this is, I believe, one of the major sources of the opposition to floating exchange rates. The people engaged in these activities are important people and they are all persuaded that they are engaged in important activities. It cannot be, they say to themselves, that these important activities arise simply from pegging exchange rates. They must have more basic roots. Hence, they say, it is simpleminded to believe that freeing exchange rates would eliminate the problem. That is what the allied advisers engaged in price control, rationing, and the like told Erhard that summer in 1948. That is why he removed price controls on a Sunday, when they were not in their offices to countermand his edicts.—Milton Friedman [16, pp. 15–16]

It is probably a very good rule of thumb to be suspicious of proposals offering simple solutions to complex problems. But is it just possible that occasionally there may be exceptions?

ARE PLANS FOR REFORM JUST NOT PRACTICAL?

The charge that they are just not practical often has been levied against many of the proposals contained in the readings in this volume. "But mere shouts of 'ridiculous,' 'preposterous,' 'utterly impractical' must not be given the value of reasoned arguments."—Fritz Machlup [32, p. 78] And there is a fortunate tendency for what is impractical or ridiculous to change over time.

A clear example of this is the question of gold policy and the flexibility of exchange rates. The present popularity of exchange rate flexibility among academic economists is a comparatively recent phenomena. It represents a radical shift in professional opinion from that held at the formation of the Bretton Woods system.[15]

A similar shift seems to be beginning also in official circles. In 1963, Senator Paul H. Douglas declared before the Joint Economic Committee:

For years I have urged the Federal Reserve, the Treasury, and our representatives on the IMF, to consider the flexible exchange rates, and I have been deeply disappointed by their refusal even to consider or study the matter. It has been an automatic reaction and, to tell the truth, I have not seemed to generate any real argument. It has been a sort of tropismatic response, even below the level of instinct.

All I can say is that I have been unable to get any lucid discussion on this subject from any representative of the Federal Reserve Board. I want to say I think they are capable of giving this a lucid discussion. I do not wish to denigrate their ability. But as this question has been put time and time again to Mr. Martin there has only been a bland parry. [36, pp. 576, 581]

By 1965, however, both the Joint Economic Committee and the House Banking and Currency Committee had asked the Administration to study the feasibility of greater exchange rate flexibility. While these requests apparently had no immediate impact on government officials, the devaluation of the pound and speculation leading to the closing of the gold pool seem to have served as a catalytic agent to official consideration of flexibility issues and alternative gold policies.

The opening paragraphs of an article in *The Wall Street Journal* shortly after the closing of the gold pool, present almost a direct answer to Leland B. Yeager's concluding question in his 1966 Congressional statement reprinted as our final reading:

The Administration would select some form of demonetization of gold if another severe international financial crisis arises.

The only question still open is precisely how to achieve this last resort—through letting the entire Treasury gold stock be gobbled up by foreign central banks or by halting all sales to them.—*The Wall Street Journal*, April 4, 1968.

The article concludes that the latter alternative is more likely.[16]

Further evidence of a break from the bind of traditional attitudes is presented in another *Wall Street Journal* article.

Previously secret testimony by a high Treasury official showed an increasingly open-minded approach to more sweeping changes in the international monetary system than those currently under way.

More flexible exchange rates, a switch to supporting the dollar by currency rather than gold operations, and creation of a new single reserve unit to replace all present and projected reserve assets were termed "worthy of study" by Frederick L. Deming, Under Secretary for Monetary Affairs.

Prior to the mid-March gold crisis, the Treasury had sternly insisted that any hint of willingness to consider alterations in current gold policy could, itself, touch off a run on the U.S. gold stock. But the weathering of the March storm and a widespread belief that the current "two-tier" gold price system is only a stopgap, has changed attitudes. Now, officials appear inclined to explore other possible improvements in the monetary system and to concede that they are doing so.—*The Wall Street Journal*, April 30, 1968.

WHAT IF AGREEMENT FOR EFFECTIVE REFORM IS NOT REACHED?

What will happen if multilateral agreement for reform cannot be secured? One possibility is a financial crisis involving a massive run on the dollar, such as the 1967 run on the pound. The proximate source of such a crisis could come from any of a number of factors. Official conversions of dollars into gold, for instance, could be prompted by purely economic reasons, such as a fear of exchange losses resulting from U.S. actions. Alternatively they could be prompted by a desire to discipline the U.S. deficit in order to diminish its potentially inflationary impact abroad or to reduce the contribution that other countries may feel they are making to the financing of U.S. policies that they may consider distasteful.

To some, the possibility of a run on the dollar is considered to be of such catastrophic dimensions that it cannot even be discussed politely. In Tobin's words, it would be "that ultimate and unmentionable calamity whose consequences are the more dreaded for never being described." [64, p. 153] However, a growing number of economists believe that such an event would not be a major catastrophe and might even prove to be a blessing in disguise.[17] A crisis would certainly prove chaotic, but in its aftermath another system would undoubtedly be created. There is no foundation to the cries that such an event would cause another world-wide depression.

As Richard Cooper has stated:

It is worth recalling that a "crisis" is defined by the dictionary as "a crucial time" and "a turning point." Any social or economic crisis involves a violent disturbance to the mental frame of reference and the conventions of behavior of the people involved in it. As such, crises are uncomfortable. But they are not things always to be avoided at absolutely any cost. The turning point can be in a desirable direction as well as an undesirable one; and the shakeup to the conventional wisdom and modes of behavior may have some value. [32, p. 18]

The official participants in the international monetary system have shown considerable cooperation in meeting short term crises, however, and to many observers the most likely result of a failure to reach effective multilateral agreement is not that the system will collapse but that it will endure too long. The lack of an efficient market adjustment mechanism may continue to contribute to excessive inflation or deflation in many countries, and, particularly for the United States, ever-increasing use of controls, selective partial devaluations of the dollar, and *ad hoc* specific programs for the balance of payments such as described by Fritz Machlup. Furthermore, there is no excuse like balance of payments difficulties to bring forth latent protectionist tendencies, as U.S. experience in 1967 and 1968 clearly indicated.

There is considerable danger from a self-feeding system of continual tightening of controls. Over time the longer run counter-productive effects of the initial restrictions would become increasingly felt, contributing to larger deficits than would otherwise have occurred. This would be compounded by the operation of Benjamin J. Cohen's Iron Law of Economic Controls: "to be effective controls must reproduce at a rate faster than that at which means are found for avoiding them." [12, p. 174] In prophetic words in 1963, the Secretary of the Treasury, Douglas C. Dillon, pointed out the costs of controls in terms of the sacrifice of other goals and predicted the outcome of attempts at partial exchange control:

Exchange controls would directly violate one of the precepts upon which our whole effort is predicated—that, in our economy, we must rely primarily upon decentralized decision-making by millions of individuals and businesses responding to market forces. Government, to be sure, must accept the responsibility for influencing these market forces in ways consistent with national objectives, but always without attempting to direct individual transactions.

Moreover, a partial system of exchange controls would soon break down as funds flowed through uncontrolled channels—spurred by the fear of still further controls. In the end, a complete system of exchange controls would be required. This would seriously prejudice the position of the dollar as the world's chief reserve currency, would tend to shrink world liquidity and reduce the volume of world trade, thus bringing in its train grave dangers of a worldwide economic recession. For these reasons, the institution of exchange controls, even though supposedly applicable only to certain types of transactions, is not practicable or acceptable policy for the United States. [36, p. 28]

A policy of attempting to "muddle through" via restrictive policies such as exchange controls would not only reduce and distort the volume of international (and domestic) trade and investment but would also impinge on other important objectives. It is ironic that the developing countries, which have so little active role in the operation of the system, have been one of the principal victims of its shortcomings. The flow of aid from the developed to the developing countries has fallen far short of the expectations at the beginning of the "development decade" of the 1960's. There is little doubt that the balance of payments troubles of several of the major aid-giving countries has been one of the important reasons for this. Not only has the nominal value of the flow of U.S. aid been reduced but the real value of such transfers has been further decreased by extensive programs of tying aid.

Unfortunately, the message of the following words by Emile Despres is as true today as when they were written in 1966.

I regard the present system, because of international cooperation, as relatively invulnerable—at least so long as a moderate deficit persists in the United States balance of payments. It is not the vulnerability of the present system but its adverse effect in reducing aid to the underdeveloped world, complicating and perhaps impairing collective defense arrangements and in hindering the international mobility of goods and capital which is the overriding problem today. The system is breeding a revived mercantilism and its apparent durability is not a source of much satisfaction to me. I regret that international cooperation, while strong enough to secure the system against crisis and breakdown, is not strong enough to reform it in a fashion conducive to free world growth, development and economic integration. [13, p. 37]

NOTES

1. We do not wish to give the impression that the closing of the gold pool has rendered destabilizing, private speculation entirely harmless. Such speculation can still affect the incentives for official holders to shift among reserve assets, for example, by affecting the private market price of gold.
2. There have been a number of similar proposals. For example, see those by Machlup [45] and Triffin [67, pp. 146–64].
3. The proposals for a guarantee of official foreign dollar balances against devaluation have generated considerable controversy. For the various arguments pro and con, see [5, pp. 156–64] and the references cited there.
4. For further discussion regarding the Despres proposal, see [22, p. 1–8].
5. Under the proposals for modified (rather than complete) exchange rate flexibility, there would still be a need for international reserves. However, the improvement in the adjustment mechanism offered by greater exchange rate flexibility would reduce the need for such reserves.
6. To policy makers in many countries, the distribution of the increased reserves

resulting from a gold price increase may be of considerable importance. The gains from such an increase would accrue to countries in proportion to their initial gold holdings and their potentiality of gold production. This means that particularly favored beneficiaries would be France, South Africa, and the Soviet Union, as well as the United States (a point properly stressed by Rueff). Coupled with the U.S. government's persistent pledges to maintain the official price of gold at $35 an ounce, these distributional effects make it very unlikely that the United States would agree to an increase in the gold price, particularly since it would impose opportunity losses on those governments that have cooperated with U.S. pleas not to convert their dollars into gold.

7. For prestige reasons, this seems to be one of the major attractions of the gold standard to President de Gaulle. See, for instance, [40].

8. The charge that such a system therefore is isolationist or nationalistic rather than internationally minded is considered below.

9. This is generally agreed by proponents and opponents alike. See, for instance, the debate between Milton Friedman and Robert V. Roosa sponsored by the American Enterprise Institute [16]. Friedman, the proponent, mentions the figure of "at least three-quarters of . . . the professional people in money and international trade" [16, p. 133] and Roosa, the opponent, "90 percent, at least, of the academic community" [16, p. 177].

10. However, not all advocates of flexible exchange rates share this view. For arguments that proposals for limited flexibility may be poor compromises, see Leland B. Yeager [78].

11. The interested reader will find a sampling of the range of common views on flexible exchange rates in [9], [11, Ch. 6], [15], [16], [39], [62], [65, pp. 82–86] and [70].

12. Econometric evidence supports this interpretation of the Canadian case. See the studies cited by Yeager [77, Ch. 24] and the later work by Officer [52, pp. 295–96].

13. One extreme form in which this argument appears is that the institution of exchange rate flexibility would generate economic warfare among countries in the form of competitive exchange rate depreciations and trade restrictions, perhaps culminating in a world wide depression. The kindest judgment we can render on this argument is that it is an example of the Arizona fallacy discussed by Friedman.

14. This is to be contrasted with the frequent destabilizing movements of private capital under the adjustable peg system, discussed by Warren L. Smith and James E. Meade in their respective readings.

15. Friedman has commented that 15 to 20 years ago one would not have found 5 per cent in favor of flexible rates. [16, p. 134]

16. One proposal that has received considerable attention recently (including the support of Senator Jacob Javits) is that the United States cease convertibility of the dollar into gold, but continue to meet its IMF obligations by instead accepting the responsibility of actively pegging the exchange rate of the dollar vis-à-vis other currencies. See, for instance, [6] and [7]. It is our opinion, however, that the additional freedom given the United States by such a move from gold to current account convertibility of the dollar is more illusory than real, as argued in [27, Ch. 3].

17. Of course, the potential benefit that *might* occur from a crisis need not be an argument in favor of attempting to precipitate one. "As for planning a crisis, that is unnecessary; we can make sensible changes in policy without one. But if one does occur, we should be ready to take advantage of it."—Leland B. Yeager [32, p. 156]

BIBLIOGRAPHY

[1] Ablin, Richard, "Fiscal Monetary Mix: A Haven for the Fixed Exchange Rate?" *National Banking Review*, Vol. 4, No. 2 (December 1966), 199–204.

[2] Aliber, Robert Z., "The Benefits and Costs of Being the World Banker: A Comment," *National Banking Review*, Vol. 2, No. 3 (March 1965), 409–10.

[3] ――――, "The Costs and Benefits of the U.S. Role as a Reserve Currency Country," *Quarterly Journal of Economics*, LXXVIII, No. 3 (August 1964), 442–56.

[4] ――――, *The Future of the Dollar as an International Currency*. New York: Frederick A. Praeger, Inc., 1966.

[5] Aubrey, Henry G., *The Dollar in World Affairs*. New York: Published for the Council on Foreign Relations by Frederick A. Praeger, Inc., 1964.

[6] Birnbaum, Eugene A., *Changing the U.S. Commitment to Gold*. Princeton: International Finance Section, Department of Economics, Princeton University, 1967.

[7] ――――, *Gold and the International Monetary System: An Orderly Reform*. Princeton: International Finance Section, Department of Economics, Princeton University, 1968.

[8] Bloomfield, Arthur I., *Monetary Policy under the International Gold Standard*. New York: Federal Reserve Bank of New York, 1959.

[9] Caves, Richard E., "Flexible Exchange Rates," *American Economic Review*, LIII, No. 2 (May 1963), 120–29.

[10] ――――, "International Liquidity: Toward a Home Repair Manual," *Review of Economics and Statistics*, XLVI, No. 2 (May 1964), 173–76.

[11] Clement, M. O., Richard L. Pfister, and Kenneth J. Rothwell, *Theoretical Issues in International Economics*. Boston: Houghton Mifflin Company, 1967, Ch. 6.

[12] Cohen, Benjamin J., "Capital Controls and the U.S. Balance of Payments: Comment," *American Economic Review*, LV, No. 1 (March 1965), 172–76.

[13] Despres, Emile, Letter to Dr. Otmar Emminger, October 3, 1966. Published in Joint Economic Committee, *New Approach to United States International Economic Policy*, 89th Cong., 2d sess., 1966. Washington, D.C.: U.S. Government Printing Office, 1966.

[14] Douglas, Paul H., *America in the Market Place*. New York: Holt, Rinehart & Winston, Inc., 1966.

[15] Friedman, Milton, "The Case for Flexible Exchange Rates," *Essays in Positive Economics*. Chicago: University of Chicago Press, 1953, pp. 157–203.

[16] ———— and Robert V. Roosa, *The Balance of Payments: Free versus Fixed Exchange Rates*. Washington, D.C.: American Enterprise Institute for Public Policy Research, 1967.

[17] Forte, Francesco, and Thomas D. Willett, "Interest-Rate Policy and External Balance," *Quarterly Journal of Economics*, LXXXIII, No. 2 (May 1969).

[18] Grubel, Herbert G., "The Benefits and Costs of Being the World Banker," *National Banking Review*, Vol. 2, No. 2 (December 1964), 189–212.

[19] ————, ed., *World Monetary Reform: Plans and Issues*. Stanford: Stanford University Press, 1963.

[20] Haberler, Gottfried, "Adjustment, Employment, and Growth," in William Fellner *et al.*, *Maintaining and Restoring Balance in International Payments*. Princeton: Princeton University Press, 1966, Ch. 6.

[21] ————, "International Monetary Problems." The Mont Pelerin Society: Aviemore Conference, 1968.

[22] ————, *Money in the International Economy*. Cambridge, Mass.: Harvard University Press, 1965.

[23] ————, "Some Remarks on Recent Discussions about the International Payments System," *Il Politico*, University of Pavia, XXX, No. 4 (1965), 750–60.

[24] ————, "The International Payments System: Postwar Trends and Prospects," in *International Payments Problems*. Washington, D. C.: American Enterprise Institute for Public Policy Research, 1966, pp. 1–19.

[25] ————, "The United States Balance of Payments," in Melvin R. Laird, ed., *Republican Papers*. Garden City, N.Y.: Doubleday & Company, Inc., 1968, pp. 429–53.

[26] ———— and Thomas D. Willett, *Presidential Measures on Balance of Payments Controls*. Washington, D.C.: American Enterprise Institute for Public Policy Research, 1968.

[27] ———— and Thomas D. Willett, *U.S. Balance of Payments Policies and International Monetary Reform*. Washington, D.C.: American Enterprise Institute for Public Policy Research, 1968.

[28] Hinshaw, Randall, ed., *Monetary Reform and the Price of Gold*. Baltimore: The Johns Hopkins Press, 1967.

[29] Ingram, James C., "A Proposal for Financial Integration in the Atlantic Community," in Joint Economic Committee, *Factors Affecting the United States Balance of Payments*, 87th Cong., 2d sess., 1962. Washington, D.C.: U.S. Government Printing Office, 1962, pp. 175–207.

[30] Johnson, Harry G., *Economic Policies Toward Less Developed Countries*. New York: Frederick A. Praeger, Inc., 1967.

[31] ———, "The Objectives of Economic Policy and the Mix of Fiscal and Monetary Policy under Fixed Exchange Rates," in William Fellner et al., *Maintaining and Restoring Balance in International Payments*. Princeton: Princeton University Press, 1966, Ch. 8.

[32] Joint Economic Committee, *Contingency Planning for U.S. International Monetary Policy*, 89th Cong., 2d sess., 1966. Washington, D.C.: U.S. Government Printing Office, 1966.

[33] ———, *Guidelines for Improving the International Monetary System*, Report, 89th Cong., first sess., 1965.

[34] ———, *New Approach to United States International Economic Policy*, 89th Cong., 2d sess., 1966. Washington, D.C.: U.S. Government Printing Office, 1966.

[35] ———, *New Plan for International Monetary Reserves*, 90th Cong., first sess., 1967. Washington, D.C.: U.S. Government Printing Office, 1967.

[36] ———, *The United States Balance of Payments*, 88th Cong., first sess., 1963. Washington, D.C.: U.S. Government Printing Office, 1963.

[37] Kafka, Alexandre, "The Current Relevance of International Liquidity for Developing Countries," *American Economic Review*, LVIII, No. 2 (May 1968).

[38] Kenen, Peter B., "Comment," *Journal of Political Economy*, Vol. 75, No. 4, Part II (August 1967), 537–39.

[39] Kindleberger, Charles P., "Flexible Exchange Rates," in Frank M. Tamagna et al., *Monetary Management*. Englewood Cliffs, N.J.: Prentice-Hall, Inc., 1963, pp. 403–25. Reprinted in Charles P. Kindleberger, *Europe and the Dollar*. Cambridge: The M.I.T. Press, 1966, Ch. 8.

[40] ———, *The Politics of International Money and World Language*. Princeton: International Finance Section, Department of Economics, Princeton University, 1967.

[41] Machlup, Fritz, "In Search of Guides for Policy," in William Fellner et al., *Maintaining and Restoring Balance in International Payments*. Princeton: Princeton University Press, 1966, Ch. 3.

[42] ———, "International Monetary Systems and the Free Market Econ-

omy," in *International Payments Problems.* Washington, D.C.: American Enterprise Institute for Public Policy Research, 1966, pp. 153–76.

[43] ———, *International Payments, Debts, and Gold.* New York: Charles Scribner's Sons, 1964.

[44] ———, *Plans for Reform of the International Monetary System.* Princeton: International Finance Section, Department of Economics, Princeton University, 1964. Reprinted in Fritz Machlup, *International Payments, Debts, and Gold.* New York: Charles Scribner's Sons, 1964, Ch. 14.

[45] ———, Statement Before the Joint Economic Committee Hearings on the 1968 Economic Report, February 19, 1968.

[46] ———, *The Need for Monetary Reserves.* Princeton: International Finance Section, Department of Economics, Princeton University, 1965.

[47] ———, and Burton G. Malkiel, ed., *International Monetary Arrangements: The Problem of Choice.* Report on the Deliberations of an International Study Group of 32 Economists. Princeton: International Finance Section, Department of Economics, Princeton University, 1964.

[48] Mundell, Robert A., "A Theory of Optimum Currency Areas," *American Economic Review,* LI, No. 4 (September 1961), 657–65. Reprinted in Robert A. Mundell, *International Economics.* New York: The Macmillan Company, 1968, Ch. 12.

[49] ———, "The Appropriate Use of Monetary and Fiscal Policy for Internal and External Stability," International Monetary Fund *Staff Papers,* IX, No. 1 (March 1962), 70–79. Reprinted in Robert A. Mundell, *International Economics.* New York: The Macmillan Company, 1968, Ch. 16.

[50] ———, *The International Monetary System: Conflict and Reform.* Montreal: Canadian Trade Committee, 1965.

[51] ———, "The Proper Division of the Burden of International Adjustment," *National Banking Review,* Vol. 3, No. 1 (September 1965), 81–87. Reprinted in Robert A. Mundell, *International Economics.* New York: The Macmillan Company, 1968, Ch. 13.

[52] Officer, Lawrence H., *An Econometric Model of Canada under the Fluctuating Exchange Rate.* Cambridge, Mass.: Harvard University Press, 1968.

[53] ——— and Thomas D. Willett, "A Note on the Stability of a Reserve-Currency System," *Quarterly Journal of Economics,* LXXXIII, (1969).

[54] Report of the Review Committee for Balance of Payments Statistics to the Bureau of the Budget, *The Balance of Payments Statistics of the*

United States. Washington, D.C.: U.S. Government Printing Office, 1965.

[55] Robbins, Lionel, *The Balance of Payments,* Stamp Memorial Lecture. London: Athlone Press, 1951.

[56] Rolfe, Sidney E., *Gold and World Power.* New York: Harper & Row, Publishers, 1966.

[57] Roosa, Robert V., *The Dollar and World Liquidity.* New York: Random House, Inc., 1967.

[58] Ruff, Gunther, *A Dollar-Reserve System as a Transitional Solution.* Princeton: International Finance Section, Department of Economics, Princeton University, 1967.

[59] Scitovsky, Tibor, *Requirements of an International Reserve System.* Princeton: International Finance Section, Department of Economics, Princeton University, 1965.

[60] ———, "The Theory of Balance-of-Payments Adjustment," *Journal of Political Economy,* Vol. 75, No. 4, Part II (August 1967), 523–31.

[61] Smith, Warren L., "Are There Enough Policy Tools?" *American Economic Review,* LV, No. 2 (May 1965), 208–20.

[62] Sohmen, Egon, *Flexible Exchange Rates: Theory and Controversy.* Chicago: University of Chicago Press, 1961.

[63] Tobin, James, "Adjustment Responsibilities of Surplus and Deficit Countries," in William Fellner *et al., Maintaining and Restoring Balance in International Payments.* Princeton: Princeton University Press, 1966, Ch. 16.

[64] ———, "Europe and the Dollar," *National Economic Policy.* New Haven: Yale University Press, 1966, Ch. 14. Reprinted from *Review of Economics and Statistics,* XLVI, No. 2 (May 1964), 123–26.

[65] Triffin, Robert, *Gold and the Dollar Crisis.* New Haven: Yale University Press, 1960.

[66] ———, *Moorgate and Wall Street,* Special Supplement (July 1965). Reprinted in Joint Economic Committee, *Guidelines for International Monetary Reform,* 89th Cong., first sess., 1965. Washington, D.C.: U.S. Government Printing Office, 1965.

[67] ———, *Our International Monetary System: Yesterday, Today, and Tomorrow.* New York: Random House, Inc., 1968.

[68] ———, *The Balance of Payments and the Foreign Investment Position of the United States.* Princeton: International Finance Section, Department of Economics, Princeton University, 1966.

[69] U.S. Treasury Department, *Maintaining the Strength of the United States Dollar in a Strong Free World Economy,* January 1968.

[70] Viner, Jacob, "Some International Aspects of Economic Stabilization," in L. D. White, ed., *The State of the Social Sciences.* Chicago: University of Chicago Press, 1956, pp. 283–98.

[71] Willett, Thomas D., "International Specie Flows and American Monetary Stability, 1834–1860," *Journal of Economic History*, XXVIII, No. 1 (March 1968), 28–50.

[72] ———, "Official versus Market Financing of International Deficits," *Kyklos* (fasc. 3, 1968).

[73] Williams, John H., *Postwar Monetary Plans and Other Essays*. New York: Alfred A. Knopf, Inc., 1947.

[74] Williamson, Jeffrey G., *American Growth and the Balance of Payments 1820–1913*. Chapel Hill: The University of North Carolina Press, 1964.

[75] ———, "Dollar Scarcity and Surplus in Historical Perspective," *American Economic Review*, LIII, No. 2 (May 1963), 519–29.

[76] Working Party No. 3 of the Economic Policy Committee of the Organisation for Economic Co-operation and Development, *Report, The Balance of Payments Adjustment Process*. Organization for Economic Co-Operation and Development, August 1966.

[77] Yeager, Leland B., *International Monetary Relations*. New York: Harper & Row, Publishers, 1966.

[78] ———, "A Skeptical View of the 'Band' Proposal," *National Banking Review*, Vol. 4, No. 3 (March 1967), 291–97.

[79] ———, *The International Monetary Mechanism*. New York: Holt, Rinehart & Winston, Inc., 1968.